Love à la française

Love à la française

What Happens When Hervé Meets Sally

Polly Platt

MEP, Inc

First Edition published in April 2008

Published and distributed by MEP Inc.
   8124 N. Ridgeway Avenue
   Skokie, IL 60076
   email: info@mep-inc.net
   telephone: 1 847 676 1596

Feedback to the author: email: polly@pollyplatt.com
                          telephone: (33) 553 64 94 75

Cover design and other drawings by Ian Heard

Layout design by David Hilditch

ISBN 978-1-60111-014-5

Library of Congress Control Number: 2007943862

Printed in Canada by Transcontinental Gagné

Illustrations

Table of Contents

Everything that precedes the union of the sexes and makes it more beautiful, and since François I, more romantic, from flirting to fashion — above all, flirting — was born in France and only has a name in French: coquetterie. For lessons in this, the elite of other nations come every day to the capital of the universe.

Brillat-Savarin, *La Physiologie du Goût*, 1826.

L'amour, c'est peut-être notre plus vraie religion, et en même temps notre plus vraie maladie mentale. (Love is perhaps our true religion, and at the same time, our veritable mental illness.)

Edgar Morin, *Amour, Poésie, Sagesse*, 2001.

I have not spent a day without loving you; I have not spent a night without embracing you... In the midst of my affairs, whether at the head of the troops or going through the camps, my adorable Josephine alone is in my heart, occupies my mind, absorbs my thoughts. If I rise to work in the middle of the night, it is to advance my sweet love's arrival by a few days.

Letter from Napoleon to Josephine, during the Italian campaign 1897, from *Napoleon*, by Vincent Cronin.

Introduction

Are French men great lovers?

This is the first question American women married to French men are asked on their trips back home, so let's address it right away. Except for one "no comment" and one "no," the answer of the dozens of Americans interviewed, whether divorced or still married, was a merry chorus of "Yessss!" They clamored to embroider on the theme of just what that means.

What, in fact, are French love, French men, French women and Frenchness all about? Why do the French marry and what do they expect from their family life? What is the history behind the different ways the sexes consider each other in France? Who are the fantastic frogs from the past who have shaped those cultural differences and given French men and women a self-conception in such contrast to that of Americans?

And what happens when Americans and French marry? Are the fireworks in the bedroom enough to make a Franco-American couple leap across the perilous divide of cultural gaps — for better or for worse, for so long as they both shall live? Is infidelity really so ho-hum commonplace in France? And if so, how does an American wife handle it? Does she feel that the meaning has gone out of her marriage and run to the divorce court, as many Americans in the U.S. do, or does she take a broader look at the French context of her husband and her family? And what are the other major pitfalls?

And finally, why and how do Franco-American relationships succeed and fail? I've looked into the past as well as the present for answers. I've only interviewed people who would have something wise to contribute, focusing on a group with more or less similar educational backgrounds, mature enough to have given their marriages a serious try, but young enough have vivid memories of the cultural aches they went through.

I'm enormously grateful to the case-history interviewees who took the trouble to go with me through the labyrinth of Franco-American joys or miseries, illusions, expectations and confusions. They have provided interesting, sometimes startling, thought-provoking observations — and some answers. They have been infinitely generous with their time and in sharing the intimacy of their lives. I'm also, privately, nervous about any regrets some of them might have, once confronted with these revelations in black and white. To offset this I've changed the names and the situations, using made-up first names and no last names at all. Where you see complete names, that is, first names plus last names, the names are real. I've used them only with permission, of course, and only where regrets seemed NA. I hope this will prevent my being strung up on a lamp post. *Love à la française* is a subject that boils the blood and quickens the pulse, and I'm ready to brave tar and feathers. I only regret that I can't publicly thank all those I spoke to for their help and that for lack of space they couldn't all be included.

Part of the pleasure of doing research for the book was finding out that the subject of love was as inflammatory for everyone else as for the guests that first evening at the "gargoyle dinner" in Chapter One. No one, but no one, is indifferent.

Part I

Frenchness

1

The Riddle

It started out a Franco-American dinner party like any other in Paris. Well, not exactly. The sumptuous living room where we gathered overlooked Notre Dame, a spectacular view you don't often get. With the Cathedral so close, the gargoyles on the façade seemed to be part of our conversation, not necessarily approving of it.

The women were American, all but one experienced Parisians by now, and the men French. The party as usual got into gear slowly, one of the couples arriving on the dot of 8:30, the rest of us straggling in after another 15 to 45 minutes, which isn't really considered late here. The traffic, you understand.

Lizzie, the newcomer, the ebullient young Midwestern wife of the punctual couple, gaped at the view and ran to the window.

"The gargoyles!" she gasped. "I can't believe it! And Charlemagne down there on his horse! Wow! What the rent must be on this place!"

The American hostess, Laura, was in the kitchen fussing over the canapés (shrimp on cucumber) which were unnecessary, as far as the French guests were concerned, but much appreciated by the Americans. Fabrice, her elegant French husband, started pouring champagne — vintage and famous.

Lizzie was shocked. "Champagne!" she cried. "At home we only have it — if we have it — for weddings, or maybe for special birthdays. It's so expensive!"

Fabrice, dark-haired, charming and handsome, a young 50, asked her politely where home was, his clever, merry black eyes taking in everything. Usually he wouldn't have passed up an opportunity to truss up a goose as she deserved, but Lizzie was a guest and a foreigner and he obviously felt sorry for her gaucheness. Poor Lizzie. Two gaffes already. I wondered how many more the evening would bring. I liked her very much. She was as fresh and true as dew at dawn. Her normal personality was ebullient — she was used to bursting into a room with loud enthusiasm — but she was usually a little more subdued with strangers. Probably her loudness here was an effort to overcome shyness. I knew she was totally befuddled in Paris, lost and uneasy. She hadn't yet understood that loudness and enthusiasm didn't work in France. Even her looks felt 'wrong.' Her straight blond hair was fastened with a barrette, like a schoolgirl's. She was a big woman, tall, with big bones and strong arms, maybe 32 but looked younger. She was what the French call *costaude*, or strong. She seemed to belong on the tennis court. Her face was handsome — big blue eyes, high cheekbones, thin lips — when she didn't spoil it with a huge grin. I'd phone her tomorrow and explain about the champagne. Early on, the doyenne of Americans in Paris, a baroness, had told me that if you can afford having people to dinner in Paris, you can afford champagne. Period. I'd pass this bit of advice on to Lizzie. And I'd caution her about mentioning money.

A roguish Frenchman joined us, introduced as Jean-Marc, a little younger than Fabrice, perhaps in his 40's. I'd met him once before at another Franco-American gathering, when he was still married to his prim American wife from Vermont. France had been too much for her. She went back to Vermont, obliged to leave without their little daughter, despite the best English-speaking lawyer in Paris. Jean-Marc and their daughter had moved back in with his mother in the posh 7th *arrondissement*.

Jean-Marc was followed by R, a French book publisher and an old friend of mine, and his glamorous dark-haired Franco-American wife, Constance, who was as outspoken as R was discreet. He was tall and lithe, his brilliant eyes a flash of blue, dancing with fun. The first thing you noticed about him was his dark bushy eyebrows. I was sure he had to comb them to keep them in place.

We all gave each other double-cheek kisses, that is, one on each cheek. Lizzie got it wrong. She aimed for R's left cheek instead of his right one. As the French always head for the right cheek, their noses collided.

"Oh, I'm so sorry!" Lizzie whinnied.

"Chère Madame, it is charming that you say you're sorry," said R, laughing, "but you will embarrass all of us in this country if you continue

"I said I'm sorry."

with it."

"The French can't say it," said Laura, arriving from the kitchen with the canapé tray. She wore a simply cut, pinkish-beige dress with a low neckline you could be sure was Chanel, and strands of silky pearls. "It would be admitting an error, which is forbidden here," she added. "So if you say 'sorry,' you embarrass them." She laughed and stroked her husband's cheek. "Fabrice and I have been squabbling about this for 10 years."

Laura was so gracious and full of fun that I couldn't imagine her ever quarreling about anything. Beautiful, almost without makeup, with thick, many-shaded blond hair, a high round forehead, a skin like smooth cream and widely spaced, deep-set, warm brown eyes, she had the kind of beauty you wanted to let your gaze rest on. Her most remarkable feature was her profile. With her large boney nose, sharp at the end, almost a beak, she could have been a Renaissance noblewoman, painted by Ghirlandaio. Laura hated her nose, but it was, of course, a rare ornament. She was the perfect complement to Fabrice's fine looks. They were the couple everyone envied and admired.

Lizzie rolled her eyes. I could see that she was about to make a comment about this "crazy country" where no one admitted mistakes. Thierry, her husband, cut her off. He was a big burly Frenchman, the kind you expect to see down a mineshaft. "It's a ballet in the States," he said. "Everyone knows whose fault it is, but they all have to say they're sorry."

Now the last couple arrived. Kate, about 45, was a psychologist who considered herself, and probably was, an expert on the French. She liked being provocative just to see what people would say. I could feel fireworks coming tonight as she sauntered into the room in skintight mauve trousers like a model on a runway, hips forward, shoulders slouched. She was exultantly artificial, from her exaggerated eyeliner to her forest of gold jewelry hanging from her wrists, neck and ears. Perhaps because of her small features — small mouth, small eyes, small nose — the only thing you remembered about her the next day was her spiky, henna-colored hair, as if your memory only recorded one of those faceless mannequins with red hair in a store window. Her husband, Geoffroy, was a banker, strictly dressed in banker's black, and a strict expression on his face; he even sat strictly. He usually loosened up with the champagne, but still, I couldn't understand what the exotic Kate saw in him. As far as I was concerned, he brought in a cold wind.

Presently we trooped into the dining room. Plates of *saumon fumé* (smoked salmon) were waiting for us with little wedges of lemon and squares of toast on many-colored Italian plates. The peach-colored tablecloth matched the dahlias in the center of the table, as well as the walls, and had a subtle shade more of pink than the *saumon fumé*. The flat silver and crystal glasses sparkled in the candlelight.

I sighed. Laura had done it again. Made us all — except Lizzie — give up any idea of daring another dinner party.

"What a beautiful table!" gushed Lizzie.

I held my breath to see if she'd comment on the napkins, each a square yard of heavy white damask with Fabrice's family coronet embroidered on them. She did. "Gosh, Fabrice," she breathed, "a crown? What are you, a king or something? An heir apparent?"

"Not crown, coronet," corrected Constance. Could I almost hear her thinking, "Dummie" or was I doing her an injustice? Constance was just French enough that I couldn't quite get a take on her. I had a few French friends, but they weren't intimate, and in general, French women were still dense with mystery for me. Not the men. The men you could get a feel for right away (no pun intended).

Fabrice laughed. "No majesties here, just a no-account count. But please, everyone, listen to this." He poured the wine (a white Burgundy) around the table as he spoke. "A friend of mine — a French friend, the kind of friend you only see at business meetings, who didn't know that I had an American wife — said a funny thing over coffee the other day. I'd like to know what you think."

We perked up and tuned in.

"He asked me," Fabrice went on, "if I knew the two worst things that could happen to a Frenchman. I said well no, so he said, 'The worst two things are a French salary and an American wife.' What do you think he meant?"

Silence. Then everyone began talking at once.

"What's wrong with an American wife?" cried Lizzie. "I thought we were supposed to be God's gift to men! Glamorous, smart, healthy, independent. Competent career women, efficient housekeepers, tender mothers —"

"Exactly," said Jean-Marc, glowering. His divorce from his American wife had been nasty and he was still upset by it. "Nothing is so deadening as perfection. If they just weren't so efficient and piously right about everything... present company excepted."

Thierry, Lizzie's red-haired Alsatian husband, who had lived in the U.S. for several years, commented that, on the contrary, American women were refreshingly natural and direct. No beating around the bush.

"If you happen to like things that are natural and direct," said Jean-Marc. "Personally, I think beating around the bush, as you call it — what we might call subtlety — is essential for any sort of harmony. Perhaps what your friend meant is that American women lack that essential quality of being sweet. Does a sweet American woman exist? French women are sweet."

This was too much for Kate. "Nonsense!" she cried. "That's the typical remark of an arrogant, insecure, macho Frenchman! French women aren't sweet! They're hard as nails! That sweetness is just part of the act!"

"Oh, Kate, for goodness sake," drawled Laura. "Surely you know what the reputation is of American women here. The French think we're overbearing ballbreakers, out to grab their money and kidnap their children to America. Maybe it's a question of turning down our volume when we're over here."

"Or maybe the French husbands should learn how to say they're sorry!" said Lizzie.

There wasn't anywhere this conversation could go without plates starting to fly. Fabrice deftly changed the subject.

But I was intrigued. I began to feel like an idiotic provincial. I have to admit that I had kind of taken for granted Lizzie's point of view — that American wives were special wonders coveted by foreign men. I'd been married to a foreigner myself, though not a Frenchman. I started asking myself questions. What was it about American women that put off these Frenchmen? Why were American women the ones in the doghouse, of all the different nationalities out there? And by the way, what did Fabrice himself think about his question? He'd been awfully quiet after he put it on the table.

And what was it about France? Why did all these Americans come here? Three million of them a year, with an estimated 165,000 residents in France and about 100,000 in Paris. How many of these were husband-hunting singles — widows, divorcées and young women with French stars in their eyes? How had the married ones met their French husbands? What were these French men like? Why did they marry Americans, and what happened to make things go sour — or if they went smoothly, how?

I decided to try and find out. As a journalist, I was naturally curious and could be a fly on the wall. As an American widow never married to a Frenchman, I was without preconceived ideas and could hope to be objective. Can a fish explain water or show you how to swim? I counted on my fellow American diners, Lizzie, Laura and Kate, to fill me in on many of the mysteries of Frenchness. I had a feeling that R, both my old friend and French, would turn out to be my mentor.

2

Why American women come to France

Why did American women come to France? And why did they want to leave home?

Plenty of reasons. With me it was curiosity and fear. Curiosity about what the insides of those medieval castles in my history books looked like, and fear that before I got there, they'd all go up in smoke in one of those wars the Europeans seemed always to be having. So the moment I was old enough, I whizzed over on summer or ski vacations from my job. On these trips I met lots of museum guides, ski instructors, mountain guides and hotel concierges. On later vacations in Paris and Vienna and Rome I went to balls and met Frenchmen, Italians, Austrians, Swedes and Englishmen; but it was a Serb living in Vienna that, finally, I married. We moved to Paris and had some wonderful years before he died.

Other Americans seemed to have made a beeline for the Eiffel Tower, which they heard was the best spot in Paris for meeting Frenchmen. Mark Meigs, of Berwyn, Pennsylvania, professor of American history at the University of Paris, sent me this email:

"I have a student who told me that she and her classmates ALL (or many) came to Paris with the idea that they would find the French man of their dreams in the elevator of the Tour Eiffel. Why they dreamed of a French man was too obvious to explain. What a *French* man would be doing in that elevator is not a question they asked themselves. This student is setting out to do interviews with people to find out where this romance idea came from. Apparently ALL the women teachers of the college program that brings these students over here are married to

Frenchmen whom they met soon after they stepped off the plane!"

It's no accident that Disney World copied a gabled, turreted 14th-century French castle with lots of towers and battlements for its French playground. French castles starred in the fairy tales we all read when we were little. They were inhabited by Prince Charmings who chose the neglected but virtuous and — underneath the soot — beautiful Cinderellas and lived happily ever after.

Prince Charming was obviously French, since he lived in a French castle. Everything we grew up with in America confirmed this and we women knew it, even if we didn't speak French and had never been to France. What we knew in our gut was that France was where women bloomed and became more beautiful than they ever knew they could be. It was where fashion had come from for centuries to make us look enticing, it was where they made perfume to make us smell marvelous, where they grew grapes for champagne so that we could properly celebrate all that. It was the country of beauty and luxury and, by the way, the country that invented romantic love.

And Paris... Paris was after all the City of Light, the most beautiful in the world. It was where the locals had philosophy discussions in cafés — Sartre thought up existentialism in one — and all-night concerts on the streets. Once a year all the museums were open until dawn. In the summer they rolled out a "beach" along the Seine, with real sand and palm trees. Oh, and the restaurants... and the palace hotels, shimmering with silks and crystal chandeliers...

As for the men. This was where men kissed married ladies' hands, where they were said to unabashedly care about beauty and art and poetry... and cooking, which they called "gastronomy." They *liked* to go to the market. They *liked* to cook — themselves — what they found there, skillfully selected.

So... France was the obvious choice for any American woman who for one reason or another wanted to leave her country and was looking for something different and exotic yet familiar (not the total Unknown, like the Orient, for example). In the 19th century it was rich, ambitious women who came looking for a title, like railroad heiress Anna Gould, who first married Count Boni de Castellane, and then, tripping over his mistresses, booted him out and bagged the Prince de Périgord, a descendant of Talleyrand, the legendary advisor to French sovereigns.

Or it was gifted rich upper class women like Edith Wharton and Mary Cassatt, who were suffocating at home. It was also rich art or literary-minded lesbians like Gertrude Stein and Natalie Barney, who were also, for obvious reasons, suffocating at home.

There has been no dearth of 20th century rich or less-rich American women married to titled Frenchmen, but they have often been women who grew up at least partly in France, or with a relative in France they visited often. To them a French husband seemed as familiar and reasonable a choice as an American. The most successful of these is the Duchesse de Mouchy, the former Joan Dillon, owner of the Haut Brion vineyards, having previously been married to a younger brother of the Grand Duke of Luxembourg. Her father, Douglas Dillon, was the American Ambassador to France.

To contemporary American women growing up in the U.S., no matter what their fortune, marrying a title would seem a good reason *not* to marry a Frenchman. It would feel uncomfortably old-fashioned, if not a downright joke; or, in the business world, a handicap. The bridegroom's title might even come as a surprise in these days of rigorous republicanism. Stephanie de La Rochefoucauld found out about hers when her husband gave her his card. The word *Comte* was crossed out.

"I could have easily not seen it," she said. "I didn't know anything about the fame of the family — the 17th-century La Rochefoucauld's *Maximes* and all that — but I might have gotten a glimmer of it the first time he took me to the family château, and told me what his ancestor told Louis XVI when he heard the gates of Versailles being rattled. It seems the King asked him, 'Is it a revolt?' And La Rochefoucauld said, 'No, Sire, it is a REVOLUTION.'"

That leaves the question of why more contemporary American women left home. Since home was more welcoming now for women artists and lesbians, and titles less prized, what spurred them to forsake everything that they knew and cared about? Adventure? An unhappy love affair? Were they misfits who didn't get along at home? For a long time I thought that it was family skeletons — an alcoholic father, a bipolar mother — that sent 20th-century American women fleeing to Paris. I still think that accounts for a lot of us, but the full truth is more stirring than any personal hurts or gripes.

In fact, I decided, Paris was the pull of the collective female unconscious. Even if they grew up without a word of French, with only the vaguest notion of where France was and no notion whatever of French history, American women knew intuitively that this was the place that would make them find out the meaning of being women, their own meaning, the place where they could blossom. The place where they didn't have to imitate men but could experiment with being completely themselves, whoever that might turn out to be, and in addition, discover what that meant. Where being women was the point. Where they were not a counterfeit afterthought.

It was the promised land. And just as hard to reach as the top of the mythical glass mountain.

3

French men on American women

A Frenchman in France is not only different from an American, but also a different kettle of fish from a Frenchman in America. In America, he is acting a part without a director, on a strange stage, making sounds that are basically meaningless to him. In France he is back where his body can move in its accustomed way, his face comes alive as he makes and hears the ancient sounds of his birthplace. So he naturally reverts to his original habits of communication, where a movement of his hand or head, or even a grunt, is understood. Sartre said he disliked Americans because they didn't move their faces, particularly their noses, when they spoke. It's easy for American women, seemingly in sync with their French husbands in the U.S., to lose track of what is going on, once in France, until they get into the swing of things — which can take years. Not surprising, therefore, if they make a bad impression on these husbands. What about other Frenchmen? What do they think of American women? Are they dazzled by their beauty and competence? By their sportiness and their sense of humor? Or do they lean towards the riddle of Fabrice's friend? In which case, just what is the problem with American women and French men?

That it was vital to hear what the Prince Charmings themselves had to say before I could proceed further became strikingly clear after the first interview. It was with one of France's most illustrious authors.

Jean-Marie Rouart of the Académie Française
The allure of the unobtainable

From the way he writes about love in his books, and from his reputation at Parisian dinner parties, I knew that Jean-Marie Rouart was the quintessential Prince Charming that the young Americans of Chapter Two yearned to swoon over in the elevator of the Eiffel Tower. I hardly hoped that he would agree to an interview, so it was no surprise that my letter proposing one wasn't answered.

When, months later, a Frenchman telephoned me, pronouncing a name that sounded vaguely like his, I thought I'd misunderstood. French men in the lofty spheres he inhabited simply didn't make phone calls like this. It must be someone wanting information about one of the used car ads I'd been answering.

So I said, "Which car are you calling about?"

Jean-Marie Rouart, novelist, biographer, playwright, journalist, was one of the youngest Frenchmen to be crowned, in 1997, with the accolade of membership in the *Académie Française*. Son and grandson of respected artists, he grew up in the midst of paintings by Manet and Berthe Morisot. He was expected to become an artist himself, but being a writer had obsessed him from early childhood. I had long admired his books, some of which are quoted later. I was all the more eager to meet him after his hearty laugh at my taking him for a used car dealer.

We were to meet at the *Café de l'Esplanade*. I found a table on the terrace with a view of the golden cupola of the Invalides. From his photos I knew that Rouart was a handsome, dark-haired 64-year old. I wondered if I would pick up on the description on his web site: "radiating tenderness and abandon like a defenseless adolescent, and at the same time an air of susceptibility and bashfulness irresistible to women of 35." I thought it more likely that as an Académicien, he would be pompous and arrogant.

When he entered the *Café de l'Esplanade*, it was with the aura of glamour and excitement of a man who had aimed high, very high, and made it, after countless failures and setbacks. No sign whatever of pomposity or arrogance. He was courteous and charming. I didn't see anything of the bashfulness or the defenseless adolescent, but he definitely had the slightly vulnerable look of a man who appeals to women, with a hint of *volupté* ("sensual pleasure" doesn't really do justice to this French word).

After a while I was struck by his troubled eyes that have spent solitary eternities exploring suicide, melancholia and the temptation of signing up for the Greek monastery barred to women on remote Mount Athos. I thought of a reviewer's description of his work as "abounding in melancholic and neurotic pleasure-seekers, one hand holding fast to a breast, the other caressing the grip of a pistol, hesitating between the red *volupté* of the bed and the black *volupté* of nothingness."

From his novels it is clear that he is a specialist in love and women as well as in words and the darker sides of life. It was women, American and French, that I had wanted to talk to him about, since an American friend of mine whom he had flirted with some time ago, told me that she had found him difficult to resist, the incarnation of the French *séducteur*. He never married. He has said that he was torn between the "Sunday turkey" and the next pretty girl.

I asked him his impressions of American women. He was guarded.

"American women have grown up in large spaces, they are perhaps less complicated than French women," he said. "They escaped the poison of Romanticism. They could be your alter ego, ride with you, ski with you, contrary to the French lady in her crinoline. But my impression is that they are afraid of carnal pleasures. Mediterranean women are tender and sensual."

I suggest that they are perhaps more sentimental than Mediterranean women?

"Perhaps... and perhaps they don't understand the importance of the unobtainable. The reality of love is in the imagination. The longer a woman tantalizes a man, keeps him waiting, the stronger is his imagination of the delights to be savored."

Did he think the marriage of a Frenchman to an American was necessarily doomed?

"Intercultural marriages, with all their social and religious differences, can turn out positively. It depends on the approach. What shocks French people is the commercialization of American marriages, of sentiment. The American organization of divorce also shocks French people. In France, a Catholic country, it is accepted that marriage is not perfect. You remember the maxim of La Rochefoucauld: *"Il y a de bons mariages, pas de delicieux."* (There are good marriages, but not delightful ones.) Here, the tradition has been to marry socially and find — perhaps — love elsewhere. Before the Revolution, no one thought about personal happiness. Then came the Romantic revolution and the individual began to insist on marrying for love. The belief that love solves all the problems in marriage is overloading the boat. Little adventures of two evenings are harmless games, flirting, with wit and repartee."

But what about if you are deeply Christian?

"Faith doesn't prevent infidelity. One can expiate guilt, if one has it, by confession. But where is the guilt? Being unfaithful to his wife doesn't imply that a man doesn't love her. It's about living, not control... what we call in French *marivaudage*. You have seen Marivaud's plays?"

I said that I had and knew what he meant.

"Then you understand the game of love... that love *is* a game. It's important in love to keep up that side, the playful side, the game aspect."

Language is of extreme importance in France, he said. "France is a literary country. It was founded by literature. Our politicians are writers -- Mitterrand, Giscard, Bayrou, de Gaulle. In the past, Montaigne, Montesquieu, Rousseau, Voltaire, Victor Hugo. Chateaubriand was a leader of the Revolution."

We talked of Balzac, Stendhal, Flaubert. "Literature is the apologist of adultery, not of marriage," he said.

I asked him what kind of women he preferred.

"I like women who live intensely," he said.

Count Albert de Mun
Americans have no *non-dit* (unsaid)

The charisma of a *grand bourgeois* like Jean-Marie Rouart is similar to that of an aristocrat. Do they have it in their genes after so many generations of ease and not working with their hands? Are they born knowing whether their lips should or should not touch the hands they kiss? Who knows? In any case, I was delighted that another distinguished charmer, Count Albert de Mun, agreed to be interviewed. Landowner, journalist, traveler, you can't forget him in Paris: such was the prominence of his great grandfather that a no.63 bus stop near the Trocodéro is named for him.

Albert de Mun is a virtuoso of The Look. Lucky you if he turns his eyes on you when you enter a room full of strangers. You are *welcomed*. He has been married twice, but not to an American. However, he knows Americans and has French friends married to Americans.

"American women have no *non-dit* — no nuances," he said. "They say what they think... they can't play the subtle game that French people love. In the beginning, Americans find it funny and mysterious, the way the French talk, but often they need to go back to the U.S., back to their own culture where everyone talks the same way.

"The problem is partly that the education is so different — they're trained to present their ideas in a different way. For us, American women don't have the intellectual potential of French women. But perhaps this is because we expect a certain train of thought.

"I guess the principal problem with Americans is that they're hooked on marriage. If they think marriage — or some kind of a permanent commitment — isn't in the cards, they pack up. While with us, marriage comes or it doesn't... it just sort of happens. Just as there is no word for 'date' in France. People have a cup of coffee, maybe go for dinner, one thing leads to another but it's not a formal 'date' with rules and expectations as in America. So there isn't the same anxiety about the kiss at the door. There is one, or there isn't..."

Olivier Todd
Americans think lovemaking is a science

I was looking forward to my interview with Olivier Todd, the novelist, biographer and journalist. A well known lady-killer, and French, despite his English name, he has been married three times, and has spent a lot of time in America, but never married an American. I wanted to ask him why not, as soon as I figured out how to make the codes work of the various doors and gates of his Left Bank building. When I finally made it to his door he received me graciously.

"In fact, there was an American I thought of marrying," he said, "but it didn't work out. I could have divorced for her. In the end, I didn't. But she phones me from America — or from wherever she is — every year on my birthday. I find that very moving. No one else does that."

But why, I persisted. Maybe Todd had one of the clues I needed.

He was evasive.

"You will have to read my autobiography, *Carte d'Identités*," he said.

I did. That didn't help, though it recounts a rich, turbulent life in dangerous places like Vietnam and Iraq. I found out that he went to California several times to see his father.

"I had a few flirtations over there, but nothing serious. I almost fell in love with a Canadian. To my horror, just in time, I realized she had that accent which I don't like. There were very few women over there that I was interested in — and vice versa — except for one. She was from Lake Tahoe. I had to stop it when she said she wanted to marry me and have a child with me. I once had an affair with an American who flabbergasted me when she told me that she had been to a hospital to 'have it done'... to be deflowered. I couldn't believe it. I'd never heard of that before."

Todd himself was "broken in," as he put it, by an older woman, a friend of his mother, when he was 13. "This is often the way it happens here and I think it is a good way, certainly better than tarts. I was never interested in prostitutes. I was lucky to have her. She taught me the vocabulary of love and was very tender. She is 94 now and living in an old people's home. I still go to see her."

I persisted with my question. Why hadn't he married an American? "In Brentwood," he said, "I was interested in an American until she got undressed. She had had all her pubic hair shaved off. She told me that this was the chic thing now in America. I was so disconcerted that I couldn't... well, you understand. I had to get dressed and go home."

I asked him what else had upset him about these women.

"Some American women seem to consider sex like a health pill for their body," he said. "I wouldn't have been surprised if they had coached me during the act in what they wanted me to do. If you reduce lovemaking to 'having sex,' like 'having a cup of tea,' where is the amorous thrill?

"Another thing that I found disconcerting over there was the women who always had a supply of condoms in their handbag — as some women now do even in France. You can't talk about things, you can't plan them carrying around condoms. It's also a matter of *pudeur*. In fact, we French — some of us — love *l'amour*, and we are often very *pudique*."

Pudeur is one of those words that doesn't translate into English. In connection with love it means discretion, reticence, a sense of wonder at the numinous which should be respected and tiptoed around in silence; a wish not to destroy something sacred by crude talk or practices. It's what the fairy tales are talking about when the traveler is given the golden key or the magic word and told never to use it. But he can't resist, and loses his soul. So you can't get a Frenchman to *talk* about lovemaking.

I asked him why the French have such a reputation as great lovers. Did it have something to do with *pudeur*?

Todd sidestepped the question adroitly. "Maybe it's like our international reputation for cooking. Everyone thinks it is extraordinary, so there must be some truth in it.

"I like Americans," he continued. "I like the way they are warm and hospitable and I like the casual way they dress — I'm sensitive to the way women dress — and that they're careful about their BO, but I don't like some aspects of the American way of life, the uniformity of some provincial towns. I don't like the way Americans think that there is a recipe for a good screw, that lovemaking is a science. It's not. It's about being attentive to the other person. Both a man and a woman have to listen to the other body, feel it in their hearts and minds.

"Also, Americans — like many French people today — rely too much on readymade food and on fast food. I don't think they understand that food and love complement each other, they go together.

"The warmest and one of the nicest feelings is having breakfast the morning after. This is the happiest time. You're accomplices, complete, in harmony, an extraordinary moment.

"The solution for a happy life, I suppose, is a couple getting on well in all ways, a harmony of the head, the heart and the body. But this fusion can not last more than two, perhaps two and a half years. At least, that is the impression one gets from reading certain sexologists and from talking to shrinks."

He paused for a while and then said, thoughtfully: "I'm not all happy with that aspect of my life. I think I would not lead the same life again. In another life I might be Italian, with four children exactly like the ones I have — but I have no clue who the mother would be. Perhaps after all, an American?"

Jean-Claude Guez
American women shouldn't be confrontational

I knew I could count on Jean-Claude Guez to put American women in a deep context from past to present. Guez is a workaholic *ingénieur* (polytechnicien), an intellectual and, now retired as a partner of Accenture, as zealous as ever as a member of several multinational boards of directors. He lived for years in Los Angeles and Chicago and has been married to his French wife for 25 years. He expressed his opinions about American women so courteously and indirectly that it was like a brilliant treatise on how to speak in the French way and be misunderstood by everyone not French.

However, I've been here a long time. In clear American language, this is what he said:

He feels that the first thing an American wife of a Frenchman should try to do is some introspection... and some work on any basic hostile reactions she has to men in general and French men in particular.

French men and women like to be together. French men enjoy women's conversation — and have, ever since women started insisting on elegant conversation back in the 17th century. If a Frenchman married a woman, he probably likes to talk to her — and he won't expect her to blow up at something he said or didn't say. This might shock him into silence for days — a cold, immovable silence which she wouldn't be able to handle. Remember, France never had women's lib movements of any serious weight. That has always been a non-issue in this country. French women found their own rights position in French society a rather long time ago... even on issues as serious as abortion.

French men are rather old-fashioned, perhaps, in not wanting to hurt their wives. Unless they're very religious, they probably won't feel that infidelity is an issue, but they know very well that it wouldn't please their wife — so they will be discreet, unless the wife has become so unbearable that they're looking for an excuse to chase her away. The depth, however, of the American woman's outrage at infidelity is something a Frenchman doesn't suspect, and she should make it clear before their marriage how she feels about it.

Tolerance for differing viewpoints from the other party, including money and politics, is absolutely vital, he said. He made these additional points:

- *Conformance to/understanding of the French way of doing things... especially on social and cultural issues, is a must in this country.*
- *Ability to read body language and to sense/understand the implicit, is critical in French society and of course, in a French couple's life.*
- *Having tolerance for/understanding of the fact that getting things done takes time here, is also vital...*
- *A wife must be... a help... not a pain. A French wife must be capable of acting autonomously and taking charge in a critical situation in the absence of her husband. She must NOT need a coach to act.*
- *Adjusting the French /U.S. differences on emotional / sex life implicit protocols is probably also a significant challenge...*
- *Renouncing typical U.S. high-volume oral fights with strong body gestures and replacing that in France with cool and soft-voice "Cartesian" arguing, is probably also another big difference to adjust to.*
- *Properly educating the children in line with French behavioral standards (far more discipline, far less freedom at the ages of 12 to 18, than in the U.S.) is also an essential criterion for long-term success.*
- *In France, the weight of the family and the elderly — who, oftentimes, live nearby — is usually much heavier than in the U.S. Accepting this responsibility is also a very important consideration.*

Benjamin Feitelson
American women are unemotional

Benjamin Feitelson is a handsome young actor in a hurry. I caught him just before he was leaving for Indochina. He threw me a few choice sentences:

"French women do a lot of talking with their eyes and facial expressions. They like things to be seductive and vague, they like a lot of circling around, nuances and innuendos... atmosphere. American women hate that. You know that expression 'cut the crap?' They want everything to be crisp and clear. I find them unemotional — there is no tear in the eye when something is sad. Italian women, for instance, are very emotional. If you walk down the street and glance at another woman, they throw the flower pot at you."

Dr. Arnold Lamazère
There should be separate intimate spaces in the bathroom.

Dr. Arnold Lamazère, a specialist in gerontology as well as a general practitioner, is an elegant man-about-town who actually visits his patients. By motorcycle. He even has a special time of day, every day, when they can reach him by phone. Needless to say, he is worshipped by his patients.

As elegant as he himself, they tend to confide in him, so he probably knows as much about their thoughts and habits as a shrink. Like most Frenchmen, he also speaks in the *non-dit* (unsaid) and in implication.

"There must be mystery in a marriage," he said. "Reserve, not telling all, is of the utmost importance, along with tenderness."

Implied: Americans are too direct, which is probably wounding, and probably misunderstood; and aggressive.

He agrees with the Japanese about the deplorable American custom of having the W.C. in the same space in the bathroom as the bathtub, which is for getting clean. It also interferes with privacy.

"For a Frenchman, it is *insupportable* (unendurable) the way Americans have the W.C. in the bathroom with the bathtub and the washbasin," he said, in an interview at his office in the 7th arrondissement. "A husband and wife each need intimate space for themselves, they mustn't invade each other's privacy."

Implied: Americans don't understand the importance of *le jardin secret* (the secret garden), or their own hidden mystery, and the part it plays in eroticism.

Charm is the key word for a Frenchman, he says. What he sees among his French patients is the women rather than the men looking for lovers.

"They need to reassure themselves, or perhaps they want to wake up their husband's ardor with a bit of jealousy. French men are hardly ever the ones to initiate a divorce — they are comfortable at home and want to stay that way, whether they have a mistress or not."

Implied: They aren't the tireless Lotharios they're made out to be. Hmm, doctor?

Thierry Lhermitte
American women have a sense of humor

The first thing you notice about Thierry Lhermitte, the matinee idol, is that he has blue eyes to drown in. The second is that he makes you laugh. The third is that he doesn't take himself seriously. He is also suave, sleek, funny, debonair, slightly cynical, seductive, occasionally brutal.

Lhermitte is France's answer to America's Brad Pitts, Harrison Fords and George Clooneys – a terribly French, terribly handsome actor who can act, and breaks up his audience in laughter whether chasing crooks (*Les Ripoux*) or imbeciles (*The Dinner Game*) or women (*The Wedding of the Century*). The New York *Daily News* promised that you'd "laugh like a hyena" at *The Dinner Game*. Comedy, making people laugh, is where his heart is. He has said that the way to seduce him (in the French sense) is to make him laugh. But he is, as well, a serious stage actor, film producer, and a passionate sportsman: a deepsea diver, a horseman, a karate black belt and a sailor. He had expected to become a mathematician. A very private *père de famille*, in 1988 he took a year off to sail around the world with his wife and children.

The film I wanted to interview him about was *Le Divorce*, where he starred with Kate Hudson and Naomi Watts. Hudson and Watts played American sisters. Watts is divorcing her French husband and Hudson, her younger sister of 19, comes to Paris to soothe her through the ordeal. Lhermitte, 48 at the time of the filming, played the philandering French uncle of Watts's husband who becomes the lover of Hudson. As a warmup to their first love tryst, Hudson does a strip, down to the sexy black underwear she has bought for the occasion. Gossip had it that Hudson was rude and nasty to Lhermitte during the filming, complaining that he was "too old" for a sex scene with her. So I was interested in his views on American women, considering this close association.

I sent him an emailed request for an interview and almost keeled over when he telephoned me himself the next day. He invited me to come out to the set where he was filming *L'Ex femme de ma vie (The Ex-Wife of my Life)*. The set was way out in one of the desolate Paris suburbs. I got lost a few times before I found it in a dreary building that was almost ramshackle. I watched a couple of scenes until he was free. There was none of the frenetic excitement often apparent on an American set. The whole thing was quiet and relaxed. After a half hour or so he showed me to a private office. He took a chair on the other side of the room, so far away that it all felt strangely disconnected. It made asking intimate questions extremely uncomfortable.

I asked him about the filming *of Le Divorce*. He said he had enjoyed it. And the American actresses? The American actresses were professional, he said. I probed. Had there been any problem with the love scene? None whatever. Period. Well, what did he think of American women now, after that experience, apart from their skill as actresses?

"I like them very much," he said. "They make the best of everything. They have an excellent sense of humor."

I dug around some more, and then gave up. This man was discreet. A gentleman. There was no way I was going to get any sensational quotes. I left him with a sense of his deep respect for his colleagues, no matter what, and a good feeling about the future of American women in France. Whether it was justified or not, I couldn't yet tell, but it was a nice feeling to have.

Pascal Baudry
A French man and an American wife are totally incompatible

Pascal Baudry's English is so perfect one almost takes him for an American. He is tall, natty, charming and passionate as well as professional about Franco-American cultural contrasts. I've often met him at Franco-American gatherings, where he sometimes gives talks that delight everyone. But he is unequivocal about his Franco-American opinion:

"An American woman should not marry a Frenchman," he said in a telephone interview. "The two are totally incompatible."

Baudry has all the credentials for such an opinion. He is an intercultural business executive trainer, a former psychoanalyst and author of a bestseller about Franco-American cultural differences, *France and America, The Other Shore*. His company takes French business executives abroad and exposes them to industrial sites and actual practices. He was married to an American himself. He has just moved back to France after having lived in the U.S. for 15 years.

"The feeling that they might get along is a mirage," he continued. "The American culture is explicit. Americans say what they mean. 'What you see is what you get' is one of their favorite expressions and it's true. They live with facts and act according to them. The French culture is implicit. An American discovers by surprise what a Frenchman means, for much remains concealed. It is hard for Americans to live with this gap between what they say and what they mean, between what the parents say and the reality of what they do, between the form of something and the content. This is true of discourse in general and in particular, of the rituals of politeness... how do they reconcile the most impolite thoughts with making others believe that they are the most polite of people? In marriage, it means that there will probably be exclusivity in the beginning... but later... we'll see about that. It depends... The American husband, on the other hand, while he may be just as unfaithful, does not intend to be, and feels guilty about it if he is. The Frenchman will simply conceal it — for it means nothing."

Somebody should write a song called *It Really Means Nothing*.

Another intercultural difference he made a point about was the "explicit clock" American women run their lives by, including their marriage. He finds it curious that American women look and dress a certain way at certain ages.

"When American women get older, they seem to just let go," he said. "They let their hair go gray, they cease to care for their skin, they dress dowdily. Not all Americans, of course. Not the Duchess of Windsor types. But in general. Whereas a Frenchwoman never lets go of her appearance. She will tint, diet, cream, swim or do tai chi chuan until her dying day, spending more and more time and — of course — money at her hairdresser's. Her wardrobe will not reflect her age. Unlike American women, who seem to stop buying new clothes at around 60 and just go on wearing the ones they bought over the years, the Frenchwoman never stops trying to keep up her appearance.

"There are so many other incompatibilities," he continued. "An American marriage is a partnership; the husband and wife support each other, linked by a contract. They are separate entities. For the French, the boundaries are more fuzzy. There is a sort of cross ownership, each owning a part of the other, which gives them the right to criticize, even ridicule each other. In marriage as well as in the rest of French life, there is no horizontal equality, but verticality. The husband is on top with the power. The French wife plays this game, knowing that, really, subtly, she is superior. The French culture is about who dominates whom, who will have the advantage. American colonists revolted against this vertical mindset when they founded the United States. They must remember this."

4

Interview with Ted Stanger

I couldn't wait to discuss these comments with Ted Stanger, the American who writes in French, author of the runaway bestseller *Sacrés Français,* of *Sacrés Américains* and of a third book recently published, *Sacrés Fonctionnaires.* Until recently he was the head of *Newsweek's* Paris office. He was married to an American and is now married to a Japanese. A Paris resident since 1993, Stanger is the American the French radio and television anchors rush to interview when they need a U.S. slant. I was hoping he would be more upbeat than my Prince Charmings about American women pleasing French husbands. He wasn't.

We talked at length in a Left Bank café near the Pantheon. When I asked him why an American wife might be the worst thing that could happen to a Frenchman, he was as happy as a marine biologist with his favorite fish. But he backed up the Prince Charmings all the way.

"A French man married to an American runs into a firestorm of collateral damage," he said. "It's a snake marrying a bear, no hope of compatibility. It's hard for him even to start a seduction because the American woman wants to know his politics first. Sixty-nine percent of Americans have to be sure a man is politically correct before they'll sleep with him — for French women it's only 10 percent. If you oppose abortion, you have no chance of getting laid in New York. An American shares her body only with a man who shares her contextual universe. A husband must confirm her place in society — in France, a society where she has historically had few rights.

"A French man doesn't give a fig for equal rights. French women don't care either, and certainly won't bore him with talking about politics. A French couple can be married for years without knowing who their spouse voted for. So you can understand that American women are shocked at how out of phase they think Frenchmen are with society. Feminism did not capture the hearts and minds of women here as it did in the States." What other problems might the couple have, I asked him. Ted looked at his watch, as if a good answer might take a few days. French husbands are best avoided entirely by American women, he said. I remembered that in *Sacrés Français*, he wrote that there are two kinds of French men, the romantic and the seducer.

"The romantic falls in love once a week in his twenties, once a month in his thirties and, after 40, once a year," he said. "Later, worn out by life and inevitable failures, his romanticism tones down and he starts worrying about his pension or the possibility of a legacy from a distant great uncle.

"The seducer, on the other hand, faithful to his style, sticks to his established routine. When he speaks to a woman, he stops at nothing. He coos, he provokes, he teases, he is sure of his game. In bed, he is the triumphant male in all his appalling glory... This Don Juan is afraid only of one thing: falling in love. In that case he might become dependent."

As for French women:

"I'm amazed at how French women have adjusted to all the calls that life makes on them," he said. "They juggle fulltime careers, homes, children and still manage some leisure time and energy and charm to be a mistress to their husband. An American woman isn't willing to put up with all this without household input from her husband."

Stanger is stupefied at what he sees French men getting away with. "The principle here is that a man is superior because he's a man. This is intolerable for an American woman. French women have a thousand-year-old priority of pleasing men, so they go along with it."

He feels that this is built into their principle of always building up their man — spoiling him the way his mother did.

"French women are particularly attentive to their men. They adapt themselves marvelously to them. They're superb at encouraging men over 45. They understand that a man of 50 or 60 is not the same as a man of 25. They're adults... they know the difference between sandals and high heels. They're careful about their looks and their grooming, with a clear relationship to their body. It's no accident that France is the country of cosmetics and perfume. French women smell good. Americans tend to smell like candy.

"I don't see many concessions to his wife by the French male, such as listening during the relationship-talks American women like to hold. This can be touchy. Resentment on the part of the woman can build up and spill over into the bedroom. But French couples are better at not feeling resentment, not letting it build up.

"Take infidelity. French men have an outrageous right to be unfaithful. An American woman's principles can't handle it. She will storm out of the house and divorce. A French woman is more practical. She'll say, Okay, you shouldn't have done it. It will cost you plenty but it's not all over."

And with all that, the French wife will still toil away at splendid meals:

"An American wife — with an American husband — gets away with slapdash meals, regardless of the harmony of the couple," he added. "Her kitchen is spotless, but her meals taste like medicine. A French kitchen is perhaps not quite so clean but things generally taste better."

5

French Women Today

Avoir du chien: avoir d'elegance, une tournure dans les manieres, un air de séduction
To have chien: chien means "dog," but to have chien means to be striking and seductive

So Fabrice's riddle was right on: there were problems for American wives of Prince Charmings. Big problems. Since the decks were stacked against them, by what mysterious abracadabra did any of them survive? Because they obviously did. Look at the couples at the gargoyle dinner. They all seemed to be getting along fine. But were they? And how come French women were so radically different?

As Jean-Benoît Nadeau pointed out in *Sixty Million Frenchmen Can't Be Wrong*, Frenchmen are themselves the natives of France. They've been there since their ancestors, the Cro-Magnons, painted the prehistoric caves in southwest France, 30,000 years ago. The past is always with them.

The American women who marry them have not been around for 30,000 years. They're not French. They're not the French women their husbands deep down are expecting at the turn of the road. Who are they, these expected women? The sex kitten (Brigitte Bardot)? The glamorous politician, tough as nails inside (Ségolène Royal)? The steamy, militant feminist author (Simone de Beauvoir)? None of these?

After figuring out why and how French women were different, the next question to answer would be how come French women were so loved, respected and admired by their men. Not that this was much of a surprise. After all, it was the exotism — the *chien* – of French women that was a big reason for all of us American women to be drawn to France in the first place. But I needed to go way back and see how they got that way, what they were like… the face of the competition.

I thought of Laura at her dinner that evening, lovely in her pinkish-beige Chanel, and Fabrice, with his merry eyes. I thought of Kate, the slinky psychologist. It was time to talk to them. I called Kate first. She'd been in France for 20 years and was also married to a Frenchman. As an intellectual, a psychologist and a self-proclaimed authority on Frenchness, she must have given the subject thought.

She invited me to come over for *un verre*, a glass of wine, around 6 pm. I was curious to see how she lived and when I did, I was sorry I had. The apartment was a disaster, dark and gloomy without charm. I guessed Kate was too busy consulting, or else bored with interiors but I wondered at Geoffroy, her husband. French men usually were keen on handsome or at least inviting interiors, and often did them up themselves.

But Kate herself was full of spirit, adorned with jangling bracelets and huge earrings. She had on tight black stovepipe trousers and a maroon velvet jacket piped in black, with silver buttons and several beaded necklaces over a black turtleneck. Nice. Her brightly henna-tinted hair seemed to drown her small face.

I asked her what it was about French women, that just the thought of them could make many Americans feel as if they had two left feet.

"French women? How should I know? I see Americans all day," she said, lounging on a brown leather couch. "Actually that's an excuse I use for the public. Geoffroy doesn't have a sister or female cousins I might cozy up to. And between you and me, I still don't speak French well enough to have a close French friend."

"Maybe you look dangerous," I suggested.

"Or maybe Geoffroy doesn't flirt enough with them to interest the ones we see at dinner parties, so that they'd invite us and give me a chance to get to know them. Or maybe I just didn't happen to meet any who were out of friends for the moment. Americans change cities, drop their old friends, make new ones wherever they are, and move on. It's different here. They don't move around. They already have the one or two friends they want, or a sister… I'm really not the one to explain the most amazing females on the planet."

"Well, give it a try. You have some ideas. You've been watching them."

She got up to get a decanter of red wine and poured us each a glass thoughtfully, before curling up on the couch again. "They have long first names. No pathetic, boring one-syllable Joans or Janes or Ruths, but Gabrielle, Penelope, Anastasia, Alexandra, Emmanuelle, Catherine,

Elizabeth — and *never* shortened to Gabbie, Pennie, Alex, Emmie, Cathie or Betsy... plus the double barreled ones, Marie-Cécile, Marie-Pierre...And then they have a string of other first names too."

"What's your point?"

"Glamour. Sophistication. Confidence." She took a long sip of wine. "And don't forget their *chien*. God, have they got *chien*."

"*Chien*, for sure. How would a pro like you define *chien*?"

"It's something women have to have in France. It's something that makes you go 'oh!' when you meet someone who has it. It's not beauty. It's part allure, part charm, part elegance; not necessarily sexy, but alluring, and striking."

Just then Geoffroy came home. He kissed my hand politely, without the ghost of a smile of welcome, and told Kate he thought she should get dressed for dinner. They were apparently going out. He didn't say it nicely at all. I wondered what he said when I wasn't there.

Kate gave him a queer look and said, "But I am dressed."

Geoffroy pursed his lips. "Ah so?" he said. He turned on his heel and went out.

Kate had just been getting interesting. I tried to get her back on the subject. "Okay, *chien*, d'accord. What else?" I said.

"If you want to know what I think, I think they're steel magnolias. More complicated, with a lot more layers, and less open."

"You mean like our Southern women? What a funny idea."

"Think about it. They're known to be master manipulators and sweet as honey while they're about it. And tough. They had to be. The macho men running this place took women's civil rights away, starting in 1500, and Napoleon put it in writing. How else should they get anywhere? But they did — and turned out to be the strongest, cleverest manipulators of all."

"Scarlett O'Hara!"

"Exactly. She was beautiful, tough, *séduisante*, devious, flirtatious, sexy, hard to get, manipulative, in control without seeming so. She would have had a field day here. And now look at them, with Ségolène Royal — a gorgeous *woman* — running for president, the first woman ever chosen by a major political party — the Socialists — as its candidate. Who says beauty doesn't matter? Woman is just another word for beauty here!"

"You're getting carried away. I can just hear you on the podium."

"Okay, of course it's not that simple. But think about their 300 years of beauty training, the bubble they live in awash with all the gorgeousness luxury can think up. Just taking care of their body — creams, masks, hair removal by wax or creams! Never by razor — then the perfuming, the hair styling and finally putting on the clothes to make that body look just right. Somehow they get the time and the money to do all that regularly. They have it in their *genes*. It's like being born with a talent for drawing."

"This wine is terribly strong," I said. "It must be 14 percent alcohol. Or more. Do you want me to leave here on my hands? Listen, you're not helping me much."

Kate stretched her legs on the couch and lay back. "These women grow up in a culture where pleasure is not only okay but something you take for granted... not like the definition of a Protestant, who is miserable if he hears that someone somewhere is enjoying himself. French women are meant to have pleasure and meant to give it. To please. You can't understand a thing about this country until you've absorbed that."

"Sounds like geishas. Come on, Kate."

"You're beginning to get it. Have you ever noticed how close the French are to the Japanese? Take the Samurai. They were all about honor, the way the French army always has been. They yelled ferociously going into battle, just like the *furia francese*. They believed in doing everything they do to perfection, like French artisans — or like the French baker folding the paper so delicately around a little cake you bought... The Japanese have the same respect for rules of conduct and politeness as the French, the same disinterest in foreigners, the same reverence for art and literature, and as for beauty, does anyone appreciate delicate beauty more than the Japanese? I could go on for hours."

I tried to bring her back to my project. "We were talking about French beauty," I said.

"Well, find a clip of Catherine Deneuve in that television ad for Chanel. Then think about Louis XIV's vision of luxury — forget his architectural and engineering projects for a moment — just think about the luxury. Then about what this means for beauty. Then look at the current crop of dazzling young movie stars, and look at the movies they're in. Movies matter here. Like food. A different kind of food, a different kind of wine."

I left and decided to follow her advice. I found the Chanel clip of Catherine Deneuve. Think of this: Catherine Deneuve at the peak of her world-famous beauty — not that she ever seems to get older — in a flowing dark gown, her long blond hair gently curled, against a totally black backdrop. She turns her inimitable green-gray eyes toward the camera, which dwells on her in such a way as to make you think you're in the same room with her. The camera comes closer as her soft, low, richly timbered voice begins to speak slowly in smooth, only slightly accented English:

"I like the idea of mystery," she says. "I don't like familiarity — it can be a mistake. I like elusive people." Slight pause. "What I really like is... intimacy." Another pause. *You* are part of her intimacy now. "How you create it is a woman's choice and a pleasure. I like Chanel No. 5, the perfume and the spray cologne. This is the pleasure... of being a woman." *Intimacy... The pleasure of being a woman...* a French woman. I don't hear much about the pleasure of being an American woman. So — of course Americans come over here to see what this pleasure is all about.

I was beginning to get Kate's message that Americans planning to poach on the territory of French women better have a good grasp of the context of these women, and to know why "French" and "beauty" seem as inseparable as Siamese twins. To understand how it all started. How it got to where it seems as if the French copyrighted the word "beauty" forever.

Not that there aren't beautiful Italians, Englishwomen, Austrians, Hungarians and yes, of course, Americans, not to mention Asians, South Americans and all the others changing the makeup of French society today. But they aren't backed up by the heavy artillery of L'Oréal, the biggest cosmetic firm in the world; of the fashion designers Karl Lagerfeld and Christian Lacroix and Christian Dior; of the perfumes Chanel No. 5, Opium (Saint Laurent) and Shalimar (Guerlain); of the jewelers Chaumet, Cartier and Boucheron. Nor did they grow up *immersed* in Paris and everything Parisian... where just saying the name of the city trails whiffs of champagne and diamonds and delectable dinners, and those other enigmas, glamour and sophistication.

What are we talking about? The world of luxury that started over 300 years ago in Paris. Paris still reigns over this world of — yes — dreams.

It was one Frenchman, Louis XIV, the Sun King, who created this world of dreams. He did it with vision, passion, talent and energy. Not to mention power. You might also call him the king of pleasure... all the pleasures you can think of, including the one called glory, or achievement. He was that rare phenomenon, a handsome ruling monarch who was a genius. You feel it immediately in Versailles, and can't help falling in love with him, as did all the ladies of his court.

After embellishing his capital with gorgeous buildings, trees, avenues, boulevards, squares, statues, street lamps and bridges, he turned his passion for beauty and style to his women, and the perfection of portable cultural goods: clothes, hairstyles, accessories and jewelry that would enhance their beauty... plus perfume, to mask the lack of hygiene. While he was at it, he concentrated on champagne and cuisine as well. The strategy was to thrill his subjects and turn them into intriguing models of luxurious living that would lure foreigners to his capital, where they in turn would be so thrilled and seduced by these splendors that they couldn't resist buying all the clothes and objects they could stuff in their luggage and take home... to be envied and later bought by other foreigners. The kingdom became a vast whirring workshop, run by the most creative and skillful artisans ever, who invented and turned out objects of such delicate, exquisite workmanship that "French style" and "made in France" came to mean "beautiful."

As for gems, the King was bored with pearls, the accepted jewel of royalty. He wanted something more original — diamonds perhaps? Diamonds weren't particularly prized then. A French merchant set off for India and came back with the 112-carat gem which has come to be known as the Hope Diamond (now in the Smithsonian). Louis paraded it on a ribbon around his neck. The $600 million he spent on diamonds during his reign put this jewel on the map and on the pedestal where it remains today — a glittering, proud token of love and commitment.

Champagne was marketed as the indispensable wine to celebrate that commitment — indispensable, in fact, to any major festivity. It was also on Louis's watch that the café, until then a sort of smoking and beer-drinking men's saloon in other countries, was turned into a decorative place of ambiance and elegance with mirrors and chandeliers, where ladies also loved to meet each other to have a sorbet and see what the other ladies were wearing. This is when chefs and coiffeurs and *couturières* first became celebrities, and the first cookbooks came out with recipes really describing quantities and techniques. You get an idea of how seriously cuisine was now being taken when you consider that Vatel, the maître d'hôtel responsible for organizing an evening for Louis XIV at Chantilly, fell on his sword when the fish didn't arrive on time for the King's dinner.

Louis had another bold stroke up his sleeve: ordering lanterns to light up his city of dreams at night, the first illuminated city in Europe, so that commerce and revelry could continue after dark and into the wee hours. It was an extravagance — all those candles! — that paid off, with Paris becoming known as the City of Light, in addition to the City of Love.

French beauty had arrived. It would be celebrated for the next three centuries in French fashion, painting, architecture, decorative arts, objets d'art, gardens and hair styles.

My old friend R, the book publisher at the gargoyle dinner, was delighted to hear about my book project and happy to be a sounding board. He had a different take on French beauty. We met at the Café des Deux Magots.

"French movies!" he said. "You can't talk about French beauty or French women without the new art form invented by the French movie camera."

Now it was his turn to drill me, passionately.

"The French camera in the 20th century!" he said. "It revealed a different exquisite beauty: that of the faces of French women. French movie directors of the 1950's and 60's such as Roger Vadim did it. They made films starring the women they loved. That was when they created the New Wave. Movies were less structured back then. The directors could be freer with how they used light and shadow and the angle of the camera. It became intimate... a caress..."

R told me about a recent documentary called *French Beauty* by Pascale Lamche, a British film producer.

"You must look at it," he said. "Meanwhile, I took some notes for you." He took out a piece of paper. "Listen to what an American critic says, Kent Jones: 'The beauty of women is an isolated phenomenon in French cinema. When the camera pauses on the face of a French actress, this is an event in itself.' And what about this: Catherine Breillat, a director, says that the director creates how you look at a woman in his film. 'It is an intimate look,' she says, 'an act of love.' An act of love!" enthused R. "Did you hear that?"

R went on:

"Breillat says that actresses are beings composed of light, and the desire and the dream of the movie director."

I thought that Louis XIV would have understood perfectly that today, the French luxury industry and the French tourist industry feed off the fame of the magic of French beauty and France's beautiful actresses; and that France has not only created these beauties, but nourishes them in a special way. Why call it commercial, when it satisfies everyone's soul so completely? Louis would have been pleased with his successors. He himself had used his duchesses to promote French clothes.

R summed it up: "A French woman is beautiful because she considers herself a work of art. She has to be the artist of herself. She can't ignore any detail. When you see her you must have the same rush of recognition that you do for any work of art."

"Heavens. How does she come up with that?"

R gave one of those careless Gallic shrugs. "They grow up in Paris seeing art all around them, so naturally they think of their own exterior as a work of art too — which the men understand, as they also grow up with art all around them. And the women know that the men understand. French men have a trained eye for beauty, therefore for fashion, so women accept being told that their trousers have the wrong cut or their shoulders are too padded for this year. In fact, they revel in the critical eye of their men!"

I wondered at this, while R paused to give a long appreciative look at one of the waitresses passing by. "And of course there is the mother," he added. "Go watch girls playing in the park and see how perfectly their jeans fit, how perfectly their pony tail is fastened, their little ears already pierced, and how they move their hips."

It was very interesting but I was beginning to feel suffocated by all this female beauty talk. What about the instructions for life we Americans were given? "Character is what counts," my father repeated all my childhood. "Beauty is only skin deep; it's what's underneath that is important. We're not here in this world for our pleasure, but to make it a better place."

I sighed and tried to think along French lines. I asked R how foreigners could get to know these French paragons of light and desire.

"By going to school with them," he laughed. Then he added, "French women are hard to get to know, for foreigners. The best place to find out about them is in French movies. They — what is that expression of yours? They tell it like it is."

6

Frenchness in French Movies

The French love movies. They go to them more than any other nation. They'll queue up for an hour in the rain for one they want to see. Later they spend hours discussing it, analyzing it, comparing it. In other words, they care about movies — French movies. They're a dream public for the film industry. The movies the French like the best are about panache, wit or séduction, otherwise known as love, or all three, with lots of dialogue and no violence, while American movies, said to be made principally for teenage boys these days, have lots of violence and practically no dialogue.

Movie stars are part of the landscape of Paris life. You run into them walking down the street or at the next table in your favorite restaurant, or you see them onstage between films. Mainstream magazines obligingly keep us up to date on their latest escapades and tragedies. *Paris Match* spread five pages on the 2006 funeral of Gérard Oury, the writer-director of 60's and 70's hits starring Bourvil and Louis de Funès, France's favorite comedy team. When actor Philippe Noiret died (November 2006), his photograph was in color on the front pages of all the dailies the next day, some taking up the whole cover. At least 10 pages of *Paris Match*, week after week, in 2001 were devoted to the stroke crippling one of the most beloved of actors, Jean-Paul Belmondo, affectionately known as Bébel. His stroke hit the French as if it had happened in their own family.

R suggested I see three movies about young women and their future husbands. The heroines in all three seem soft as well as beautiful. Not cold or aggressive but tender, vulnerable. The roles they play show their clever, flinty sides as well. At first they seem disinterested in their admirer.

His mating dance, with much flapping of wings, takes a long time to get a reaction. The heroines' sense of stillness and sweetness seems immutable. You can't imagine them raising their voices, much less shouting. But watch out. French women are the best screamers of all, if they feel betrayed or slighted by a lover, or if someone has cheated them at the office. In France, it's a woman's good right to scream — or cry, for that matter — if she has a reason. I was told several times while researching this book that one of the things French men miss in American women is exactly that. They much prefer passionate emotional tirades to cold Puritanical restraint. It may seem to be an odd form of seduction, but it's emotional, involving and inclusive, rather than denying and exclusive.

Let's take a closer look at their roles.

1. Written as a play in 1834 and slicked up for a modern audience into a merry, fast-paced movie in 2005, *Il ne faut jurer de rien (You shouldn't swear to anything)* gives Melanie Doutey, as Cécile, the heroine, the role of resisting and finally ensnaring Valentin, played by the devastating heart-throb, Jean Dujardin, who has the best smile on the European side of the pond. Valentin is a sworn bachelor and a disillusioned, licentious philanderer like the play's author, Alfred de Musset, who spent much of his time in brothels. Valentin's uncle, a fabric merchant with social ambitions, presses him to marry Cécile, the only daughter of a baroness with a big château. The baroness, a cash-poor widow, has bartered her daughter for free access to the uncle's textiles. Valentin, deeply in debt but loath to the idea of marriage and certain of his charm, agrees, on the condition that if Cécile succumbs to his advances during the courtship, the wedding is off and the uncle must pay him 10,000 francs. Valentin has just 30 hours to seduce this young woman, whom he discovers to be a beauty and a gem of innocence. He looks forward with glee and overbearing confidence to this pleasant task. He has not taken into account the wiles, skills, grit and steely resolve of Cécile.

Faking a carriage accident near her château and passing himself off as a Habsburg prince, he puts his charm and ingenuity into his attempts at embracing her. Cécile puts hers into resisting him. Whenever he makes a pass, she manages to avoid it, feigning not to notice, or rebuffing it pertly. Then she dazzles him with more charm until the next pass. She doesn't hesitate to show her skill at fencing and shooting. Way ahead of her time à la George Sand, she smokes a cigarillo and wears a pants suit and top hat to the local fair. Valentin begins to succumb to her spell, but up until the last minute, he is decided to deflower her ruthlessly and cash in on his wager with his uncle. He tricks her into coming to a party in a brothel.

At the brothel, Cécile ensnares him in his own trap. She tells him that he is acting absurdly, that she loves him and he loves her, what is he waiting for? Valentin caves in. He falls in love with her, overcomes his aversion to marriage, and the movie waltzes to a happy end at a ball at the château, with everyone celebrating, including the Madam and the easy ladies of her brothel.

2. Valentine, Sophie Marceau's character in *L'Etudiante (The Student)* is in the midst of excruciating studies for one of France's toughest graduate degrees, known as an *agrégation*, or *agreg*. Edouard, the hero (Vincent Lindon) is studying music composition at the Conservatoire. He plays the piano in a rock band to pay the rent for his studio. Valentine's beauty stirs him when they share a skilift by accident. Spotting her later in a Paris Métro station, he tracks her into a subway car. She rolls her eyes in disdain. He is persistent, determined to see her again. Most women can't resist at least inspecting such an admirer. Finally she agrees to meet him for dinner at his usual restaurant, a crowded student hangout. Arriving before him, she is careful to hide in *les toilettes* until a few minutes after he shows up.

Edouard and Valentine fall in love. Valentine's pre-exam studies suffer, which makes her irritable. After she moves into Edouard's studio, she pushes the wrong button on his answering machine and hears him talking with his friend Charley, recorded by mistake, complaining about her nervousness and single-minded ambition. She explodes. She takes a taxi to the ballroom where he's playing the piano on live television. She storms into the ballroom, screams insults at him, throws the studio keys at the piano and storms out. Then she refuses to see anyone for five days, until after the exam. Edouard, more passionate than ever since her tantrum, tracks her down to the library at the Sorbonne, minutes before she is to go before the panel of judges waiting to examine her. He rages at her about her vile character and about how much he loves her. Valentine manages to keep her cool and passes the exam. The lovers are reunited.

3. No one could seem softer and more demure and fragile than Judith Godrèche as Mathilde, a young noblewoman during the reign of Louis XVI, in the luscious, malicious film, *Ridicule*. Mathilde is under the thumb of her father to the point of being engaged to a decrepit old aristocrat in

order to pay off her father's debts. She seems to be rather demure and colorless, until we see her in a diver's suit experimenting with how long she can be underwater in a well. As it turns out she's studying hydrostatics.

Enter Grégoire (Charles Berling), a poor young landowner of the minor nobility from Les Dombes in the provinces. Grégoire has galloped 400 miles north to Versailles to beg for help from the king's ministers in draining his mosquito-infested swamps. His project falls on deaf ministerial ears. Grégoire understands that the King himself is his last hope, and that his only path to him is by way of the bed of the dangerously voluptuous court intriguer, the Comtesse de Blayac, played by Fanny Ardant at her steamiest. His heart belongs to Mathilde, and Mathilde, still engaged, is giving him clear signals; but Grégoire, with nothing to offer her, is too honest to respond. He decides to go back home to Les Dombes for a visit to think things over. As he's saddling his horse to leave, Mathilde takes matters into her own hands. She throws her arms around Grégoire and kisses him ardently. Nevertheless, he gallops off. Without telling him, Mathilde breaks her engagement while he's gone. Blayac gets to him first when he's back, but Mathilde, overlooking his Blayac dalliance as swamp duty, goes back with him to live in Les Dombes.

The lesson Americans were to take home from these three, I guessed, was that old-fashioned softness and wiles were still very much à la mode for girls in France today, but that a girl's repertoire also included 21st century brashness, should the situation absolutely call for it.

And after the wedding bells? What were French marriages like in real life? Were French wives really as broad-minded as Mathilde in *Ridicule*, who understood that Grégoire's nocturnal assignations with Comtesse Blayac had nothing to do with his heart?

I asked R about this.

"The answers are as varied as sands on the beach," he said. "But there are general lines. Have a look at another film, *Tout pour plaire (Everything to please)*; it's all there."

This film, cool and speed-paced, is about three elegant, bourgeoise Parisians in their mid-thirties: Juliette (Mathilde Seigner), a prickly single lawyer with a lively wit, who likes to sound tough about men and use coarse language, and her two friends who have both been married for 15 years: Florence, a graphic designer, and Marie, a doctor. The friends meet regularly shopping for clothes in upmarket shops and having expensive health and beauty treatments: sauna, swimming, manicures, depilations, sometimes lunching on vegetables and oysters.

Marie (Judith Godrèche, whom we saw in *Ridicule*) has a delicious marriage to Pierre, an artist. When, despite the Pill, she discovers that she's pregnant, she flips at the thought of the added exhaustion and expense of another child, as, along with her medical practice, she pays all the bills and does everything for their two children and the household. Pierre, who doesn't sell his paintings, adds nothing to the till and doesn't see the problem. At a party, Marie flirts with Xavier, a film director. She takes a walk with him on the beach, but later, after one kiss in his beach house, says this isn't what she wants and goes home to Pierre. She lies to Pierre that there was no kiss. Pierre, mollified, finally sees the problem with the pregnancy, promises to help her more and sell his paintings.

Florence (Anne Parillaud) is long-suffering with her tyrannical boss, Caligula; her uncommunicative, workaholic husband, Julien; and her dour son, Ludovic. Caligula finally gives her a project. When he takes it away, she quits her job and throws a fit at Caligula, though he has meanwhile decided to give her back the project.

The three friends have this discussion about the lost project:

"Who did he give the project to?" Juliette asks.

"Someone else at the office," says Florence.

"He's sleeping with her, of course," says Juliette.

"Oh, no — he's married."

"Then you can be sure he's sleeping with her," says Juliette.

"You mean you think all married men sleep around?"

"Yes, except ones who have a real reason not to, such as being a tetraplegic or in a deep coma. As long as they don't leave their wives, they think they're being faithful."

Florence discovers that indeed, Julien, her own husband, has a mistress. This triggers another fit. Florence leaves him in a fury, taking Ludovic, though Julien protests that he loves her, begs her to stay and wants to take her on a trip to Spain. He says he has worked so hard in order to keep up their standard of living; and that he has a mistress to forget her coldness to him.

Juliette, unmarried and jilted, takes a book to the sandbox in a park, advised that this is the best hunting ground for an unattached divorcé. She meets Benoît, there with his little boy. Over a glass of wine at a café, Benoît, attractive and charming, tells her he has been divorced for three years and has no plans to marry again, since he has nothing but suffering to show for his 15 years of daily marital devotion. He's through with suffering.

"Women demand a lot these days," he says. "And they reproach us for everything."

Juliette ignores this signal and falls in love. The romance ends in a kingsize bed at a splendid château-hotel in the country. They're both still more or less blissfully asleep in each other's arms, when Benoît's cell phone rings. He makes plans for the following Wednesday without checking with Juliette. Juliette, now wide awake, finds that unacceptable.

Benoît is confused. "Why? What's the matter? We're not married, as far as I know…"

"No, but…" says Juliette.

"But, what?" says Benoît. "That's the whole point. That's why we've been having such a good time — we see each other, we talk, we screw — and it's great because we're not in love."

"Oh? I didn't know we were so cool. In other words, all this doesn't mean a thing to you?"

"I didn't say that!"

"*Tu ne m'aimes pas?*" (You don't love me?)

"*Mais si, je t'aime beaucoup!*" (But yes, I like you a lot!)

"*Beaucoup! Tu m'aimes beaucoup!*" Juliette jumps out of bed, furious. "That's for domesticated animals, cats and dogs! You f— me three times a week for weeks and weeks and are nice to me — that means to me that you're in love!"

Benoît points out that he has always been clear. "It's you who imagine things," Benoît sighs. "So now it begins, the infernal cycle of reproaches."

Juliette, dressed and packed, slams the door and leaves the hotel in a rage.

I arranged to meet R in a café after I'd seen the movies. Waiting for him I thought about the mystery and magic of the French language. Juliette's castle in the air had been blown away by a single word: *beaucoup*. It usually meant more of something; when added to *aimer*, it denied the poetry and the passion of love. The phrase became simply a friendly "I like you." Love in France reigned supreme, alone. It was the sun of words. It was or it wasn't, but no qualifiers were allowed. *"Je t'aime,"* was the ultimate gift.

R arrived in a rush, his hair and bushy eyebrows a bit disheveled.

"Exasperating author? Deadlines overrun?" I asked.

"It's novel-prize time — you know, the Goncourt season, everyone on edge," he said. He smoothed his eyebrows and ordered a glass of wine.

"First of all," I said, "I always heard that French women weren't friends, just rivals, never did things together and never talked about anything personal with each other, just politics and more politics. However, in *Tout pour plaire*, they meet all the time and discuss their love problems and everything else."

R laughed. "Yes, in fact Mathilde Seigner gave an interview saying she was worried about the scenario when she first saw it, that she and the two other actresses would be having jealousy scenes. Nothing of the sort happened, but I don't think these kinds of friendships are very common yet, here. Women are more likely to meet in some kind of association connected with their careers... editors in a literary circle, for instance. But it is indeed another sign of change... or *rupture*, in Sarkozy-talk. For younger women, times are really changing. If they're married, they can make enough money to jump ship and these days, there's no stigma if they do. They've always been free to lose their tempers, but formerly they couldn't afford to lose their husbands. They were stuck."

"In other words," I pursued, "French wives run to the divorce court if they find out their husband is unfaithful — just like Americans."

R shook his head violently. "No, not the same at all! Most would melt after a pleading like Julien's. Look how long it took Ségolène Royal to boot out François Hollande. They'd been together as if married for 30 years and had four children together. But it took years, a presidential campaign and the media trumpeting Hollande's new love from the housetops before she threw him out. What is new in the film is Florence dumping a solid and seemingly devoted husband and father, a good wage earner who still loves her, without any obvious dreadful vices like alcohol or gambling, and without another man waiting for her in the wings."

"What about Juliette?"

"Also a new idea. Formerly, she would have stuck to Benoît and waited around, hoping, for commitment. But Juliette is right. Men aren't so keen on commitment nowadays. She might have waited around forever."

7

La séduction

It was time to call Laura. Gorgeous Laura, with her graceful, elegant husband, had simply smiled mysteriously when Fabrice brought up his riddle.

Laura would have plenty to say about French men and how American women could make them happy. I had the naïve Lizzie much on my mind, the more I thought about her and her attractive Alsatian, home where everyone knew his secret name after years abroad, and about the comments of my Prince Charmings. Thierry must be deliriously happy to be back.

Laura invited me to their apartment for tea. I nodded to the gargoyles and thought they looked less mischievous today.

She told me that she and Fabrice had first met on the water — Laura was superstitious about that, it meant permanence, she said — when she was taking sailing lessons in Brittany. She'd come to France for the Civilization course at the Sorbonne. Fabrice was a summer instructor between his semesters at the Ecole Polytechnique.

"It all boils down to one sentence," she said. "Put the men first, way in front of the children. And do whatever they want."

"But Laura..." I was shocked. "That's impossible for American women."

"Well, it's part of the deal. They can like it or lump it. They'll never have the French touch... they'll never be as pretty and exquisite as Madame de Pompadour, they'll never be a sexy intellectual like Ninon de Lenclos or a gorgeous wit like Madame de Montespan, so they might as well face it that French women today descend from them, and that many have the allure of all of these sirens at once. So the Americans must do what they can, which is whatever their husband wants. And try to be as much like those women as possible."

"Come on, Laura. You're selling American women short. They can be just as brilliant and sexy and exquisite as anyone. Well, maybe not always exquisite. But your ghosts of the past, for heaven's sake, you can't be serious."

"Glorious ghosts. There's nothing more important for Americans to bone up on, if they want to survive a French marriage. Think about it. What are they getting in exchange? What makes Paris different? People blather on about the quality of life and the beauty of old stones, but it's love that it's all about. It's where men talk about love, and make love. Poetically. Tenderly, and vigorously. In Paris you trip over lovers on the bridges, on the park benches, even on the bus. Love is the French national passion, along with soccer. It's in the magazines and movies and books as well as on the street."

She got up and brought me a framed photo of Fabrice.

"Look at those dancing eyes. A wife needs to keep those eyes dancing. Whatever it takes. I really do think that there should be a law that before an American marries a Frenchman and produces French children, she has to pass an exam in the history of French women. How for the last 300 years they have bamboozled rough and tough macho men into a rigorous finishing school and polished them like priceless gems before, finally, they surrender. I was lucky. I had taken that Civilization course and was pretty prepared for all this before I met Fabrice... surrendering, by the way, doesn't mean being vanquished, far from it. It has always meant complicity. It's a delicate meshing of men who are both macho and sensitive, trained to be that way by strong women, and women who don't let their toughness show so that it gets in the way of bliss. So that men always want women around — a French man, alone in public? Not unless he is racing to a train for a country weekend, where there will be lots of women — and the women feel better when they're together."

I had to admit it was true that among the big surprises that hit foreigners in Paris between the eyes was men and women mixing everywhere. Barbara Leonard, an American software writer who has lived in France for 14 years, told me that she is always amazed that her French companion wants to do everything with her. They met at a cycling club. "It was a passion for both of us," she said, "and everywhere we went we took our bicycles. Now I have a health problem that prevents me from doing all the cycling, so he has pretty much given it up too. He wants to be with me."

I talked this over with R.

"Laura is right," he said. "France is different. Where else are women not excluded from male activities? Like everything else, it started with Louis XIV. His two great passions, besides building and hunting, were women and war, so he took his harem to the battle front with him – his Queen, his ex-mistress, Louise de La Vallière, and his present mistress, Athénaïs de Montespan. All in the same carriage and no comfort stops on the way. Just think of the misery of those poor women as the carriage rattled over the ruts..."

R also thought that American fiancées of Frenchmen should have to pass an exam in French history.

"Ridiculous," I said, groaning inside at what I thought he was getting at. "I guess what you and Laura are really saying is that I should put Laura's glorious ghosts in this book I'm working on. But just mention the word 'history' and people fall asleep. So how do I keep them awake?"

"Easy. You simply start with the scandals. For instance, the aphrodisiacs Madame de Montespan used to lure the Sun King back to her bed. It was a mixture of the dust of desiccated moles, the blood of bats and the spittle of toads — and it worked. But — it gave Louis XIV a terrible headache. When he found out what she'd done he was so furious he almost sent her to the Bastille. As for the number of inconvenient rivals poisoned by various members of his court — don't you think American women would be interested in this? Of course, you must get passionate about the French past yourself."

"That's what worries me! Research! Time!"

R went on, "And you must know — feel in your gut! — that history is you — and me — history is relevant! Why do you think the French game of seduction is so irresistible? Because of three centuries of *salonnières*. Brilliant women, CEO's, really, the way they organized their daily receptions and dinners, and what people talked about and how they talked... They schooled French men in the rules and arts of love and their ornaments: the fine points of etiquette, *courtoisie*, style and fashion, the aesthetics of gastronomy... oh don't get me started on the *salonnières*! Extraordinary women!"

I didn't dream of getting him started on *salonnières*, about whom my grip was extremely shaky. I opted instead for *séduction*, one of R's favorite subjects. It was the first chance I'd had to really get him going on it. Alas, he said he had no time and had to rush back to the Goncourt excitement. But he grinned and gave me a great paragraph before he ran off:

"*Séduction* here is a game where both parties are winners, but only if they know the rules. Hence the difference of the French word *séduction* from the English: it simply means to please, no unpleasant undertones of trickery. After amour, it is the most compelling word in the language. Look at the ads — the word seduce is used for everything from vacuum cleaners to beauty creams.

"Have you seen the new television ad showing a handsome, elegant couple, sitting at a table playing chess? From time to time between moves they look soulfully at each other. A swooning aria from *Tosca* is sung quietly in the background. Camera zooms to a huge red mouth and then back to the chess table. What is this ad about? Opera? Philosophy? Chess, maybe? No. Nail polish. But you sell it with love. *Séduction!*"

He gave my arm a little squeeze. "We French men enjoy the dance of seduction. If it doesn't lead to the bedroom we just shrug it off, but still enjoy the dance."

There was no doubt, I thought, that everyday exchanges between French men and women, often strangers who would never meet again, had the fizz of seduction. Flirting French meant acknowledging the opposite sex in a nuanced, tender way – no leers! — whether it was the grocer, the post office clerk or the concierge. They did as much business as possible, whether in a bank or at a market, with the opposite sex. They thought it spiced the routine transactions of life and made everything more fun. Often there was no business involved at all, but the sudden awareness of intense appreciation in an all-enveloping Look. It happened to me on the Pont de la Concorde. I was on my rusty old bicycle, pedaling as fast as I could, when I noticed a shiny Lexus convertible with the top down in the next lane, going slowly. A tanned Richard Gere without the gray hair gave me a long, devastating Look. "Madame," he said, caressingly, "what a beautiful bicycle."

My daughter-in-law, Emmanuelle Dalyac, still feels dazed and dreamy remembering an encounter years ago on the Boulevard Saint Michel, when she was 18. "He was good looking, a bit older, maybe 30," she said. "He was walking towards me. Suddenly he stopped in front of me, covering me with appreciation from tip to toe and said, '*Mademoiselle, si vous dites un mot, je vous épouserai.*' (Mademoiselle, if you say just one word, I will marry you.)"

It was a neighbor she had passed on the street several times who finally stopped Joan Morgan in the local FNAC . She didn't know him, but of him – that he was married and that he was noted for his womanizing as for the films he'd directed. "Where have we met?" he asked her, with the full bedroom-eyes Look that said clearly, "Was it my place or yours?"

"Don't worry," said Joan, an old hand at French teasing. "Nothing happened."

"Did he drop the ball? Of course not," she said, telling me about it. "He bowed and said, 'The honor would have been all mine.'"

Sometimes it can get a little uncomfortable, if it's too close to home, but still it can give a fizz to the day. Alison, a friend of mine, told me about this exchange:

"There's a very nice couple on the ground floor in our building. He's a former minister, now semi-retired, as he told me. He's attractive, though too bourge for my taste (wears a loden coat, among other things), is always very nice to me, as is his wife. We ran into each other at the door this morning, began to natter, about age. He said it sometimes happens that he comes on to a woman who is 30, because he still feels like he did at 30.

"Translation: I cheat on my wife, like all Frenchmen.

"I didn't flinch, so he went on to say that he's 67, and that 67, to a 20-year old, is an old man.

"Translation: I'm announcing my age, you must admit I don't look a day over 50. — True, but still not my style.

"I said, regretting the words the moment they were out of my mouth, but in the habit of flattering men when you can, just because I like men, 'Oh, vous savez, cela depend des femmes.'

"Translation in his mind: Why doncha come on up and see me some time?

"I am sure he will appear at my door one day, on some pretext, probably wearing only his loden coat. Oh dear!"

Don't discount the supermarket for the day's lift. Polly Lyman, a divorcée who moved to Paris two years ago, emailed me about one of these encounters:

At the Carrefour supermarket at Auteuil, in the checkout lane for home delivery, in front of me was a tall handsome man, clearly just back from vacation. He was wearing Bermudas and topsiders, a polo shirt and a great tan. Tousled hair. I was trying to check out his domestic status by analyzing what he was buying. We were jostling and bumping a bit because of bulky items in our respective carts. Anyway, I did notice a wedding ring on his finger, so he was off-limits. However, when it was my turn to go to the delivery desk, they said, "What else can we do for you, Madame? Vous êtes avec le monsieur, n'est-ce pas?" (You are with Monsieur, no doubt?) I replied in my best stage sigh and engaging smile, "Non, hélas!"

Mr. Tousled Hair was flattered and amused, and gave me a complicitous nod as he headed out the door.

It was a great little moment of connecting. (I would NEVER have done that in puritanical New England, especially not as a divorced woman). I guess part of it is that in France it feels as though it's your duty to show appreciation of beauty or something pleasing.

These exchanges create a sort of magnetic tension between people. The door is wide open for the next step, which probably doesn't happen, but in any case, everyone's spirits soar."

Alice-Gray Gregory, a pretty blonde now back home in Charleston, S.C., after a couple of years in Paris, told me that The Look is what she misses most in the U.S. "Of course, in France, if you're lucky enough to be on the receiving end of a Look, you never smile or start a conversation, but that acknowledgment, that unspoken way of saying, 'I admire the way you look and carry yourself,' can leave you floating on air the rest of the day. It's a way of really noticing the people around you, of being aware of who they are. It's rarely practiced in the U.S. And without that, life is surprisingly diminished."

R had added this sentence as he was leaving: "We like seduction best when there is love. There was a brief period in the 1960's and 1970's when the sudden surfacing of the Pill made sex the rage and downgraded love. Ah, but love is back now, with a vengeance!"

In time you realize that this really is the country of Love; that Love, every aspect of it, is in the air the French breathe. They marinate in an erotic bath of it all day — and night. They never tire of talking, reading, and writing about it, anymore than they tire of dining, its close relative. It affects visiting foreigners. On the Métro I overheard a young American man trying to kiss a resisting American girl. "But it's okay to kiss here, Rosie," he said, "the French expect us to." After a while it gets to you. It's like the surf of the sea, always foaming, its waves sometimes breaking over the whole country, such as is happening right now, as I write — and it's not even Valentine's Day. Jewelers, parfumeurs, fashion designers, artists, writers, film producers have taken up the theme of amour. Chanel is featuring a handbag covered with hearts. One of Sonia Rykiel's latest fashion shows features dresses with **LM** (pronounced like *elle aime*, she loves) in big letters across the front. Dior has a brooch of rubies in the shape of a heart with a Cupid's bow of diamonds piercing it. The Palais Benedictine in Fécamp (Normandy) was showing 20 paintings of the late artist Niki de Saint Phalle for an exhibition about love called *"Vive L'Amour!"* ("Long Live Love!") A recent popular movie in France also making waves in the U.S. is a collection of 18 scenes of love in Paris, shot by 18 different French directors, called *Paris, je t'aime*. At the Parc de La Villette, a huge complex at the northern edge of Paris, including a science museum, a music auditorium, an outdoor cinema, gardens and workshops, the city of Paris was running an exhibition called, *"L'Amour, comment ça va?"* ("Love, How Are You?"). This is an excerpt from the exhibition's catalogue:

> *Desire's discreet relative, Love, makes it possible to live together differently, as well as to seek out and build social relations and environments which allow everyone their living space... Although Love is a shared dream of desire, and a form of suffering, it is also an energy that weaves and creates.*

Paris's preoccupation with Amour doesn't stop at La Villette. Posters all over the city show the Eiffel Tower silhouetted against what looks like a full moon, with the caption *"Paris protège l'amour"* (Paris Protects Love). In small print it gives the telephone number for information about AIDS. The moon in fact represents a condom.

The rest of France is just as delighted with Love and seduction as the capital. Last week in the Dordogne village of Eymet (population 4,000), the little library's fourth annual Poetry Evening was organized by its delightful librarian, Marie-Christine Raymond. I wouldn't have missed it for the world. About 29 people, 22 women and seven men, all local, sat in a circle and listened to poetry readings by several of the other participants. The poems were all about — guess what! — love. Everyone was French, except me. Monsieur Jacques Sauvaget, a retired carpenter, read a poem by Baudelaire. A young hairdresser with a baby in a sling around her neck read a poem by Verlaine. A schoolteacher read one of the songs by the great troubadour of the Middle Ages, Bernard de Ventadour, *J'ai tant d'amour au coeur* (I have so much love in my heart).

Don't think for a moment that the magazines and Sunday supplements are being left out of this tidal wave of love. Never have there been so many articles about happy and unhappy couples, happy and unhappy families, and mostly not very happy singles and — dependable lure for female readers for hundreds of years — how to attract and keep the right man in your life, or how to rev up your partner's flagging passion... in other words, the art of seducing the French male.

It takes a while to find out that life in France is in fact based on the French concept of seduction. Not just social life, but all communication with other people, that is, with both sexes, your own and the other.

"If you don't make an effort to be *séduisant* (seductive) with the man or woman you're talking to, you're insulting them," said Danielle, an advertising account executive. "You're expected to do your best to please them by your appearance, your behavior and your choice of language. This is why, if you've made the effort to dress nicely, you get better service when you go out to shop or dine."

"Frenchmen aren't afraid of love," said Dara Teste, who grew up in Connecticut and now, divorced from a Frenchman, sells antique books. "People put love on a high pedestal here. Men don't hesitate to talk of love among themselves — and not in a dirty way. They're at home with their sensitive side. They can wear pink shirts and can carry around a portfolio full of drawings without anyone turning a hair. Even SNCF train conductors wear designer uniforms, the latest by Christian Lacroix. In the U.S. you get the impression that for most men, the model is still the exclusively masculine Marlboro Man — but that they don't dare admit it with women, and so they're confused about how to be with them."

"French boys are a million times sexier than American boys," said Diana Holmes, a former model with the perfect measurements and, it seems, the perfect French husband. "Probably the French are the sexiest of all. The way they look at you. The way they treat you. American men are more, well, respectful. French men are more carnal — and more human."

Mary Ellen was dreamy-eyed when she told me, "He always gives me a foot massage before we make love. You have no idea... And he never talks about 'having sex.' French men don't 'have sex.' They make love."

"Latins in general and Frenchmen in particular do cartwheels around Americans in bed," said Sophie. "The whole thing has to do with whether they give pleasure to the woman or not."

Priscilla was poetic. "I love the maleness of men, French men. Their wide shoulders, their deep voice, their beard, their Adam's apple, their sex: that all this is part of a man who is interested in love, who isn't afraid of women, who can make love and, most amazing, talk about love... a man who reveals me to myself... and allows me to deepen his existence as male..."

Shelby Marcus-Ocana, a glamorous academic administrator, is divorced from a Frenchman. She has reflected deeply on the subject of "the French lover." Herewith her views:

There is a plethora of myths circulating in regards to the amorous talents of Frenchmen. "The French Lover" is seen as a redundancy, and many of my female compatriots will attest to the pants-dropping effect of English spoken with a strong French accent. I've been pondering this idée reçue lately, trying to put a finger on what exactly makes the Frenchman so, um, bedable.

Shelby continues:
Caveat: what follows are gross generalizations unique to me. While not a sexual ethnologist, I have done a fair amount of hands-on, empirical research in this field. I do not consider myself an expert and am still in the data-collection stage of my research.

Seductive Tool No. 1:
I think I'm handsome; so should you

To us American women, the average Frenchman is just that: physically average. Observe the French actors who are continually cast in heart-throb roles: Gérard Depardieu, Vincent Lindon, Jean-Paul Belmondo, Daniel Auteuil. None of these men possess the physical attributes of say, a Brad Pitt or George Clooney, yet all three of them have bedded some of the most beautiful women in France, both on-screen and off. How did they do it? Sheer confidence. There is nothing more seductive than a man who thinks he is worthy of your attentions.

Even if he is 5'5"
Self-image is a reflection of France itself. You've got a small country the size of the state of Texas here, yet it is one notch down from the United States in terms of international relations, with a permanent seat on the United Nations Security Council. Just as France revels in its self-importance — President Chirac once proclaimed France "a beacon for the human race."

Seductive Tool No. 2:
You are the most beautiful woman in the world

Frenchmen do not hesitate to tell you how beautiful you are. It is not necessarily used as a pick-up line; it can be a mere observation proffered as fact. Once I was riding the Métro, daydreaming and minding my own business. The train arrived at my destination; as I rose to exit the car, the very normal-looking, neither swarthy nor lascivious man across from me spoke up: "Mademoiselle," he said, "Je voulais vous dire que vous êtes ravissante." (Miss, I wanted to tell you you are ravishing.) There was no subtext to his statement, he was merely sharing his observation. Whether it is true or not, I cannot confirm. But the unencumbered freedom with which the Frenchman shares his thoughts about how he perceives you is powerful stuff.

Seductive Tool No. 3:
The actual act

Frenchmen love to make love. As often as possible.

Cordelia confirms Shelby's *"Seductive Tool No. 1"*.

"There is nothing like the intensity of a determined Frenchman when he's seen a woman who pleases him, if he is an experienced seducer," said Cordelia. "I'm a happily married woman with no interest in cheating on my husband, but one time when he was away and I was invited to a dinner in Paris without him, one of the other guests began hypnotizing me before dinner. He wasn't particularly good looking, but he had long eyelashes and sensitive lips. He was placed next to me at dinner and kept it up all through dinner, talking first about inane things like turning grape juice into wine... and then somehow he got on the subject of Flaubert and Madame Bovary, and how Napoleon had seduced Marie Walenska and how Madame Récamier had succumbed to Chateaubriand... I can't explain it, but he wove a sort of spell... I had to think up some excuse and run home to safety right after dinner. I had a hard time getting to sleep. He had somehow wormed his way into my soul."

So, what are these French men like that love women — and have been shaped by them? How can an adventurous American girl get to know them?

You arrive in France on a blisteringly hot July day, and on the streets of central Paris, the men are wearing suits. Dark suits. An American from New York is confused to find himself the only man in Paris wearing a pale blue seersucker suit. No tee shirts to be seen, except on tourists. You soon realize that these men on the street look different from what you're used to. A surprising number of them are handsome in a smooth, virile Sean-Connery sort of way. Think of the flamboyant new president, Nicolas Sarkozy, and François Fillon, the prime minister; or think Dominique de Villepin, the former prime minister, a tall macho power type and a poet, with full, sensitive lips and a mop of casually messy, voluptuously wavy, graying hair. For the under-35's, two- or three-day beards are still in, but we're talking here about the over-35's. These men are elegant and groomed, they've been through grueling schooling, with bright eyes to show for it. They're tall (except for Sarkozy) and confident, as befits the heirs to a culture that has contributed decisively to civilization's art, science and technology, not to mention style… and the art of love.

After a few days you're struck by the courtesy of Frenchmen… strangers you've never met, even boys of 15. They hold doors open for you, if you're a woman. They talk quietly in buses and on the Métro, and offer you their seat, if you look as if you need it, or even if you don't. The other day, a bomb scare at the Montparnasse train station blocked off the usual taxi area so that I had to go out in the street to hail one. Chaos. I was giving up hope when a man who did manage to get one offered me his.

At the open market on Saturday or Sunday, particularly the organic one on the boulevard Raspail, you see them buying vegetables and fruit, usually with a woman companion. It's the men who choose the best leeks and pears, and balance a melon from hand to hand, just like Gérard Depardieu in *Green Card*, when he shows Andie MacDowell how to go marketing.

French men will tell you that good food and good love go together. I guess you've heard about the great French chefs. They're nearly all men.

If you're undaunted by the comments of my Prince Charmings, and are curious about meeting one of these poetic *gallants*, it's perfectly possible — almost anywhere but in the elevator of the Eiffel Tower. The best is if you have a friend who can take you to a party. The next best thing to do is to pick a café in a business district and go there regularly. But almost any other place in Paris has possibilities. Waiting in line for an opera ticket, browsing in a (French) bookstore or at an art gallery opening, marching in street demonstrations (*manifs*), doing whatever it is you like to do. Matchmaking sites on the Internet are popular — 15 million French people are said to use them — but chancy. Tales abound about the frauds and pranksters. (The most popular is Meetic.com.)

Or, why not at the shore? "I met my husband on the beach," said Rosanne. "A handsome *ingénieur* with curly dark hair and dimples. It was at Arcachon, near Bordeaux. I was hunting around in the sand for a ring I'd lost. I found it — but as I'd noticed him watching me, I kept on looking for it until he came over and asked if he could help. Bingo. We were married a year later."

The pleasantest way to meet someone is through complicity — joining a group that shares your zest for choral singing or squash or scrabble or birdwatching, whatever.

The surest way is to get a dog. This could be a bit of a burden, but, I promise you, the French are dog-mad and half of Paris will stop to admire him — "*Oh le petit toutou, qu'il est beau!*" — and while they're at it, admire you, too.

It's better if your dog is beautiful, but you don't have to be. Ted Stanger points out in *Sacrés Français* that even ugly women get to play the seduction game in France. It's a matter of knowing you're fascinating, often producing that most reassuring phenomenon in France already mentioned, The Look, from an admiring man. French women are just as adept at this game as French men. Up to the age of 70, or even 80, these superb creatures magically untouched by Time (is it the creams? Facelifts? Botox?) can startle newly-arrived American men with The Look, compelling and boldly confirming their allure and at the same time suggesting a vast and varied palette of experience.

Visiting Paris, Charlie Crummer, an American physicist at the University of California, Santa Cruz, was curious to try out The Look on a beautiful Frenchwoman himself. This is what he emailed me:

> "*I was walking back to my hotel in the Marais. The street was empty as I approached a lighted area. Empty, that is, except for a couple walking toward me. It was a man and a stunning woman. Without smiling I gazed at her as I would any beautiful work of art.*
>
> *She noticed, smiled and walked up to me (This just doesn't happen!).*
>
> "Est-ce que vous êtes venu pour l'exposition?" *(Did you come for the exhibition?) the woman asked me.*
>
> "Non, je ne savais rien d'une exposition," *I said.*
>
> "*Really! In that case, go over there," she said, pointing, "and have a glass of wine and some peanuts, and look at the paintings. The artist is there and he's very nice."*
>
> *That was it. She and her friend and I walked in. They went on by*

themselves and I had some peanuts and wine and saw some more beautiful
art. I'm still enchanted by that moment."

There is one imperative for these encounters: seriously attractive
grooming. Not flashy or gaudy, but leaning towards the conventional.
Sporty classical, casual but solid, with understated chic is safest. Always
wear showy earrings, day and evening. And a thin gold necklace, with
or without a pendant. High spike heels and a jacket with well-cut jeans
or trousers not keeping any secrets about your curves. If you're massively
overweight, slim down before you come. In general, Frenchmen don't
go for fat women. Many like Titianesque curves, but not obesity. Why do
you think French women diet all the time? The competition is fierce out
there.

Here's what the magazines say about actually meeting one of these
bachelors — echoed by the men themselves. In a café, look available, but
don't look around. Read a book or a newspaper. In France there is nothing
remotely shameful about being picked up. On the contrary, it's proof of
your *chien*. It may be that he takes one look at you and it hits him between
the eyes that you're the one. If so, bravo. But the next steps have to be
more difficult for him. Whatever you do, don't cheat him out of the
preliminaries. Courting, the chase, overcoming obstacles is what it's been
all about for hundreds of years. The poet, the intellectual and the warrior
in every Frenchman is faithfully recorded by French authors: love is first
of all in the mind. Witty, *soignée*, you make him fight for every inch,
creating your own *carte de Tendre* (see illustration page 76), that map of
anguish and rapture designed by the clever *Précieuses* in the 17th century,
with the Hill of Despair, the Valley of Hope and so on. Remember that
the famous beauty and the most skillful coquette of the 19th century,
Juliette Récamier, broke all the valiant hearts from Bernadotte to
Metternich without succumbing until she met the love of her life,
Chateaubriand. They were lovers for 32 years, until they both died in
1849, but after his first advances, she kept him waiting for six months.

Things have speeded up a bit today, but not as much as you might
think. Frenchmen will tell you that a great deal of the pleasure of love is
to be found in the chase. "The Frenchman's heart is naturally romantic,"
writes Jean-Marie Rouart, in *Adieu à la France qui s'en va.* "He wants to
conquer the ideal woman... he dreams of killing dragons and risking his
life for her... A woman must always present obstacles." Or this, from the
pen of Eric Emmanuel Schmitt in *Odette Toulemonde* : "Why was he still
dreaming of Donatella 15 years later, when he had possessed dozens of

women in between? Doubtless because she stayed mysterious, wrapped in her enigma... the greatest womanizers are mystics who prefer what women withhold to what they abandon to them..."

It is true that the most striking thing about the relations between the sexes in France is that they've worked out how to be together and love every minute of it. It is also true that feminism never caught on as in the U.S., and that the new freedoms and publicity given to what happens between the sheets has had little effect on Frenchmen. Still, while in the past this was unthinkable, now what they know about women's newly acquired power and success in business, and their expectations of sexual performance, have made some younger Frenchmen nervous to the point of skittishness. The least suggestion of aggressiveness sends them straight out the door, as you saw in Chapter Six with Benoît in the film, *Tout pour plaire*.

If you've spotted a quarry in that café and nothing seems to be happening, you may have to — very softly — nudge things along a little. A modern version of the drop-your-handkerchief-routine, for instance — a big conspicuous earring or even a cell phone. He finds it and brings it to you, rolling his eyes cheerfully. He invites you to have an espresso. You accept, saying that would be nice but you only have a minute. You sip your espresso slowly, listening to him intently, hardly talking yourself, your eyes meeting his only for a few swift seconds. You encourage him to talk about himself (usually not difficult) and pay close attention to what he says. With deft — but not too obvious — questioning, his type and tastes should become evident.

However, if he questions you a little too persistently, and listens extremely intently, this might be the sort of wolf you want to avoid. At all costs. If he starts out by telling you that you're beautiful, that is really a watch-out red light.

I was alerted to this danger by Michel Vicidomini, a suave man about town whose Italian name (though he is French) means, sort of, I-Conquered-and-Dominated.

"Seducing a woman is easy," said Michel, over a very expensive dinner at the Hôtel Costes. Michel is a handsome, divorced real estate agent who, at 50, has had plenty of time to practice what he preaches. "First, you tell her she's beautiful. Then you listen. Most men don't listen to women. They don't want to have problems they can't solve, so they avoid listening. Therefore, men who do listen have a free field. Women love it, they fall for it every time."

Please don't get the idea that French men have a Don-Juan complex

— that they're out to conquer and quit a woman, and move on to the next one. As Ted Stanger pointed out in Chapter Four, they are more like Casanova, sincerely, tenderly in love each time — until the next.

After your espresso with your new friend, you leave without asking his name or giving him yours. Believe me, he will be there at the same time the next day. But you won't be. You skip a day, and spend it pondering his conversation. What does he like to do? Does he like his women petite and fragile, needing protection, or strong and independent? Be a chameleon. Practice being indifferent and mysterious but nevertheless delightful. Show up at the same place and time two days after you met him. If he's not there yet, follow the example of Sophie Marceau in L'Etudiante (Chapter Six) and hide in les toilettes until you're sure he's there. Don't ever arrive early at a rendezvous, and never before him. After several espressos together, he may ask you out for dinner. For goodness sake, don't talk politics or show off, if you're not an intellectual. Even if you are.

Especially if you are. Maryse Vaillant, psychiatrist, author of "Comment aiment les femmes, du désir et des hommes" (How Women Love: Desire and Men), writes that she was surprised to discover how many successful, competent French career women of the 21st century hid the scope of their brains even from their husbands, and how much they depended on having husbands, even inferior ones, to feel successful as women. In case you feel that having the wit to shut up demeans you, take heart from Madame Vaillant. She says that the genius of women lies in what they bring to men. "Women cause the men be born to themselves," she said in an interview. "They are the real creators."

After dinner, let him pick up the bill. If he doesn't, that's another red light. He won't expect you to share. French people don't share restaurant bills.

Pay attention to whether he opens the taxi door for you, or the door of his car. If not, drop him. He has no "education," as the French say. He has no manners. He's not for you.

Kate had gone into the whole French courtship scene carefully for her seminar groups.

"What happens next probably depends on his age," she said. "The younger he is, the longer the courtship will be. It won't be the precisely programmed steps to the altar of the American courtship, which is, roughly, the first date, then going steady, then the noble moment when he bends his knee and pops the question, then the wedding. With the French, don't expect any of that. Marriage just sort of happens. There is no word in French for a 'date.' The future couple hangs around with friends, they see a movie together with friends, he is casually invited to her sister's birthday party, maybe he even invites her to dinner once or twice. At some point they end up at his place, he cooks dinner for her... and then... somehow, they're at the local city hall getting married. By the way, French women's magazines are beginning to talk about dinner 'dates,' which they spell *déite*."

This is pretty much how it went with a Swedish niece of mine, a pretty and awfully bright blonde of 29. I'll call her Maria.

"I was taking a sabbatical from my law practice to spend a year in France, but I didn't know anyone," she said. "What to do? I asked around and ended up joining a *vendange* group grape harvesting in Burgundy. I had the best time, met lots of really nice young French people. After the *vendange*, they invited me to all their parties in Paris. At one of them there was a young Frenchman called Pierre, he was about 30. I found him wonderfully handsome and charming. He left the party pretty soon, but gave me a long really lovely Look. The same thing happened at several other parties. Finally he asked me out to dinner.

"He was very gallant, treating me with great respect, always opening doors for me, even the door to his car. They never do that in Sweden. But — he never made a move. It was most odd. I couldn't imagine what was going on. Finally, after two or three months, I decided to ask him. I said that I liked him very much, I would be leaving Paris in a few months and it seemed to me we were losing time. He told me that he had recently broken off a relationship of several years, and wasn't sure he had anything to give me yet. Then he told me that he had such respect for me that he didn't want to start something unless he was really ready. So then... well, then, he kissed me and... we had a wonderful few months together. We broke up when I went home to Sweden, back to my practice, and he left for a special job he was offered in New York. Last summer he came to see me in Sweden. My mother really liked him. So that's where we are now."

Maria made her risky move knowing in her gut that it was the time to do it. If she had done it sooner, quite likely she wouldn't have seen him again. Very French. It's more difficult for a foreigner to gauge the moment. The more Zen you are, the safer. That is, give no hint of possessiveness or of needing him. In general, it's better not to sleep with him the first night. Never reproach him, never leave your toothbrush at his place. R told me that the two errors that women make are expecting that the first night of love anoints them as the fiancée, and, secondly, being curiously distant if he doesn't call for a few weeks. It's a good idea to take a trip somewhere alone from time to time, if only to show how independent you are. Even if he likes petite, fragile girls, he likes them independent. But independent *à la française*, that is, not brassily, aggressively independent.

"I never heard anything so hypocritical and unnatural," said Jenny, from Cincinnati, hearing my recital. "Artificial! I certainly won't ever be so fake with a man, I don't care what he thinks. I will always be myself. And if he doesn't like it, then he's not the husband for me."

Probably not a French husband for Jenny, in any case. Artifice is what France is all about, the art of style in everything, in this case the art of seduction. France's great expert on style in seducing men is — or was, no one knows if she is still alive — Madame Claude. I'd have liked to interview her, but she retired after she did time in the pokey, and her whereabouts are a mystery.

Born Fernande Grudet, Madame Claude ran a call girl service in Paris in the 60's and 70's, of such renown that thanks to the power of her clients, it was said that she became almost an arm of the French state. She often found the girls on her list in the *Gotha* or *Who's Who*. They earned between 8,000 and 9,000 euros a month (30% went in Madame Claude's pocket) plus presents — mink coats, jewelry and cars. She was particular about whom she took on, and fussy about their training. Sometimes she had them remodeled. Even more important were their manners and culture. They were taught how to talk about art and politics... shades of the Comtesse de Loynes preparing to launch her salon?

I asked Kate if she knew any of Madame Claude's little tricks.

"Madame Claude!" she said. "Those 'little tricks' must have worked — her girls ended up with ex-crowned heads or movie stars. I guess she'll never go out of date. Well, one of the tricks was during dinner on the first date, let your hand slide onto his sleeve."

"Did you ever try it?"

"Oh, please! A writer for the *Tatler* in London wrote that such techniques would never work in England, where men were only attracted to women who reminded them of their dogs. She said that once when she tried sliding her hand on her date's arm, he said, 'What's the matter? Is there a spot on my sleeve?'"

"What else?"

"Learn how to be a good cook. Work up lots of exciting dishes. But do you know what she felt was the most important in holding a husband?"

"Tell."

"More important than *anything* was fine lingerie. Silky, lacy, black or colored and matching bras and panties."

Lingerie and department stores seem to agree with this, with zillions of them heaped on row after row of counters, lacy, satiny and silky in every imaginable color, along with bras, skimpy panties and thongs. Have a look at the counters full of them at Bon Marché, on the Left Bank, or the Galéries Lafayette.

In fact, exotic underwear is in as never before. In celebration of the centennial of the first use of the term *brassière* – the bra itself was invented in 1889, in Paris, of course – lingerie stores are offering these dream underclothes not only in tulle, satin, lace, and sometimes all three, sometimes trimmed with velvet, but even in new colors like orange and petunia. A recent issue of the very conservative, not to say prudish, *Madame Figaro* showed nine full-page color photos of the new-rage bras and matching panties so skimpy as to be hardly panties, but not skimpy enough to be called a thong (*un string*). The panties might have a narrow skirt of ruffles or be wider and laced up the side. One of them was a cream-colored satin panty girdle — yes really, a girdle — with garters, edged in black velvet.

Madame Figaro calls these pages "an ode to hyperfemininity, a love of lingerie with a tiny bit of nostalgia, and very daring."

If you believe *Madame Figaro*, Madame Claude and Chantal Thomass, the queen of French lingerie design, these are the clothes a Frenchwoman cares most about, goes way over her budget for, and that give her the quiet confidence she is famous for. I was finally convinced of this when visiting my neighbor in the Dordogne, a farmer's wife with a 24-year-old daughter, and saw her clothesline hung with about 12 lacy black bras and panties.

And by the way, the next time you have to undress for a French doctor, he'll not only notice your lingerie but give you a big compliment on it, if it's pretty. Don't be offended! Enjoy it. In *Docteur, puis-je vous voir… avant six mois?*, Nicole de Buron mentions the importance of pretty lingerie in a hospital. This holds for wherever you might have to undress, including the gym. The underthings that the ladies reveal in the dressing rooms at the Club Interallié and the Polo Club could be the models in any of the big designers' showrooms.

Now you're ready for the Paris romance of a divorced American woman of 52 that is full of lessons that Madame Claude would have approved of. You'll see why you must always be ready for the marvelous unknown… groomed, perfumed and dressed perfectly from the inside out, beginning with the silky, matching, black lace underwear. You saw what happened to Bridget Jones. Well, that embarrassment was in London. In France it would be unforgivable.

Still marveling at her good fortune, Jane R. emailed me:

Not long ago I was at a party, another of the mixed Franco-American parties I often go to. I had a dinner partner of total charm, about my age, plus he was tall and lanky with a long narrow face, aquiline nose and warm brown eyes with crinkle lines. He was not one of those monologue men who expect you to crank them up when they run down. Nor was he the type you warned me about whose listening was so rapt as to be suspicious. He not only asked questions but pursued the answers. The questions were personal without being indiscreet. As if he was really talking to me. Have you seen Foucault's Pendulum? Are you interested in the Infinite? Have you ever been to India? Why not? You're interested in George Sand, then of course you've been to the Romantic Museum? No? We must go together some time, it is extremely interesting... subtly showing that he wouldn't mind seeing me again, and that he was (or least was giving the conscious impression of being) — for the moment, anyway — unattached. We discovered that we lived near each other. We had already agreed that we liked to walk home after a party, if it wasn't too far. So he asked if he could walk me home. Did I say no? Of course not. Did I suspect that it would be an adventure in itself? Of course not. He took my arm so that our bodies were close. It felt good. At almost every block he asked me if I had heard of the Resistant who was shot on this street, or he would tell me a tale of what happened to his grandfather right here 60 years ago. A cross street was named for his great, great grandfather, Marshal Comte Maurice de Saxe; so he told me about that, and then asked me about my grandfathers and great grandfathers. I cooked up tales of Sitting Bull and Pocahontas which seemed to please him. About half way home he stopped in the middle of a deserted street and told me with a sweep of his arm that this was the spot where his ancestor, a Huguenot, had been knifed by one of Catherine de Medici's assassins during the Saint Bartholomew massacre. Suddenly he took me in his arms and gave me a long, profoundly moving kiss. Oddly enough, it seemed appropriate. So of course I kissed him back. When we reached my door I felt we had known each other all our lives. I lifted my face for a couple of bisous. What I got was not bisous but another deep, searching, profoundly moving kiss on the mouth. I almost swooned. Did he expect to be invited up for a nightcap? Did he want to be? It was a moot point.

I wasn't inviting anyone at that hour for a "nightcap" that I had only known for three hours. Besides, I had dressed in a hurry for the party and the apartment was a nightmare of mess.
He said he would call the next day, but he didn't. He hasn't called back at all. What on earth happened?

I wrote back:

Dear Jane,
Lots of things could have happened. He could have heard from an old girlfriend meanwhile or he could have a problem or an illness he didn't want to tell you about. But most likely, it's that you didn't invite him up. The second deep kiss at the door suggests that. Frenchmen often expect that one thing implies the rest. In other words he thought you were weird to accept the kisses and not continue the pleasure. If you had refused the kisses, it's quite possible he would have been fired up for the chase.

What I wanted to ask her was if she understood all his references… to George Sand, to the St. Bartholomew's Massacre… and to the Comte de Saxe. I began to see that what Laura and R meant by the relevance of history.

8

The rebel innovators

In the Middle Ages, French husbands were free to beat their wives as often and as hard as they pleased. Husbands could banish wives to prisons or convents for adultery, or oblige them to shave their heads and chase a chicken around in the street, stark naked. Or they could lock them in a wooden cage on a pulley called an *accabussade*, which would be dunked in the river like a crayfish trap. They could even murder them. Wow.

But in the 18th century, David Hume, the Scottish philosopher, was amazed to arrive in Paris and find that the world of men he was used to was full of — women! No exclusive men's clubs. Or bars. Women went on shoots with men, sat in coffeehouses with them. Talked politics with them both before and *after* dinner. "France is the country for women!" he exclaimed.

What had happened? How did those slaves of the Middle Ages turn into the exotic creatures of today that we American women grow up admiring from afar, with a kind of awe and yearning – which we don't quite admit — for their innate style, their charm, their wit and their allure... these goddesses who were the women my Prince Charmings expect at the turn in the road and who have it all, luminaries in public and mothers of *familles nombreuses* at home? Women like Clara Gaymard, head of General Electric Europe, mother of eight; Christine Lagarde, former head of Baker & McKenzie, the largest international law firm in the world, and then minister of finance in the Sarkozy government, mother of two; Anne Lauvergeon, the head of Aveva, the civil and military nuclear energy group, with 70,000 employees under her, mother of two; and Ségolène Royal, the first woman ever chosen to be the candidate of a major French political party (the Socialists in 2007) for President of France, mother of four... all of them slim and stylish and gorgeous enough to be on the cover of *Vogue*. Ségolène Royal, the beauty queen of them all, was, in fact, shown in a bikini (at 53) in *Paris Match* during the presidential campaign. Looking great.

How had these women come so far from the era of chasing chickens around naked? Laura, R and I sat down over a glass of wine one day in Laura's apartment and talked about them, and what should go in the book.

"What happened was Love, romantic Love! Everything followed from that," R said.

He got up and began to pace the room while he expounded, looking out of the window from time to time as if the medieval kings on the facade of Notre Dame were helping him with what he wanted to tell us.

"Abélard, then after him, Eleanor, *la divine duchesse*! Of Aquitaine, of course. They did it! Since them, Love trumps everything in France — even war, even intellectual brilliance. Think of Pierre Abélard! Talk about history! He was born in 1079 — almost 1,000 years ago! — and was the most brilliant thinker of his time, one of the most brilliant thinkers of all time, a theologian, a dialectician, a philosopher, poet and writer, he was one of the founders of scholasticism, he was the forerunner of Thomas Aquinas — he is regarded as the founder of the University of Paris — he was more adulated than a football or movie star today, over 5,000 people would flock to hear him wherever he spoke — "

R stopped pacing, for emphasis and pointed his finger at me. "And why is he still famous today? Because of all that? Not a bit of it. Because of his *love affair* with Héloïse!"

He sank back into his chair. He paused, took a sip of wine and leaned forward in enthusiasm. "Probably the greatest real love affair of all time! Do you know the details? No? But it's better than any TV serial — I published a book on Héloïse and Abélard last year — it's got everything. Passion! The idolized Abélard, 39 years old, making the 17-year-old virgin, Héloïse, pregnant, her uncle sending thugs for revenge, to castrate and emasculate him — what a story!"

R jumped up again in excitement. I could see that it was a moment when he longed for a cigarette — which he gave up 20 years ago. I wished everyone who went to sleep when "history" was mentioned could hear him now.

"Abélard died in 1142, 20 years after the birth of Eleanor, Duchess of Aquitaine, heiress to what is now most of southwest France. She must have heard him speak in Paris when she was Queen of France — already at 15! — before she went Crusading, and probably was affected by his story with Héloïse... hence her own huge contribution to the history of Love. Which wouldn't have happened without her amazing father... And *this* is where it all started! France!"

Eleanor was the first of the women who transformed French society.

Eleanor of Aquitaine (1122 - 1204)
Warrior queen, poet and 12th century Emily Post

First there were the troubadours. Eleanor's grandfather, Duke William IX of Aquitaine (1064-1127), was the first on record. He composed and sang songs of love. How come? Perhaps he heard them from the Moors on his travels to Spain. Probably he was enchanted by the artistic delights and the poetic and voluptuous life he found in Byzantium during the First Crusade. His son, Eleanor's father, Duke William X (1075-1137) was also a Crusader and an alumnus of the wonders of Byzantium — and an even more talented troubadour and composer of lyrics and songs, as well as famously lecherous. His court at Poitiers, as I've written elsewhere, was a joyous place, sunny and elegant, cultivated and exhilarating, with musicians, artists and poets.

Eleanor, that staggering 12-century comet of exploding energy, inherited his charm and passion for the opposite sex, as well as his artistic talent. As Queen of France she was culturally starved in the dreary Louvre of the mid-12th century with her pious husband, Louis VII, though she was probably as enthralled by Abélard, if not by his seminars on universals, as the rest of Paris. She was certainly too young to appreciate universals.

During the Second Crusade with Louis VII, she woke up in glorious Constantinople (now called Istanbul) with its gardens and fountains, its architectural splendors and dazzling court, not to mention her glamorous uncle, Raymond of Toulouse, reigning sovereign of Antioch. That was it for Louis. Eleanor dumped him and France for the future King of England, Henry II, carefully holding onto her heritage of Aquitaine and Poitou. She set about creating courts in London and Poitiers as splendid and cultivated as in Constantinople. She composed songs and tales with troubadours and poets. She had 11 children, she led her soldiers in battle herself, even at 80 she rode ceaselessly around Aquitaine and Poitou to save her heritage from marauding French barons; but it is as a Muse that she is immortal, for it was she who brought personal, individual romantic love to the West.

Troubadours like Eleanor's father and Guiraut de Borneilh sang of a generalized romantic love, "what the eyes have made welcome to the heart." But it wasn't until Eleanor ordered the story of Tristram and Isolde translated from the Latin into French that love was personalized, and became, for the first time, as the historian Joseph Campbell put it, "the beginning of a distinctive Western consciousness, the romantic idea of the choice of the individual as an ideal to be lived for, which became a social system in the West." The historian Pierre Gaxotte calls this earthshaker "the gratuitous and magnificent gift of France to the Western world."

As the Crusades continued, emptying the castles of their lords and masters, the ladies were left in control of the restless and wild young knights around them. While the knights hounded them crudely for love, the ladies saw their chance to demand an overhaul of crass and coarse behavior. Led by the steely Eleanor, they imposed rituals and codes of courting, and organized "courts of love," where the knights could appeal if the results of their wooing were disappointing. Courtly behavior and chivalry were born — and the first glimmers of a generalized female power some time in the far, misty future.

Christine de Pisan (1364 - 1432)
The outraged pen of a soothsayer's daughter

These rumbles of female power were not underestimated by the leaders of the male bastions of power, the Church and the Sorbonne. Their propagandists went to work, representing women as an incarnation of Eve, an instrument of the Evil One and the cause of man's exile from Eden. In his long satirical poem, *Le Roman de la rose* (*The Story of the Rose*), the popular 13th-century writer Jean de Meung, enemy of women and *courtoisie*, denounced female iniquity in a resounding vitriolic roar.

It took an exceptional woman to try to drown out Jean de Meung. Christine de Pisan was an exception in any age. Her rebuttals in 1402 — the first French feminist tract — stirred up a scandal, as did her red-hot poem of outrage at Joan of Arc's being burned at the stake in 1431.

So — who was this amazing woman?

Christine de Pisan was the daughter of Charles V's court astrologer, who, unfortunately for him and his family, neglected to foretell the death of the King in 1380. He lost his post and died soon after, as, in battle, did Christine's husband, leaving her with three small children and not a centime to feed them with. She began to write. The courts of England and Milan were so thrilled with her work that they each tried to hire her, but the Duc de Bourgogne, Jean de Berry, also a fan, offered her his patronage to stay in France, making her France's first self-supporting woman author.

Madame de Rambouillet (1588 - 1665)
Muse of literature and manners

Half Italian, Catherine de Vivonne grew up in Italian elegance and *raffinement* in Rome. With her marriage to the Marquis de Rambouillet in 1600 she moved to France and found a wretched kingdom still staggering from the Hundred Years War with England (1337-1453), the manners and morals as battered as the corpses on the battlefield, the courtly etiquette established by Eleanor of Aquitaine a wisp of memory. Men at court, decked out in finery, cleaned their nails and ears in public. Their conversation was loud and bawdy. As for respect for women, the usual adjective applied to the French court in the 16th century was "depraved."

Madame de Rambouillet was revolted. She rolled up her sleeves and went to work. First she wanted to raise the level of language. She had the money, the position and the connections to launch a literary circle, a huge ballroom to hold it in — known to history as the *salon bleu* — and the intellect, enthusiasm, tact, perfect taste and gaiety for promoting it. At the same time she wanted to redesign French society itself: the way people of *le beau monde* met, how they behaved, how they talked together. So she invited keen, articulate men with roaming minds and a few decorative women to come and discuss all subjects under the sun according to her strict rules of delicacy and urbanity. They read each other's verses and plays, hashed them over and fine-tuned them. Pascal, Molière, Bossuet and Racine supped and discoursed at her table. Corneille read all his plays there. The salon was the intellectual pinball machine where ideas ricocheted, collided, collapsed or rose again, enhanced; where poets, novelists and playwrights were discovered... and where eloquence blossomed into the flower of French culture: conversation.

Gradually, alongside the emergence of this new literature, manners and elegant language became an obsession with a coterie of the Marquise's friends mentioned earlier, *Les Précieuses*. They continued the debates of Eleanor's "courts of love" on questions like "Is love compatible with marriage?" illustrating them eloquently with the , an allegorical map of the path an aspiring lover should follow to conquer the heart of his beloved, avoiding the dangerous Ocean of Passion and Lake of Indifference, on through the sweet, calm villages of Pretty Verses and Love-letters.

Madame de Rambouillet did nothing less than revolutionize French society and, creating the first salon, revived French literature. For the next 300 years, French salons were the temples of taste and aesthetic excellence, the centers of the political, intellectual, literary and artistic life of France — itself the artistic pace-setter for all of Europe. They were the prerogative of women, under the control of a woman. By the end of the 16th century, French women had been gradually stripped of all their medieval civil rights. They had to wait for the 20th century to get them back. But with the salons, they turned the tables of power and influence. They domesticated, civilized and dominated men — without seeming to

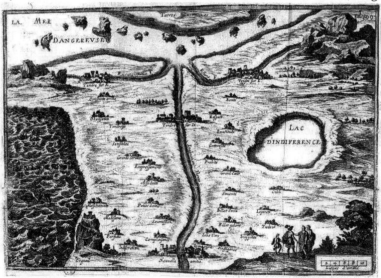

Carte de Tendre

17th century map, by les Précieuses, of the imaginary country of Love, where the lover must find a path to the heart of his lady through various dangers and trials. After braving the **Dangerous Seas of Passion and Hostility** *and the* **Lake of Indifference***, he reaches the villages of* **Sweet Verses, Sensibility, Perseverence, Generosity, Respect** *and* **Moderation** *... and is worthy of his lady's heart.*

do so.

Ninon de Lenclos (1620 - 1705)
Knowledge and *volupté*

Ninon de Lenclos was a famously gorgeous young noblewoman with a brain and a talent for playing the lute... which she exchanged for the primrose path. She made sin irresistible for everybody. She turned her house into a salon, where the bright talk larded with eroticism was soon labeled philosophical libertinage. Her favors were often free and always bestowed only on people she really liked who respected her dignity. She became a rich social star. Even the Court of the Sun King received her, though the Queen Mother demurred at first. Among her illustrious friends and admirers were the Great Condé and Queen Christine of Sweden, who, like Ninon, liked to travel in masculine clothes. In her forties, Ninon opened a school of good taste for young women.

Her lifestyle, the pleasures she reveled in, spiced with sharp wit and leavened with dignity, helped tone down the shame associated with adultery for the ladies of the Court. To certain groups of aristocrats like the circle of the young Marquis de Lafayette 100 years later, being faithful to a spouse began to seem ridiculous.

Madame de Maintenon (1635 - 1719)
The Cinderella of all time

The romance of the plain but virtuous governess/nurse/stenographer who marries the boss has been a story teller's gold mine for centuries. But the penniless governess who captures the handsome, glamorous, absolute King of the most powerful nation in Europe? The Sun King himself? Who would imagine such a fantasy?

Françoise d'Aubigné, known to history as Madame de Maintenon, pulled it off. She did it, first of all, with her immense culture and her wit. Louis XIV loved to talk and to laugh. Let's not forget her charm. Stunning beauty was not part of the deal, though she was good looking. Her secret weapons were her genuine love of children — Louis adored his children — and her wisdom and composure.

I can hear you history buffs hooting, "Wit? Laughter? That dreary old religious bigot who convinced the King to revoke the Edict of Nantes and massacre all those Protestant Huguenots?"

No, she was not dreary at all, not a religious bigot, and, according to serious historians, not implicated at all — at all! — in the Revocation of the Edict of Nantes. This is the spin that has sizzled down to us from her enemies at court, sick with jealousy. One can understand them. She was, actually, a clever, fun-loving young woman who came up from nowhere with appalling hardships, whose probity was unquestioned and whose religious faith was deep... and who was definitely not on her knees praying all day.

Françoise was born in a prison. Her father, a minor nobleman and blackguard who probably murdered his first wife, was in prison for debts. Françoise was dumped in a convent school. At 16, handsome and intelligent but not gorgeous and with no dowry, this gregarious girl who loved parties had but one ambition: not to be stuck in a nunnery. The only other alternatives offered her were marriage to a cripple 36 years older than she, Paul Scarron, or the street. She grabbed Paul Scarron. He was poor, with a body shaped like a Z, and probably impotent to boot, but there was nothing crippled about his mind. He had been a fixture of literary Paris for years, a writer and poet known for his biting, often malicious wit. He was in excruciating pain. He often screamed most of the night, with Françoise sitting up next to him, helping him as best she could. He showed his appreciation by giving her lessons in repartee, in literature and philosophy, and in Spanish and Italian. Françoise's wit and gaiety were soon the talk of the Marais. Poets, intellectuals and nobles flocked to the Scarron salon, including Racine, the Duc de la Rochefoucauld, Cardinal de Retz, Ninon de Lenclos, Madame de Rambouillet, the Marquise de Sévigné and the capricious friend who, with huge irony, became the godmother of her destiny, the Marquise de Montespan. Yes — her again! — she of the aphrodisiacs, who put toads' spittle in Louis's soup to get him back to her bed when his ardor was fading.

Scarron died eight years later, leaving nothing but debts. Shortly thereafter, the beautiful Athénaïs de Montespan, as bewitching as she was frivolous and madly in love with the King, had the first of her babies with him and desperately needed a nurse to take charge of the infant instantly after birth. It would have to be a special nurse who could be trusted to keep this secret from Athénaïs's dangerously jealous husband. Who but her poverty-stricken, dignified friend Françoise, who would be only too glad of an extra income?

So in 1669, the penniless orphan, now 34, became the governess of an almost annual flow of royal babies — seven in fact — and mistress of a house of her own, a coach and servants. The King was at first not pleased at this choice of governess. He felt she disapproved of his liaison with a married woman, as in fact she did. But he was touched by her genuine despair at the death of one of the infants. After that he began to like her. In 1673, when it seemed safe, he decided to recognize two of these children, and put them — with their governess — in rooms near his, first in Saint Germain, then in Versailles. It became his habit to chat daily with the children and then with Françoise. At first they talked about one of her charges, the Duc du Maine, a little boy of precocious charm whom they both adored. Gradually these conversations got longer and longer and became a habit.

Louis, an absolute monarch, was well trained by Cardinal Mazarin in the rigors of government. His word was law and his look could be terrifying, but he ruled like a concerned CEO-General who believed in concertation. He bothered about all the details of his ministers and their portfolios, of his generals at the front, of his people and their complaints, and of his courtiers and their problems. He concerned himself with the sizes and shapes of the new buildings, canals, bridges, gardens, fountains and the huge aqueduct burgeoning in Versailles, but never shared his concerns with his friends or mistresses, nor let women into his council of ministers. He felt the loss of the solid, calm friend he had had in his mother; Françoise turned out to be just the wise, reliable companion he needed.

Madame de Sévigné, that indefatigable letter writer, didn't fail to notice.

"His Majesty frequently spends two hours at a time in Maintenon's apartments," she wrote to her daughter, "conversing in so friendly and natural a manner as to make it the most desirable spot in the world... She has introduced him to a new land heretofore unknown to him, which is friendly intercourse and conversation without restraint or chicanery; he seems charmed by it."

Louis was falling in love with her and, impressed with her principles and belief in God, began to put his baroque lovelife in order. He stopped his affairs with Athénaïs de Montespan and with another more recent conquest.

With the sudden death of his shy Queen in 1683, Louis's life changed radically. He was free to marry again. A foreign princess? One of the local duchesses? He conferred with his ministers; his succession was secured, there was no need for risking a civil war with another royal baby. Louis at last could marry whom he loved. He loved Françoise. When he told her of his decision, she thought he was joking and almost fainted. According to her diaries quoted in *L'Allée du Roi*, she remembered how, after the death of Scarron and before she took charge of the royal children, she had asked the man she then loved, the Marquis de Villarceaux, if, should his wife die, he would marry her. He had snorted in disdain at a Villarceaux marrying someone of such inferior birth. The Sun King saw it differently. When she said, "Sire, according to the world, the greatest king on earth can't marry the widow of Monsieur Scarron!" Louis replied, "According to the world, it is I who make and unmake nobility. One is always well born when distinguished by me."

They were married in a secret ceremony in 1684. These two newlyweds in their forties were in love with each other. For the first time, the letters of Françoise bubbled with joy and light-heartedness. Louis was never far from her side for long, and wrote her tender letters from the front about how much he loved her. In Versailles, he told her he couldn't be without her presence for more than an hour. He would send her notes several times a day. He spent whole afternoons in her salon going over government business while she did needlework.

She continued to be the lover and support of the King until his death in 1713. Gradually he took her into his confidence about affairs of state and often followed her advice. He greatly appreciated the school for indigent young ladies which she started in nearby Saint-Cyr. On his deathbed in 1713, he told her that he had loved her more than any other woman.

Francoise's share in the complex makeup of French femininity is an awesome mix of tenderness, charm, discretion, integrity, altruism, depth of feeling for children of all ages and an overarching religious faith. Most elusive and commanding of all is her triumph in turning a confirmed Lothario into a faithful, pious husband.

Madame de Pompadour (1721 - 1764)
Beauty, taste, delicacy and style

Even as a little girl, Jeanne-Antoinette de Pompadour, born Mademoiselle Poisson (Miss Fish) was determined to become the mistress of the next King, Louis XV. Her mother — yes, really — encouraged her, educating her at an Ursuline convent, organizing voice lessons by Jeloitte, the star of the Paris opera, and elocution lessons from a dramatist. Pretty and graceful with perfect manners, she learned about taste and conversation from the 18th century's most famous *salonnière*, Madame Geoffrin. Why shouldn't she attract the handsome young King, yet another lusty Bourbon?

Her big moment came during a masked ball in honor of the Dauphin's wedding. The King went as a yew tree. Jeanne-Antoinette, tipped off, also went as a yew tree. They tangled in each other's branches. The King was amused and intrigued. They were inseparable thereafter, first as lovers for five years and then, her health too delicate to continue on that level, 10 years more as close friends until she died. Uncontested is her good taste and her happy influence on literature and the arts, including the painters Boucher, Nattier and Watteau, not to mention many wonders of 18th century French furniture, *objets d'art* and styles of dress. We have her and her brother, the director of the King's buildings, to thank for these glories of France: the Place de la Concorde, the Ecole Militaire, and the Petit Trianon. The Elysée Palace, where she lived much of the time, reverted to the crown and is now the residence of the Presidents of France.

She was a petite jewel of a woman who based her career on the ability to please and entertain men. Thus she was able to dominate artisans and workshops, and redecorate the whole kingdom with her delicate artistic exquisiteness and taste. The flavor of Louis XV's reign is the flavor of Madame de Pompadour. As his great grandfather Louis XIV intended, the qualities that would secure the quintessential Frenchness of French women, the magic that would lure women from foreign lands were gaining momentum.

Jeanne Detourbey, Comtesse de Loynes (1836 - 1900?)
From orphanage to cultural umpire

If Françoise d'Aubigné and Miss Fish shot up to social heights from very far down, they at least started out as a Mademoiselle, or a member of the lowest nobility. Jeanne Detourbey climbed up from the absolute pits.

She began life miserably in an orphanage in the Champagne country near Rheims in 1833. She seems to have had a particularly sweet and loyal nature. She was lovely looking, with magnificent eyes, small delicate features and tiny feet. She had charm. She had a pleasing voice. She was intelligent. Her most precious gift, she knew, was her dignity, her innate certainty of being a lady as well as looking like one. A shame to be washing bottles for a champagne grower!

Like a Midwestern American today, yearning for the bright lights of New York, Jeanne washed the bottles and dreamed of Paris. One day she stuffed her rags into a satchel and hitched a ride on a haywagon. Her orphanage street smarts served her well in Paris as she made the rounds

Jeanne Detourbey, Comtesse de Loynes
Portrait by Eugene Amaury-Duval   *(photo: Lessing archives)*

of the theaters, seeking the eye of a director. Indeed, the director of the theater Porte Saint Martin did give her a script to try out; finding no talent but delighted by her charm, he assigned her to his bed instead. And treated her well.

Her next benefactor was a few steps up the ladder, Emile de Girardin, an eminent publisher. Jeanne was on her way, not considered as a by-the-hour whore but as a member of the demi-monde. Girardin brought a stream of politicians and journalists to the apartment he gave her. Jeanne listened as they argued and stormed and hatched out plans and projects. Why shouldn't she set up a salon of her own? But for that she needed time, money, position and culture.

The money came soon. Ernest Baroche, a friend of Emile de Girardin, had plenty. He fell in love with her and then had the bad luck to be killed in the Franco-Prussian war of 1870. She mourned — he was the first of two loves of her life — but dried her tears when she learned that he had left her everything he owned, including a sugar refinery. In due course she met the head of the refinery, an aristocrat of the Ancien Régime, Count Edgar de Loynes. He was at her feet in no time. He married her in a civil ceremony, which so horrified his parents that he agreed to annul it. Jeanne let him go, but kept the title. She now had the legal rank and social position to go with her riches.

She set about preparing what she was determined to make — and did make — the most distinguished salon in Paris. For becoming a *salonnière*, a woman's rank didn't matter. She must be rich and charming, on her toes culturally, strong as an ox to keep to her schedule of receiving groups for afternoon teas and evening dinners. She must be a networker, tirelessly refreshing her guest list while at the same time warding off competing *salonnières* liable to poach her major attractions. She must not neglect her kitchen, nor her wardrobe. But — and this is the point for American women to consider today — France was socially mobile. Any woman with chutzpah, who understood the game, could lob herself into this power over the social and political life of France.

Jeanne now had everything for a great *salonnière* except culture. Once she had found an appropriately impressive house on the Champs-Elysées and a great chef for the exquisite dinners she would give there at least twice a week, she begged — and bagged — five of the most illustrious men of the century to educate her. The poet and critic Sainte-Beuve, though trembling with bad health, taught her about literature. Hippolyte Taine gave her lessons in history and philosophy; with Ernest Renan, the century's great philologist, she studied linguistics, philosophy and civilizations, also vocal style and timber; and with Théophile Gautier, she studied poetry. Perhaps her greatest celebrity coup was persuading Gustave Flaubert to coach her in prose excellence. All these men were under her spell; with Flaubert it went farther than the antechamber. This genius-giant had an eye all his life for pretty women. His taste for passionate and very short love affairs — so that he could get back to his beloved village of Croisset, near Rouen — was another boost for Jeanne.

From 1860 to 1895, the great of the 19th century trooped to her house, some of them every day. The themes were often political, but depended on whoever was there... Guy de Maupassant, Raymond Poincaré, Gounod, Jules Verne, Georges Clemenceau. Jeanne received them seated on a pink ottoman near the fire in her salon, always with a bouquet of violets at her waist.

In a way, the *salonnières* foreshadowed the first feminists, but with the great difference that they were not in competition with men. They didn't feel the need to be. They wanted to stock their minds and sharpen their wits. Their vision was to create a great renaissance of art and literature, competing with Italy, and they were determined to import Italian manners for French men. They aimed high — and they achieved both their goals.

George Sand (1804 - 1876)
The first modern woman: artist, mother, activist, lover

In 1833, at a literary salon in Paris packed with power people and mighty pens, George Sand rose to read aloud from *Lélia*, her second novel. Petite, plain rather than pretty but with haunting black velvet eyes, her luxuriant dark hair pulled back in a knot, she wore an elegant black velvet pantsuit 100 years in advance of its time. Her script was also 100 years ahead of its time. She was 29.

"A woman today," she read, "is not allowed to think freely, to have control over her property or to enjoy her body. It is easier to accuse a woman of frigidity than to give her pleasure. A respectable woman has the choice of resignation or suicide."

There was an uproar. The critics booed. No one had ever written of such taboos before. One of them said her book was good only for reading in the W.C. Another told her he was giving her a lot of space in his newspaper column the next day. When she tried to thank him, he said: "Don't thank me. I'm dragging you in the mud. Your book is execrable. It will sell beautifully — like manure. By the kilo!"

Strong stuff. But Sand held fast. No wonder the bestsellling philosopher, Bernard-Henri Lévy calls her "the first modern woman." She was an artist and an activist, and a passionately devoted mother. Born in 1804, the year Napoleon was crowned Emperor, her life was a blazing technicolor blueprint for women shackled with the Napoleonic civil code. The code gave them the legal status of children; their husbands had life and death power over them.

Sand had always been an unfettered spirit. It went with growing up as an only child in a big house with a permissive grandmother, an absent-minded tutor and the whole county of Berry, 125 miles south of Paris, to roam around in with her local friends, the children of peasants. When still a little girl called Aurore Dupin, George Sand knew that she was different.

She was different first of all because of her bizarre background, part royal, part gutter. The Fates must have cackled merrily when mixing up her genes. Her father, Maurice Dupin de Francueil, was an aristocrat, a brilliant officer in Napoleon's army. Her paternal grandmother was the illegitimate daughter of Field-Marshal Count Maurice de Saxe, himself the illegitimate son of the King of Poland. Sand's mother — are you ready for this? — was a camp follower, that is, a sort of army groupie. So George Sand had the blood of the most exalted and the most ignoble social classes. Who can be surprised at her extraordinary life?

After the sudden death of Sand's father in a riding accident when she was four, her grandmother won her custody. When her grandmother died, Sand, at 16, was the only heir. She married quickly. Baron Dudevant turned out to be an intellectual and physical sloth whose one pursuit was hunting — wild boars and chambermaids. After eight years and a son and a daughter, she made an arrangement with him that left her free to leave the château at Nohant for several months of the year and live in Paris.

She stumbled on her talent for writing while searching for ways of increasing her income to cover Paris expenses. She had always loved spinning tales. She began by contributing to newspapers, coached by the editor of *Le Figaro*. After the publication of a book she wrote with Jules Sandeau, her new lover, she wrote her books alone, every night of her life, from midnight until 6 a.m., no matter how the evening had been spent, whether at the theater, with friends, or in passion. It did not always please her lovers that she would get up from an embrace and go straight to her writing table. The words simply flowed in a torrent of 90 novels, countless essays and pamphlets, a three-volume autobiography and 26 volumes of correspondence with her scores of friends.

She wanted to be known as a writer, not a "woman writer." She took half the name of Sandeau and added George, partly for a male smoke screen, and also because it meant "farmer" in berrichon, the Berry dialect. She never explained why she dropped the "s" of the French name "Georges."

First Trip to the Stars with Alfred de Musset

Sandeau was too lazy to last long. The poet Alfred de Musset — Yes, him again! — was the first with the passion, tenderness and experience to "take her to the stars," as she put it. "She is the most feminine woman of any I ever knew," he wrote. She met him in 1833 at a dinner given by their mutual friend, the critic Sainte-Beuve, for contributors to the magazine *La Revue des Deux Mondes*. She was 29 and had just finished her second novel, *Lélia*, which was to amaze and excite her public even more than *Indiana*. Musset, at 23, had set Paris on fire with *Contes d'Espagne et d'Italie*. He was a dandy and a womanizer, known for his excesses of alcohol and opium, and also as one of the most brilliant conversationalists of Paris. At that dinner, he talked. Sand, all her life conscious of having little *esprit*, or conversational wit, listened.

These two who would seem to have little in common — Sand preferred milk to alcohol — were delighted with each other. She was charmed by his poetry. He was charmed by her novels. They corresponded. Sand thought she wasn't interested in him except as a friend, until in one of his letters Musset struck a brilliant chord: he said she should take pity on him, that he loved her to desperation and was like a "pitiful child." All her life Sand loved nursing people and taking care of children. She felt that being a mother was the essential element of being a woman, the one thing that really set women apart from men. Being invited to mother this poetic genius proved irresistible. She wrote him a coded invitation to a tryst. He responded with a coded poem which, if you skipped every second line, was a declaration of carnal desire. It ended with "When?" She sent back one word: "Tonight."

They spent the next two years in an uproar of passion gradually destroyed by Musset's addiction to brothels and drugs. A trip to Venice, intended as romantic bliss in that blissful city, was a horror of illness, Venetian thugs and the debauchery of Musset.

In their first days of rapture, Musset told her that, famous as they both were, passionate as they were, prolific writers that they were, they would be remembered as two of history's greatest lovers. He was wrong. Sand would qualify, but the lover linked to her in the history books would be Chopin.

In the two years between the famous liaisons, Sand led a frenetic life of writing, mothering, loving and political action with the republican friends of one of her lovers, men who would later all have boulevards in Paris named for them: Arago, Ledru-Rollin, Raspail, Barbès.

Frédéric Chopin

Sand first met Chopin in 1837 soon after he arrived in Paris. He was 28, the son of a Polish mother and a French father. A musician herself, Sand spotted his genius instantly. She was intoxicated with his music and the delicacy of his touch. She wrote in her journal that he had a very sweet smile, eyes that were lively rather than melancholy, and that he had the noble air of a great lord in exile. This was her man for a trip to the stars. However, he was frail. He coughed. She saw that he was shy. Perhaps, even, he had given his heart to someone else. Though it was her nature, when given the right signals, to head straight for the fire and flames, she saw that this was one time to go slowly.

In fact, there were no signals from him at first. Chopin's first impression of her, dressed in trousers and smoking a cigar, was negative. He wrote home to Poland that he had met the famous novelist George Sand and found her displeasing. Was she a man or a woman?

When they met again in October 1837, Chopin changed his mind. He wrote in his diary: "I've seen her again... She looked deeply into my eyes while I was playing. The music was a little sad, legends of the Danube: my heart danced with her in the country. And her eyes in my eyes, dark eyes, unusual eyes, what did they say? My heart was taken! I've seen her twice since. She loves me. Aurore! What a charming name!"

After a trip to Majorca as ill-fated as her earlier one to Venice, they settled in Nohant in 1838. Sand nursed him continually. The years were rich in musical creation. That first summer in Nohant he composed his Sonata in B flat minor, the second Nocturne and three Mazurkas. He valued Sand's musical taste, and wrote home that she was a "fine listener" who understood his interior life and helped him to get his themes on paper. Chopin was in love with Sand, as much as he could be with anyone, and wrote in his journal, *"Pour toi, Aurore, je ramperais sur le sol, rien ne me serait de trop, je te donnerais tout! Un regard, une caresse de toi..."* (For you, Aurore, I would crawl on the ground, nothing would be too much, I would give you everything! A look, a kiss from you...)

Sand felt a great tenderness for him, but she had understood in Majorca that Chopin's health could not permit the pleasures of physical love. She nursed him, she mothered him, she encouraged him, she was next to him at the piano with all her sensibility, but she refused to endanger his health. With time he became gloomy and jealous. He would freeze her with long silences. Also, nothing about country life pleased him. He was less and less able to bear Sand's boisterous political friends.

Chopin left Nohant in 1847. His tuberculosis finally killed him in 1849. Did he realize that he owed her several years of his life? That without her he would not have composed many of his masterpieces? Who knows? Gratitude is a painful load to bear.

The frenzied fugue of Sand's life continued without Chopin. In the years 1847 and 1848, she exhausted her last energy promoting the overthrow of King Louis-Philippe with tracts, speeches and bulletins. She impressed the famous Franco-American observer, Tocqueville, who was prejudiced against her. She continued battling for women's rights and administrating Nohant, its farmers, their leases and crops, supervising the house, always teeming with family and friends; supporting them all when they were in trouble or needed money, intervening for them with the authorities. Every night, without let up, she worked on her novels and plays to pay for it all, and found time somehow for the current ruler of her heart. There was never a dearth of candidates. Her last love was an artist, Charles Marshal, whom she wrote three months before her death at 72: *"Je t'embrasse et je t'aime toujours."*

After her funeral, Flaubert wrote, "I cried my eyes out *(j'ai pleuré comme un veau)*... one would have had to know her as I knew her to realize... the immensity of tenderness in this genius... She will always be one of the lustres of France and a unique glory."

And yet, and yet. To this day, if you mention her name to the people of her neighborhood in the Berry, you may get the response, "Oh, George Sand! That scandalous woman! We weren't allowed to mention her name when we were growing up!"

But in the center of the town closest to Nohant, La Châtre, you can find a statue of her dominating the town square.

For the historian, Académicien and former minister, Alain Decaux, the 19th century is "The Century of George Sand." Why? Interviewed by *Le Figaro*, he said, "Because she was widely read and wrote enormously in all the genres, not only fighting for liberating women from their legal inferiority, but also for their private rights, writing about sexual relations and the injustice of a woman raped every night by her husband. She scandalized her readers, which made them pay attention and led to the evolution we know today."

Coco Chanel (1883 - 1971)
The genius

Gabrielle Chanel's father, the son of an impoverished peasant from the Auvergne, was an itinerant merchant. He hawked pots and pans at various town fairs in *la France profonde*, the Auvergne and the Midi, trailed by Gabrielle's lovesick and asthmatic mother and an ever-increasing number of children born en route. When there were five, the mother died. The girls were put in a convent-orphanage school. The boys were farmed out to relatives.

All her life Gabrielle gilded these unglamorous tracks beyond recognition. She was more or less truthful about learning how to sew from her Aunt Julia, her mother's sister. Aunt Julia had married well and had real skill and imagination in designing and decorating hats, which Gabrielle absorbed, so that after leaving the convent she got a job as a seamstress in Moulins, in Provence.

Coco's First Look at Taste

At night she sang in a café. Her husky voice was toneless, but her looks were striking. A rich playboy-infantry officer, Etienne Balsan, fell in love with her. Desperate to move up in the world, she saw that his boudoir would take her farther than her voice. Like Jeanne de Loynes, she knew that being a kept woman was her only option and needed only be a first step. She went to live with Etienne at his château in Compiègne, where he was breeding race horses. Gabrielle, now called Coco, had her first look at opulence and taste. Etienne's house, impeccably run by a competent staff, was always full of his military and horseracing pals and their extravagantly dressed mistresses.

Coco kept her eyes open. She absorbed proper housekeeping and etiquette and mused about the corseted dresses cramping the mistresses and the freer, more practical yet elegant attire of the men. Even as she dressed primly in her great longing to be taken for a bourgeoise, she began to have the ideas about making dresses — men's clothes made for women — which would later have women storming her stores.

Coco was restless. She had too much energy and ambition to party on and on with Etienne and his idle horsey crowd. The hats she made for herself were sensational — simple but with exciting shapes — and were not just noticed but coveted by Etienne's guests. Coco considered them a business trump. Etienne was not one to flout society's rules — mistresses were not supposed to be seen working — but he let Coco set up a milliner's shop in his ground floor apartment in Paris.

The hats caught on. Soon she needed a real boutique of her own. Etienne was averse to doling out real sums of money except for his horses. Coco fumed and fussed. Finally an English friend of Etienne's, Arthur (Boy) Capel, a shipping and coal millionaire, intrigued by her style, offered to back her. He leased a shop for her at 31 rue Cambon, now a Chanel address throbbing with history. Boy Capel and Coco Chanel fell in love. Thus began what turned into the love of Chanel's life.

Unlike Etienne, Capel didn't hesitate to introduce her to his aristocratic lady friends, the social lights she would need as clients. Coco began to feel not only loved, but secure and accepted. The next years were probably the happiest of her life. With Capel backing her, she went from hats to dresses and expanded first to Deauville and then Biarritz, where in 1915 she had her first grand opening as a couturière. World War I (1914 -1918) was kind to her. Paul Poiret, her main fashion competition, was laboring for the French army, leaving the field wide open. Chanel pressed her advantage. Poiret had begun loosening corsets? Chanel threw them out. Poiret had begun showing shoes? Chanel showed ankles. She made loose, simple clothes women flocked to buy, using a new, inexpensive material held in contempt until Chanel discovered it: jersey.

Coco was now on the map, with 300 employees at her three stores. Only one thing was missing: the march to the altar with Boy which would finally make her respectable, her "irregular" life past and forgotten. But Boy also had a past to erase. To compensate for being illegitimate, in 1919 he married into an eminent Scottish family. Chanel was devastated. She was sure he would come back to her, not, alas, as the husband she longed for, but at least as her lover. In 1920 he was driving from Paris to the Midi, either to join Coco — which she was sure of, all her life — at the house she'd rented for them there, or to join his wife at the house he owned. We'll never know which. He had an automobile accident on the way and was killed instantly.

Coco was beyond sorrow, somewhere in the limbo where people go who are so cruelly hurt that they are hardly alive. She met a man who was also stricken, for a different reason, Grand Duke Dimitri Pavlovitch Romanov, a nephew of the last tsar, Nicolas II. He had been one of the accomplices of Prince Youssoupov in the murder of Rasputin. The Communists had stolen his country; he feared that he had also lost his soul. The mood of this lonely man exactly matched Chanel's. Though she was 10 years older, the two mourners understood each other perfectly. They were lovers for a year. What did they talk about? Perfume. Boy Capel had given Chanel the means to build a successful business. Grand Duke Dimitri would make possible the stepping stone to real empire: a fabulous, stable perfume.

Chanel's genius included a modern flair for marketing. She knew that perfume, as a sales bait for clothes, screamed for attention. The chemistry of a stable scent had not yet been invented. In those days, a woman who wanted to smell wonderful all night long at a party had to drench herself with perfume while getting dressed, and people would swoon from the vapors when she arrived. Coco's ambition was to create a perfume that would last indefinitely from just two dabs behind the ears. Dimitri was able to introduce her to Ernest Beaux, a brilliant chemist and "nose," the son of an employee of the tsar who had been involved with creating the court's perfumes. Beaux, working closely with Chanel in mysterious secrecy in a Provence lab, produced the first fixed scent in France, and the first not from a recognizable flower. In fact, it had 81 ingredients. Coco had her breakthrough. From dozens of examples Beaux had composed, he gave her five phials of mixtures to choose from. She shook her head at all but one. What to call it? "It will be launched on the fifth day of the fifth month of the year — let it be called Number Five," she said. Instead of the fancy decorated *flacons* in use until then, she put her precious Chanel No. 5 in a plain square bottle. "What's inside the bottle matters more than the bottle," she said. What was inside that bottle was to bring her millions of dollars and remain the golden goose of her house.

In 1938 began years she and the Chanel empire would rather forget. She retired to Switzerland and sat out World War II, mostly, it appears, on the lap of a Nazi Gestapo chief. It is said that after the war, only the personal intervention of Churchill saved her from prison and the shaved head of a collaborationist.

In 1954, at the age of 70, she made a comeback and again revolutionized fashion with her soft cardigan suit that every American woman had to have, if not genuine, then a copy. One of her greatest coups was to mix strands of junk jewelry with real gems. Another was introducing for the first time the small handbag with a shoulder strap, often a chain.

Chanel's message to women is to live their lives according to their own dreams; or, more specifically, to dream big, to live every moment fully and be alert to grab the chance when it comes. She is saying that to love is good, the more love the better, don't worry about the pain it could bring before it happens. Don't look back. Be feminine, be elegant, be yourself. When you think of Coco, think of pearls, strings and strings of fake pearls. They were hidden in the top bureau drawers for a while but now they're back. They always will be. They're part of Chanel's legacy of French femininity: how to achieve it, how to spot style, how to develop *chien*.

Sand and Chanel, Chanel and Sand: two giants born at the beginning and near the end of the 19th century respectively, bracketing it like two towering *chiens de faïence*. Both lives were roller coasters of triumphs and heartbreaks. Both women outraged their conventional contemporaries.

Their names are still household words. Neither was considered beautiful or pretty. Cecil Beaton, the iconic fashion photographer, noted in his diary that Chanel was "no beauty, but by her allure she put all other women in the shade."

It's called *chien*. They both had it. Masses of it.

Now you can see the improbable: that Chanel, born a pauper, and Sand, born to ease, had much in common. Between the two of them, with their to-hell-with-what-people-think rage for freedom — freedom of movement, freedom of loving — they shredded centuries of corsets and taboos. They revolutionized the way the world looked at women and how women looked at themselves. They were both artists and workaholics at their art. They ushered in the liberated woman of the 20th century. They did it without alienating men.

With George Sand something else that was new and exciting was stirring: social conscience. She was an activist not only for herself and her family but for women in general. A feminist, a direct spiritual descendant of Christine de Pisan, she was independent in heart, body and mind. A modern woman, indeed!

Brigitte Bardot (1934 —)
Sensual delight on film

In recent years she has only been involved with dogs, and animals in general, but the film star that Brigitte Bardot was in the 1950's hit the world like Venus shot from a scallop shell. To many, she was all flesh and no brain, but the world was ready for flesh after a long dreary war. For Americans, she was so terribly *je ne sais quoi*, such a charming lady yet so... *sexy*. So... *French*. Roger Vadim, her director husband, understood that it was her intrinsic bourgeois modesty that made the sight of her marital antics so novel and strange and... refreshing. Tame, compared to today's boudoir scenes, but revolutionary at the time. *And God Created Woman*, the film that rocketed her to stardom, is as flimsy in plot as what some consider Bardot's inability to act; nevertheless it hit a planetary feminine chord and proved to be a watershed. Films were never the same after it.

"That ease with her body... that uninhibited sensual pleasure. It's so different with us Americans, lots of us, anyway," said Nelly, age 31. "We're not supposed to think about our bodies. It never occurred to me to have even a facial in the U.S. That was like being vain and frivolous, things my mother was very firm in condemning. You'd think all this would have changed with Women's Lib, the sexual revolution, the Pill and so on. It hasn't, though publicly, everything has changed."

Sex and the City couldn't have happened without Bardot, nor could Kate Hudson's torrid striptease for Thierry Lhermitte, her French lover in the movie, *Le Divorce*. Hudson showed real chutzpah in undressing down to her garter belt. I asked Diane Johnson, author of the book, whose idea the garter belt was and she said right away, "Thierry thought it would be great." French men love their women clad only in just that. French women know this, and if they have plans — or hopes — for the evening, dress accordingly. In *Nous ne savons pas aimer* (*We Don't Know How to Love*), Académicien Jean-Marie Rouart's narrator writes that after picking up a woman in a Montparnasse bar, he was surprised, when she undressed, to see that she was all prepared, wearing a black garter belt with lace frills.

This garter-belt culture is one of the hurdles for American women settling in France, giving them a panicky feeling, as if they're skidding into the style of a hooker, or their idea of a hooker. French ladies learned about it from courtisanes like Ninon de Lenclos in the 17th century. They have an instinct of the fine line between voluptuous and lewd. They're the champions of nuance. It helps that they have hundreds of years of tradition behind them. The sensuous phenomenon of Bardot was just one more link in the chain.

Part II

Bumps on the Road

9

Gastronomy, negativism, and blame rejection

I was getting closer to what Frenchness was, why American women set out for France, and what the general way to a Frenchman's heart was. I wasn't much closer to the reason why, having found it, American women lost it... or to the reason for them, as wives, being the nemesis of Frenchmen, if they were. Obviously I needed to talk to these women themselves; and to their French husbands. But first I wanted to know what cultural volcanoes American women were up against.

Perhaps Annette Lyons, an American psychoanalyst who had been practicing in Paris for 15 years, could tell me. I went to see her in her apartment in the Marais.

"Can you imagine," she said, "the number of desperate American women who come through here, successful lawyers, doctors, you name it... they marry a Frenchman with stars in their eyes... and they lose their soul. To survive here, you have to accept things you'd never, never do at home."

I asked her what she meant by their losing their soul, and what things they had to do which they would never accept at home.

"You'll have to ask them," she said.

I asked R. He hooted and reminded me that he was French and thought French. It was true that Constance, his wife, was half American, but the other half was French, and as the daughter of a diplomat she had lived in so many places, and had always spoken such good French that the French scene was no problem for her.

"She has all the qualities that charm Frenchmen about Americans," he said. "Direct, to the point, no subterfuge, competent, enthusiastic... above all a positive, can-do attitude, but civilized, that is, with eyes and ears and wit."

"But aren't we all like that?" I said.

R laughed. "What I see in the typical American woman who comes over here is that she's proud and headstrong, probably spoiled by an adoring father. He whispered to her all her childhood that the world is her oyster, gobble it as she likes. She hears that France is the place where women are goddesses, and then packs her bags. Goldilocks has found her chair. She will fall in love with her French Romeo... he courts her with *foie gras*, wraps her in silks by Lacroix, makes love to her night and day and says yes to all her demands and whims. At first."

He asked me if I followed. I said that, indeed, he was a little biased. "But don't stop," I added.

"Well, then, as a wife," he went on, "she plummets to earth. Oysters and foie gras for Christmas, period. If French women are goddesses, nevertheless, the country, the business, the arts, the whole thing is run by machos. They — how do you say? — they brook no quarter. Explain grievances? She has *grievances* in God's best country? Alone, she will have to survive a barrage of shocks. She'll have to deal with the taboos. Her husband will have become a kaleidoscope of the unexpected while she tries to turn herself inside out to go with the flow and learn the language. Her new countrymen are Cartesian pessimists and speak in double negatives. She feels attacked. She deflates. She becomes a pale silhouette of the local charmers. She loses the glow and zest that had made her husband marvel when they met. If the Big Bad Thing happens that she can't overlook, she divorces. Or perhaps she's trapped. French families — I am sorry to say — are famous for throwing up a firewall of legal reasons why French children shouldn't be allowed out of the country. So she's free and divorced but stuck; or, if she leaves, she's childless. If she's smart, she sticks it out, counts her battle scars and goes to work on herself. With a stupendous effort and investment, thanks to grit and her husband's example, mostly in the *non-dit* (unsaid), she becomes a new sort of marvel, a blend of hothouse French exquisiteness and nuance, and sporty American candor. It would be folly to quit now. Even without oysters."

"Have you known many of those?" I asked.

He laughed. "Yes, it happens. usually with Americans who were steeped in the language and lore of the country before they came. It makes sense. It's like being told that if you take that path through the woods, you might find a tiger asleep on it, blocking your way — so go another way. Don't step on its tail and you'll be fine. But someone has to tell you."

What were the taboos and shocks and grievances, I asked him.

R joked that to find out the details of the disagreements and shocks and taboos I'd have to marry a Frenchman myself.

I decided to start with Lizzie and her reactions to France.

We first saw Lizzie at Laura's dinner, marveling at the gargoyles and the champagne, shortly after she arrived in France. She didn't meet Thierry on the Eiffel Tower but in Philadelphia. They'd lived in America for four years before coming to France. I'd met her before at another party soon after she arrived, an effusive young woman who loved to laugh, a big hearty melodious laugh. Her whole appearance and attitude then was one of energy. She talked in exclamation points. She'd just moved into the apartment Thierry's parents had bought them in suburban Neuilly, which Lizzie still pronounced "Nooly." At Laura's dinner party she was clearly fighting hard to keep her sense of humor, and maybe losing the battle. The exuberance was not so much subdued as artificial.

I thought that getting together with Laura, a happy wife and an old hand at Paris who lapped up everything French, and Kate, who had a cool eye and was good at explaining why things were the way they were, might help Lizzie to get her exuberance back, as well as help her to open up — and let me in on her problems. I was also personally interested in the Franco-American marriages of Laura and Kate. They had both initially declined to be interviewed for this book. I was curious why.

Laura was delighted with the idea of a little meeting with Lizzie. She was always ready to help people. Kate balked at first. She said that after all, this was her professional field, she should really charge us. But then she decided it would be interesting to hear the problems of someone "normal" who wasn't screaming or moaning about committing suicide. Lizzie was happy at the idea.

I arrived first. We sat down in Lizzie's small but pleasant living room, mostly furnished by IKEA. It was on the ground floor and faced a garden. I asked her about her background, how she got here.

"I'm from Nebraska," she said. "As Bill Bryson wrote of Des Moines, 'somebody has to be.'"

Her father was a farmer, as his own father and grandfather had been before him. His schooling stopped at the eighth grade. Her mother died young, and it was from her stepmother that Lizzie first heard the name

France.

"For some reason she loved France and wanted me to, too. The first present she ever gave me was for my sixth birthday, a soft little black velvet poodle," she said. "He was so cute and cuddly! She told me his name was Fifi and that he was French, whatever that meant. She papered my walls with a paper called Francine and told me to study hard so that I could get a scholarship to a college in the East, and learn about France. This had been her dream, and I was elected to live it out. I did long to get out of Nebraska — but I had complexes about the East and anyway, I didn't really like my stepmother that much. So I did the opposite. I went to the University of Nebraska instead and studied business. And also got over my East Coast complex — there were some smoothies from there in my school who really weren't worth having a complex about! I got a scholarship to the Wharton School in Philadelphia."

She met Thierry in a pastry shop near Wharton.

"He didn't know what all the cakes were and there wasn't anyone else much around to ask, so he asked me. Well, that's what he says. But I'd seen him before, in the halls, and noticed that he looked different and that maybe he was looking at me — in fact, I was sure he was. When he spoke to me, of course I heard his accent and flipped! Some sort of foreigner! Maybe a real Frenchie! I have to admit my black velvet Fifi had made me curious about them."

Thierry, a big gruff Alsatian with red hair, wasn't exactly the model Frenchman on the order of Maurice Chevalier or Charles Boyer that Lizzie's stepmother had in mind, but he thrilled Lizzie nevertheless.

"He gave me a big rush — how could I not fall for him? My only little flirt until then had been with an Austrian ski instructor in Aspen. What a great skier! You can't imagine. The grace he had, and faster than the wind! That was fun. But he drank too much and I have to admit that hanging out with him was — well, all he could talk about was deep snow and mushy snow and different kinds of ski wax. What I don't know about ski waxes! He wasn't that good in bed, either, though Austrians are supposed to be brilliant in that department. It was just, you know, a soccer match."

"A soccer match?" I queried.

"You know — straight to the goal and no hands. But Thierry! He had so much in his head, I thought it would never all come out, not in a thousand years. Besides being a fabulous lover. He started talking about marriage practically right away! Do you think he was lonely? I don't know. But — France. That seemed pretty weird. To tell you the truth, I could hardly have told you where it was on the map. Louis XIV? Forget it. But Marie Antoinette — those wigs! I'd seen pictures of them — and she had her head cut off? Of course I didn't have a clue that everything would be crazier than living in an igloo... and I didn't want to leave my father, the farm, everything. Thierry said we could live in Philadelphia or New Haven or somewhere — not New York, everyone said you couldn't bring up children in New York... and if we got married, I guess you had to think about kids. He promised me we wouldn't live in France, just go on visits. And he talked about the Alps — I didn't know there were Alps in France — great skiing, he said. So we got married and Thierry got a good job in St. Louis and everything was fine. We had a little boy and a little girl. He was a very sweet husband and father! But then, three years later, he was head-hunted by AXA. That big French multinational? He said we'd have to go to France for a bit but after that, it could be anywhere in the world. He said it was too good to turn down. Well, so here we are."

Laura and Kate, good friends, arrived together. Lovely and serene, Laura sailed in with that perfect French *look* in jeans, a white scalloped blouse and stiletto heels. Kate was in her daytime, non-slinky, professional look of black trousers, black turtleneck, high heels, and several long, beaded necklaces.

Lizzie got up to let them in. She gave Laura one awkward kiss on the cheek and laughed nervously.

"Ever since cracking noses with that friend of yours at your party, I get it all wrong," she said. "Can't we just shake hands — or nothing — like at home?"

Kate laughed and slipped into her professional jargon. "It's nice to actually touch people when you say hello — touch their hand, touch their cheek, be close. That's what the French miss most when they come to the U.S., they feel sensorially deprived. We Americans make ourselves into little islands, cut off. We won't let people inside the two-foot bubble of air surrounding us."

"Think about it, Lizzie," said Laura, "it's much friendlier to touch people, kissing or shaking hands all around the room, not just dismissing them with a wave and a vague 'hi'."

Kate stood up. "Come on, let's do a role play," she said. She asked Lizzie to come and talk to her as if they were at a cocktail party.

With Lizzie about two feet away, Kate then moved in much closer and continued to chat about the weather with their heads about six inches apart.

"Doesn't this make you uncomfortable, being so close?" Kate asked then.

"Claustrophobic," said Lizzie.

"Well, then, think about it. With our two-foot-thick bubble of air surrounding us, we Americans are enraged by people who dare to invade it. For instance, French people coming towards us on the sidewalk. American managers in my groups fuss about the 'bloody rude French.' A software designer even growled, 'They not only bump into me, they try to push me into the street!' But the French don't have a bubble of space around them. So, of course, when they pass you on the street, they don't allow for yours — or theirs. Germans have the same reaction as Americans, only more so. The bubble of air around them is often three feet thick. Imagine the shock and confusion of Chancellor Merkel when George Bush, whom she hardly knew, came up behind her and began giving her a neck rub."

Lizzie looked electrified.

Laura broke in. "God, Kate, you sound like Psychology 101 at Wellesley."

"Hush, Laura," said Kate. "That was a great course. Not Psych 101 but Kate III, Introduction to Cross-Cultural Living. Let's see. I like to begin this sort of meeting with a French marvel. Difficult to choose, as there are so many, I'm sure you'd agree, Laura. A 'marvel' is to remind us that we're in France in order to love it, appreciate it, and adjust and be effective members of the community, and transform the hell we're going through. In other words, we want to be positive. But we're not here to knock America, either. Laura, why don't you give us a marvel, since you don't like me playing Teacher?"

Laura beamed. She sat up straighter and pushed her hair back.

"Love to!" she said. "For instance, the politeness of French men. Even strangers! Not to be believed when you first get here. The way they open doors for you — even the car door — and carry your duffle bag, *sans gêne*. The way they look at you, as if you're a chocolate éclair, and will set you straight if your skirt is too short or your jacket too long for this year. And — what a pleasure to see them at a big dinner party at an embassy — the way, if they're placed at a small table of ten or so, they go around and introduce themselves and shake or kiss hands, first with all the women at their table, and then with the men. Americans just sit and gawk at the people they don't know. Well, I have to say, I love French manners."

"Byzantine, but don't quote me," said Kate.

"Of course," said Laura. "It took them 1,000 years to work them out."

Lizzie gave us a glass of Coke from a side table as we settled in. Kate took out a notebook with a list of cross-cultural marital problems Lizzie might want to talk about.

"For today, select two," she said. "Blame rejection, repression of children, overly strict discipline, negativism, criticism, racism, gastronomy, lying, husband tyranny, narcissism, marriage contract, mothers-in-law, infidelity —"

"That sounds like a list of contagious diseases," said Laura.

"And all bearable with a little cross-cultural acupuncture," said Kate.

"When I arrived," said Laura, "an old-timer American took me in hand and said to think of the two things that poisoned my life here most, and the two things that put me in raptures. I spent so much time thinking of the raptures that I forgot all about the poisons."

Lizzie let out a yelp. "Forgot all about them! When they hit you in the face all day!"

"Tell us about them," I said.

Lizzie fairly erupted. "The no no no's I get all day! And never 'I'm sorry!' And food!" said Lizzie. "Eating! It's eat eat eat here! All these big complicated meals! Thierry didn't mind sandwiches for lunch in the U.S. — but here, it's a three-course meal — twice a day! His idea of a perfect evening — here — is to sit *immobile* in a good restaurant for three hours!"

"All right, so, three: gastronomy, negativism and blame rejection," said Kate. "Dining, Lizzie, is a sacrament in France. Thierry is back home, where food *matters*... how it looks, how it's presented, how it *tastes*. You had better learn how to spoil him with taste thrills. If you don't, someone else will. His mother probably cooked blissful meals."

"His mother!" said Lizzie. "When she comes for lunch, she brings the food."

"You see," said Kate. "Did you know that the top three-star French chefs have the status of movie stars? And they write books."

"And commit suicide from the strain," said Laura. "Like Bernard Loiseau, who did. Apparently he was worried sick that he might lose one of his Michelin stars. It turned out that he hadn't — but he was already dead."

"Just imagine," said Kate. "They have to come up with sublime new recipes all the time, plus direct a platoon of subchefs and waiters, supervise the restaurant dining room, charm the customers, create and invest in frozen food delights, write books, check the proofs for mistakes... They always need loans to expand and are in constant anxiety about whether they can pay them back. Really, Lizzie, you need to adopt a posture of awe of the gastronomy culture here."

Lizzie wasn't convinced. "There's a lot of pizza takeout being ordered by French women, I can tell you — anyway the younger generation."

Kate didn't want to accept this. "Let's move on to negativism," she said. "When did you first notice it?"

"Practically when we got off the plane and I began seeing all these thin-lipped Frenchmen with the corners of their mouth turned down — like a horseshoe with all the luck falling out! That's the way they look on the street — all the luck gone. It's depressing! Thierry is beginning to look like that too. He wasn't like that in the States. He was really gung-ho about everything."

Kate made some notes. "Second lesson for today: his country is as much a part of a marriage as the husband himself, particularly this one, with its very strong culture — culture in the sense of the shared system of how a unit of people operates on all levels. You know the word *terroir*? It's one of those big many-layered French words. It bubbles with meanings — soil, rural roots, place, tradition, a hundred things — like soul, for instance — and brings tears to a Frenchman's eyes. Thierry is *home* again. Imagine what that means. In this culture, it's not a question of love me, love my dog, but of love me, love my *patrie*. Seriously, Lizzie. This is *crucial* to your marriage."

"But how can he change so much? For instance, with his mother. I mean he practically jumps when she asks him to do something. We had to live with his parents in Paris when we first got here, until this place was ready — I almost went bonkers —"

"No mothers-in-law today, we need a whole week for that," interrupted Kate. "Laura, what about handling the abominable no's?"

Laura threw out her arms and whooped. This was her *casus belli*. She had resolved it with Fabrice through tedious negotiation and relished any opportunity to share her triumph... step by step. It would take a while. I went to get another Coke.

"French babies are born saying *non*," she said. "Being negative is their thing. Grownups have a love affair with it. Negative is good, positive is soppy. It starts in school — teachers pounce on their pupils for the tiniest mistake. And they insult them. My daughter Janet's best friend was told that her marks were terrible because she was too fat! Talk about negative feedback! Soothing words? A compliment? You're kidding. Even when something is very positive, they say it in the negative. Something 'not bad' means it's very good. A woman said to be 'not beautiful' means she's a fright of ugliness. But Americans are cheerleaders! We'll put a positive twist on almost anything! We say that someone revoltingly ugly 'has a good heart' or a 'lovely disposition.' If she is difficult and nasty, then she is 'insecure.' The child with terrible grades 'will do better next time'... while my kids tell me their French school pals tremble at coming home with a bad report card. They might miss a week of dinners, their computer might be seized, or even — horrors — their ski vacation might be canceled."

Lizzie was transfixed. "So what do I do with Thierry?"

"You have to know that he *can* say yes," said Laura. "Instead of getting mad when he grunts *NON* to your wonderful new idea, you have to sit him down and quietly go over your points one by one. Listen to this. I've been working on Fabrice for 15 years. Do you remember the children's story about a locomotive, *The Little Engine That Could*? And how it puffs and puffs to get up a steep mountain and it's just so hard, and the little engine keeps saying 'I think I can, I think I can, I think I can' — and it does! It actually makes it to the top of the mountain. Well, I read the story to the kids, and every once in a while I'd repeat it to Fabrice when he was in one of his black *non* holes, and do you know what? About a month ago he told me he'd begun to see the point of American 'positive thinking.' I was blown away. He actually said to me, 'You've given me hope, to think I can really do things that seem impossible.'"

Kate got up, did a twirl around her chair, and clapped.

"Laura, that is sensational," she said. "He ought to give executive seminars. Really. The work place in France needs him! It's deadening! I got here from Chicago, accustomed to pats on the back — did anyone here ever tell me anything nice? I can tell you, it makes the stress that much worse when you have a deadline."

"You see why I'm quite happy not to work here," said Laura.

Kate began gathering up her things. "I'll have to fly in a few minutes. Well, Lizzie, after all those years being positive in America, Thierry should be a pushover for moving to yes. Do you feel better about it?"

Lizzie didn't say anything for a while. She got up to fix a flower falling out of a vase. She said, finally, "But what about not saying he's sorry?"

"Ignore it," said Kate. "The French can't make a mistake, it's not culturally acceptable, so how can they say they're sorry for something they didn't do? So just drop 'I'm sorry' out of your head. And while you're at it, banish the word 'crazy.' Nothing is less crazy than France."

"*You* have to make an effort," said Laura. "No one is going to wave a magic wand. If this place is magical, it's because it's different, it takes work to get your mind and heart around it, to even perceive that it *is* the most magical. It's like going through the sound barrier. Boom, a new way of looking at everything. So now — I have to run too — shall we meet again next week? Kate? My place?"

"Lizzie," said Kate, half way out the door, "have you ever moaned cruelly about France in front of Thierry — when you were out for dinner at one of those restaurants he likes, with his friends, for instance? Yes? Well, can you imagine how that upset him? That insult would cancel 10 years of his saying 'I'm sorry.'"

As we separated I decided to get some more ideas on the things we'd talked about.

I ran into José Vidal at a cocktail party. José is a Spanish-Frenchman who travels a great deal, especially between Spain, France and America. He is profoundly Latin. I asked him about the U.S. He rolled his eyes and groaned.

"How do I *feel*? It's always a shock for me, arriving in America," he said. "Everyone is so separate, like trees in a forest. *Moi*, I must feel close to people, I must greet them with a handshake, cheek-kisses — skin on skin, warmth. I must be able to *feel* them. In a few days I get used to it. But then the bear-hugging starts. This is a shocking thing, for a Frenchman — this person who grabs you and throws his arms around you, *crushing* you like a boa — you wonder what he wants, what he will do next. Perhaps one will be suffocated? I do not like this custom. It is not gracious. It does not have warmth. There is no feel of skin. It is brutal. Dominating. Bullying, like the U.S."

José had more to say about New York. "No skin touching — and we can't even use our eyes to look at women. The Look — penetrating, seizing the whole being of the admired woman, bathing her in ardor — does not exist in America. If you give an American woman The Look, she calls the police. My senses are screaming after two days in New York. And my poor wife — you cannot imagine what she goes through — no men looking at her! At first she thinks she must have on shoes that do not match, or a lace slip peeking out below her skirt... With no men staring at her, she wonders if she is a woman."

Lizzie's tales of her mother-in-law had also impressed me. Bringing her own food to lunch with her son? Were we Americans really such boors in the kitchen?

I decided to attend a ladies' lunch in Paris, where Amélie, who lives in Lyon, and whose French family tree goes back for centuries in the

Loire Valley, was asked to tell about her two years in California with her American husband and their two little children. Amélie was fascinated by the local attitude to cooking.

"The women I met seemed to look on cooking as secondary," she said, "as if it's not really a part of their life, and sometimes as if it's, well, beneath them. Or even as if it's a punishment. While for us, it is absolutely central. Above all, it's a pleasure. Preparing and making a meal that gives other people pleasure — family or friends — and sitting with them around a table enjoying it together is one of our great joys.

"One afternoon, the wife who was bringing my children home from school — she was doing the car pool that week — happened to come into my kitchen. 'You're cooking? From *scratch?*' she asked in amazement. The next day she came by and again found me in the kitchen. 'You're cooking again? But you were cooking yesterday!'"

Amélie said that the only American she got to know well during her California stay was an unmarried intellectual of about 55. She was "very *soignée*, beautifully dressed, like a Frenchwoman" but also had never seen anyone really cooking in a kitchen.

"She asked me a million questions — how I did that sauce, what was that pot for, things that in France we grow up with like the alphabet.

"Every time she came for dinner, she arrived well ahead of time to see what I was doing in the kitchen. One time I made a zucchini *au gratin*, really very simple, you just fry the zucchini and then cover them with grated cheese and put the dish in the oven for a while, but she watched and queried every step as if it were translating hieroglyphics.

"Sometimes I saw the kitchens of some of the mothers of my children's school friends. They were sublime, with shelves and shelves of cookbooks. Yet no one ever seemed to use them."

10

Bossy husbands

Laura's roomy, luminous apartment was even more splendid, if possible, in the daytime than in the evening. Outside, the sculpted saints of the Cathedral facade chanted of eternity to the July tourist mobs below. Inside, the furniture was a cheering welcome to the world of elegance, a mixture of Louis XVI tables and commodes with bright ormolu handles and deep comfortable armchairs and sofas, some in white, some in bright colors. Much thought, as well as taste — and let's face it, money — had gone into this room. The same could be said for Laura's outfit, a peach-colored jacket over a simple white blouse and black, *moulant* (form-fitting) trousers, and slender high-heeled pumps. Her chic was classic and totally French, and beyond the grasp of most of us in the American community... as it was of Lizzie.

Lizzie's jeans didn't fit, were too short and the wrong cut. Instead of high heels, or at least slender pumps, she had on running shoes. She flopped on the couch, explaining that she'd bicycled over from "Nooly." Kate, in her professional black again, asked her what she wanted to talk about today.

"His mother! Wait till I tell you what happened last weekend!"

"I said we needed a week for mothers-in-law. Not today."

Laura told Kate that Lizzie needed to let off steam.

Lizzie burst out, "I hate to say this, because after all she's Thierry's mother, but I might just kill her some day. I'm 32 years old and she treats me either like a slave or a four-year-old. When we were living with her after we moved back, I was the *maid* who was told to bring the food in to the dining room for dinner, and change the plates — and do the dishes! Now that we're in our own house, she comes over and runs her finger over the furniture checking for dust! Anyway, that's not what I wanted you to help me with."

Lizzie was brimming over with a family drama. She'd just come in specially for our meeting from Normandy, where Jacqueline, her mother-in-law, had found a summer rental for the family. They had moved out there last weekend. Jacqueline had also hired a cook for the summer, which, Lizzie admitted, was nice of her. The cook was Spanish and was enormously fat, with the biggest breasts she'd ever seen, which is the focus of the story. "Balloons!" said Lizzie.

The cook came to Neuilly for the departure. Jacqueline introduced them. Then the cook got in the back seat with the au pair girl and the two children, one of them on the au pair's lap, and all the children's paraphernalia — the stroller and so on — that didn't fit into the trunk. Lizzie was up front with Thierry. Matthieu, 6, suddenly remembered his bicycle. Lizzie told him there wasn't any room for it. Matthieu started crying. Jacqueline was standing by the car, ready to wave goodbye. She tried to soothe Matthieu, but he just cried louder.

Thierry, the cook and the bicycle

So Thierry got out, carried the bicycle to the car and jammed it in the back, with the handlebars just a millimeter from the cook's huge boobs. Lizzie had a fit. She pleaded with Thierry. "That's dangerous, please don't take the bike, if you have to stop suddenly you'll impale the poor cook's breasts!" Thierry began to start the car.

Lizzie appealed to Jacqueline. "Please," she said, "he'll listen to you, please convince him not to take the bike!"

Jacqueline's answer, which froze Lizzie and which she was still trying to digest, was: "He's over 21 and vaccinated; he knows what he's doing."

"Can you imagine?" said Lizzie now. "She was ready to sacrifice that poor woman's breasts because of a whining child!"

"Well, did Thierry have to stop suddenly?" said Kate.

"No, but if he had —"

"So he was right. Matthieu was happy and the boobs were unharmed."

"But Jacqueline's attitude — what about female solidarity? What about taking unnecessary risks in hurting people less fortunate than you?"

"That's how she kept Thierry's father happy," said Laura. "Never argue. Don't forget, the bicycle belonged to Thierry's son. Sons take all, here."

"Never argue!" said Lizzie. "I can't live like that. I'm supposed to turn myself into a sort of cuddly stuffed teddy bear, is that it? I thought marriage was about being a partner! What's going on here?"

Kate clicked in with her professional voice: "What's going on is not to expect explanations, or equality. Just accept, and normally you discover that those peremptory decisions turn out to have a reason that isn't immediately apparent. You know, really, this story is about American women being spoiled. They're used to always having their way. Thierry had all the information he needed to decide if it was dangerous or not — he knew the road, he knew how much control he had over his car. Most of all, he was the male, he was in charge. You just had emotion."

This was too much for Laura. "I don't agree that we're spoiled — no one spoiled me, I can tell you. Spinach not eaten for dinner was served cold for breakfast. And if Fabrice treated me like that..."

"Oh, Philadelphia," groaned Kate. "Puritan hairshirts. The rest of us aren't like that, and Frenchmen in general aren't like Fabrice. And I'll bet he has plenty of downsides."

Laura frowned and looked as if she was going to retort, but didn't. Lizzie sighed and groaned some more. She got up to open a window, sat down, drank some coke. "Well, tell me what I should have done at a restaurant last week, then," she said.

"Is it another mother-in-law story? No time," said Kate.

"No, it's a domineering-husband story. It's almost as if he's become a control freak. Thierry was never like that in the U.S."

"You keep saying that," said Laura. "It can't have come on so suddenly. You were at home, in your own comforting pond of St. Louis and didn't notice, probably. So, what happened last week?"

"Thierry took me to a little bistro — a really simple restaurant, for dinner. The waiter was dark and handsome, not very tall. I love Italy and Italians. I said something trivial to Thierry, like, 'The waiter must be Italian, he has that sultry smoldering look.' So what did Thierry say? He told me, 'No, he's French. But just don't ask him!' Why not, for goodness sake? The nerve of it!

"I kept my cool, for once, but I wasn't having that. I mean, who decides what I say? Is he some kind of ventriloquist or something? I finished my *blanquette de veau* and then caught the eye of the head waiter. He came over and I asked him, 'Please, we're having a discussion, could you tell me if our waiter is Italian?' Whereupon he said 'Why yes, in a way — he's Corsican.' So we were both right. And do you know what Thierry said then? He was *furious*. He said, 'I asked you not to ask him.' I said, 'But I didn't! I asked the head waiter!' 'Same thing!' he said. I was bowled over. Now I ask you, why shouldn't I ask a harmless question like that? As if it was an insult! And... honestly, who is he to tell me who I can talk to?"

Laura said that wasn't the point at all.

"The point is that in France, it's rude to talk to waiters at a restaurant. A couple from Tulsa staying with us last summer did that, asking the waiter questions about where he was from and what were the interesting local sights they should see. I remember feeling uncomfortable and Fabrice's face getting a twitch near his right eye, the way it does when he's angry or embarrassed. Waiting on table is a respected profession here. It's not for college students trying to earn an extra euro. You can't chat with your waiters anymore than you can chat with bank clerks or tax inspectors."

Kate started dialing on her cell phone, explaining to someone that she was late. Then she said, "If a Frenchman lays down the law in a public situation — like the one at the bistro — it's probably because of a question of propriety or status. Americans usually don't factor in either of these considerations. So, if the American wife is confused and annoyed about what's happening, it's best to trust her husband and shut up. And don't bring it up later at home. They hate that. Just forget it. Also, the

111

French don't like being asked about their background, and a Corsican might be offended to be taken for an Italian. But that's also not the point. The real point for me is as I told you before, just accept. Do what he says. He's always right, anyway 99 percent of the time. Don't expect an explanation. It doesn't come. Issuing orders, not explaining goes with the territory of being a French male. Accept it now and save yourself pain later."

"Is that what you do with Geoffroy?" said Laura, a little archly, I thought.

"Of course," Kate snapped, getting up to go. "If I didn't..." She turned to Lizzie. "Try to bring us a marvel about France next time. Be positive."

"Wait," said Laura. "I've got a killer warm-up for the mothers-in-law meeting. Just listen to this. An American I want to bring to the next meeting, she's called Judith, told me she was all set to go on vacation to Greece with Xavier, her husband, when her mother-in-law said she wanted to come too. Judith told Xavier that she wasn't going if his mother came along. For once she wanted to have two whole weeks alone with him, without her. So guess what? Xavier went to Greece with his mother — and Judith stayed home!"

Kate laughed. "Serves Judith right — imagine coming out and saying such a thing!"

On the way home I thought again about that mother of Thierry. I would have reacted exactly like Lizzie.

11

Social gaffes

Lizzie had to go to America, so our next meeting, after the summer, would be our last. Laura came with the two other Americans she had mentioned last time, both wives of Frenchmen: Judith, the wife who missed going to Greece with her husband, and Evelyn, a friend of Judith. Kate arrived last. We gathered in Lizzie's garden under the shade of a walnut tree. Two walnuts promptly fell on my head. Lizzie's children were on a walk with the American au pair girl.

Judith and Evelyn, both slim and dark haired, looked terribly casual-chic French, Judith in jeans and t-shirt, Evelyn in a skirt, both in pumps. They had been in France for 15 years or more. They described themselves as adjusted and well-oiled parts of the French system: happy cogs, but still, they did pause sometimes and register that some things here were, well, troubling. The idea of airing all this wasn't "French bashing!" We all agreed on that. It was simply comparing some "anomalies."

We introduced ourselves. Judith told us that she was 43, had been a physical therapist when she met Xavier, a doctor, at a professional convention in New York. She was from Chicago; they had three teenage children, and she was trying to get a work permit here.

Evelyn, 45, was a freelance journalist, had four children, also all teenagers, and had lived in Versailles for 19 years. She stunned us all when she said she met Henri, a banker, at a hotel during a pilgrimage to Santiago de Compostela. I noted that she had the sturdy legs of an athlete.

"You don't mean you walked all the way from Chartres to northern Spain?" asked Laura.

"Henri walked, well, half the way. I took the train with some friends to Souillac and went on horseback from there. Actually, I was on a magazine assignment, but Henri was really on a pilgrimage. French Catholics do that. Thousands of them, every year."

We digested that for a while and then Laura told us there was nothing to tell, much, about her background. She had grown up outside Philadelphia, been to Foxcroft boarding school —

"With your *horse*?" threw in Kate.

"Don't be silly, Kate. And then I went to Penn and after that did some fund raising — I'm hopelessly bad at that — for what they call worthy projects, then took a year off to visit France, and met Fabrice at a sailing camp."

Lizzie wanted to know about the embroidered crown on the napkins at dinner that night.

"It's the coronet of a French count," said Laura. "Don't worry about it — they do that here instead of embroidering linen with initials, as they do in the U.S. — but it's probably good for you to know about names starting with a *de* — it's called a *particule*. It usually means that that person is a member of the nobility. Either the old, *Ancien Régime* or the more recent Napoleonic nobility. The important thing is not to use it if you're just referring to the last name."

"What's that supposed to mean?" said Lizzie.

"Well, if you're mentioning a Frenchman everyone is always talking about, Alexis de Tocqueville, and you say Tocqueville said such and such, that's fine. Just don't say, 'de Tocqueville said such and such.' Say Monsieur de Tocqueville or the Count de Tocqueville, or simply, Tocqueville. Kate, your turn."

"I know people who never use other people's 'de,'" said Kate, with a yawn and a little smirk at Laura, whose name had a 'de,' which Kate's didn't. "They think it's anti-republican."

Laura was unruffled. I guess she was used to handling jealousy, if that's what it was, but I was nervous at the undercurrents swirling around.

"Lots of people have lots of ways of behaving outside the box," Laura said. "Let's not confuse Lizzie."

"That sounds like perverted snobbery to me," said Judith. "Kate, do tell us about yourself."

Kate told us she was from Santa Barbara, California, had a Ph.D. in psychology and said she had spent "some time" as a student at the Jung Institute near Zurich. She met Geoffroy ice skating in front of the Hotel de Ville in Paris. "I fell and he picked me up, simple as that," she said.

We all raised our eyebrows and she added, "Well, let's just say I knew what to do then."

"Did you ever not know what to do?" Laura asked. Laura had a funny sardonic smile which wasn't like her, but Kate didn't seem to notice.

"Never as well as you, dear," she said.

Lizzie passed around glasses of tomato juice and tonic water, along with little pieces of paper for jotting down subjects we wanted to talk about, then collected them and read out the topics: criticism, visiting American parents, children's education, privacy, etiquette rules, class differences, unsignaled danger, racism, endless school vacations, mothers-in-law, marriage contracts. No one mentioned infidelity. I guessed I wasn't going to hear about it in a group. Everyone wanted to talk about having been emotionally battered to a pulp by critical husbands, with whom, nevertheless, they said they were happy. It seemed like a lot of things to be upset by. Were other nationalities so bothered by the French? Was this at the bottom of the riddle?

"Lizzie, what's the good news you were going to bring us?" said Laura.

Lizzie laughed. "No screens on the doors in France — and no flies or mosquitoes! All summer long! I couldn't believe it."

"Good point," said Kate. "We've all gotten so used to it that we take it for granted. Who has a marvel?"

"I have a humdinger," said Evelyn. "Do you know that some French words are masculine in the singular and feminine in the plural? Just three, but two of them are among the glories of French: *amour* and *délice...* love and delight. Imagine! Their most magical words!"

"Sounds like oysters, except that oysters change back and forth," said Judith. "Has anyone here seen oysters having sex?"

"Please, Judith," said Kate, "French oysters don't 'have sex', they make love, like French human beings." She drew a deep breath and switched themes. "So, spouse criticism today — "

Château reality check

"First, can I bring up something really bugging me?" said Evelyn. "One of the people we met at our club invited us for the weekend — to what turns out to be his family château. I don't have a clue about château codes, particularly the don'ts. Please help, someone!"

Laura had paragraphs and paragraphs to say about them.

"Just be glad you didn't marry into one of those families," she said. "The châteaux that are lived in, and not hotels, are huge and hideously uncomfortable. You'd be spending the winter freezing and the summer slicing vegetables for 20 people at meals — extended family, friends, you name it. Your bed will be agony. Single beds. The bathroom is down the hall. If it's winter, you may freeze to death with thin blankets. No central heating, of course. Always take your own hot water bottle. The summer may be excruciatingly hot — forget about air conditioning."

"Yes, but the rules?" said Evelyn.

"Just copy your hostess."

Evelyn looked dubious but said nothing as Kate took over again with her professor's cough.

"Shall we get back on the page? You have to keep in mind that criticizing — *critiquer* — isn't negative in France. Negative or positive isn't the point. The point is that it's a national addiction, like soccer. You dribble a few words and then drive with a devastating remark, and someone else butts in, grabs it and dribbles some more before he too kicks a long one..."

"Oh, come on Kate, that's gobbledygook," said Laura.

"*Critiquer* in America is a first cousin of *non*, but not here," said Kate, ignoring Laura. "Here it's the unofficial French religion, as well as the national sport. Teachers in school are constantly after children to hone their *esprit critique*. Parents massacre their kids at the dinner table if they don't get it right. By the time they're grown up, they've perfected it — which means that everything and everyone is scrutinized, analyzed, picked apart and put back together. The idea is that if you don't know how a thing works, you don't understand it and can't make it work for you. Like a watch. This country is about intellectual agility."

"Maybe," said Evelyn, "but after a while it's depressing that nothing is ever just plain good — there's always a 'but.' No one is really nice, period. Henri has to assassinate everyone."

"It really is depressing," said Laura. "I can't bear the way holes are punched in everyone. Part of being positive and optimistic in America is thinking well of people until you're obliged to admit they're serial killers or pedophiles. I've fought Fabrice so hard about this that he doesn't do it anymore — and he even says it makes him feel better. I don't let my children criticize everything and everyone negatively all the time either. *Esprit critique*, all right. We have to learn it —"

"Counter attack!" said Kate.

"No!" said Laura. "Handle it positively! We Americans don't like hurting people's feelings and I don't see why we should. I think one of our duties in being here is standing up for the best of America — and being positive is one of our best qualities."

"Oh, God," said Kate, "you sound like Mary Poppins."

Judith squeaked in agreement with Laura. "Half the time this so-called criticism is just plain nagging! I left a faucet dripping, I cooked the fish too long, I forgot to take the key of the car totally out of the ignition, I spilled milk on the rug, I talked too much at dinner the night before with some friends. If I didn't have a Herculean ego, I'd have been flattened into a puddle of grease long ago."

Evelyn banged her glass down on the table. "Right! And what about their friendly-insult criticisms? A so-called friend at a party recently said in a manner he no doubt thought was charming and provocative — rather than insulting — that my new hairdo had given me a *coup de vieux* and no one would f— me any more. What am I supposed to do with that?"

Kate laughed. "Do what Nicole de Buron had her character do in one of her books. Hit back. Say, 'Well you were always so ugly I'm sure no girl ever let you pick her up.'"

"I don't agree at all," said Laura. "I think you should smile and tell him to come to the hairdresser with you the next time."

Kate made a sort of clucking sound. "Oh, you're taking all this too seriously... a Frenchman is just acting according to his cultural imperatives — using his *esprit critique*. And did you consider... couldn't an American husband be just as fussy?"

We all disagreed. American husbands wouldn't be so sharp, so unrelenting. They'd negotiate. You left the headlights on, so he'd get a week of not emptying the garbage. That way, the wife's mistake would turn into a boon for the husband. It would make the wife more careful and the husband, instead of being annoyed, would have something to whistle about.

"I guess it depends on whether French husbands empty the garbage," said Judith.

"What's the third hermaphrodite word?" asked Laura.

"I can't remember," said Evelyn.

"About criticism." Kate was trying to wind things up. "Maybe husbands and friends are sometimes a little too frank, but the amazing thing about French strangers is that they're not. You can lose your car keys in the gutter or fall down on a step and no one will say, 'You should be more careful!' They'll just help you. And they'll never be indiscreet. I got a huge frightful shiner bumping into a sharp wall — and no one at the café where I always have breakfast said a thing."

"They thought your husband was beating you," Laura laughed.

Kate gathered her things ready to leave. Evelyn, Judith and Lizzie all talked at once about things they'd wanted covered before we parted.

Parental visits

Lizzie had just had a visit from her parents.

"Thierry gets upset that my stepmother wears too-loud colors and fancy-colored glasses with decorated rims. My dad wears pink shorts in town in the summer. They expect dinner at 6 pm. They sit down at the dining room table and wait for it. That's the way it is in Omaha. You tell them, 'But Dad, we don't eat till 8 or 8:30 and sometimes 9 pm, when Thierry gets home from work.' They can't get used to that."

"Tell them about the dress code here," said Laura, "and for heaven's sake, give them dinner early."

Coddled sons

Evelyn erupted. "When Antoine turned of age, I told him he was 18 now and would have to take care of his own clothes, washing them and so forth. He was aghast. 'Mom, I can't!' he said. The way French mothers coddle their sons is not to be believed. They may still be living the life of luxury at home until they're 30. And if they're not, it's still Mom they expect to do everything. Go to any train station in Paris on Friday afternoon and you'll see young French men with a duffle bag of laundry to take home to Mom."

"That's the way the mothers want it," said Kate. "It keeps them in power and it keeps the families together for good."

Danger

Lizzie grabbed the floor again with something the rest of us had long since gotten used to and forgotten about.

"Accidents! I'm supposed to live in a country with no fire escapes on lots of buildings, no fire extinguishers — and often no bars on the windows! Thierry says I exaggerate — I can't get him to listen to me about this at all — but the carelessness! Of officials, and workers — with these horrible accidents. I have a friend whose mother fell out of a bathroom window in the country... It had a horizontal bar which wasn't properly secured. The bathroom was on the second floor, and when she was trying to hang something out the window, she leaned on the bar. It gave way, and she fell out. Fell out! And broke her neck!"

We all looked at each other, trying to take this in, until Judith said, "Well, listen to this. I was helping prepare a buffet dinner for one of the

French associations I belong to. It was at the house of our president. She sent me up to the attic to get some extra plates. I couldn't see a thing up there in the dark. I stumbled around looking for the light switch. And then — suddenly my foot went out into pure space — I fell through the trap door to the floor below."

She paused a moment and drew a deep breath, remembering.

"I broke my back. I had to lie on my back in a rigid corset for three months at the hospital. I didn't know till I got out if I'd ever walk again. The worst was being away from my little baby. He was only four months old. Xavier had a terrible time finding someone to take care of him."

Kate shrugged. "France relies on its clever citizens," she said, "to figure out open manholes, shaky ladders, misleading road signs, open trapdoors. People aren't coddled and treated like babies, as in England."

She seemed to have an excuse for everything French. I wasn't the only one who had noticed.

Lizzie let out a sort of whoop. "Hey, whose side are you on, Kate? Judith was practically crippled for life by that hostess's negligence and you sound as if it's her fault for not noticing a trap door in the dark!"

Kate sat up as if she were suddenly uncoiled. "My business is to make people comfortable in France! Statistics show that it's easier for Americans to get used to Japan than to France! I'm trying to prevent nervous breakdowns and homicides. There are two sides to everything and if I don't present the French side, how are newcomers going to get it? French people can't give it to them. It's like trying to get a snake to explain how he molts."

Lizzie was not to be put off. I was delighted to see that she was finding her feet: "If you ask me," she said, standing up and wagging her finger at Kate, "what this country needs is a few good American lawsuits!"

"The lawyers here aren't paid enough to attract people clever enough to try their cases properly. It will never happen," said Kate. "And if it does, watch out. Goodbye, la *douce France*. They'll make tough American trial lawyers look like Little Red Riding Hood. Listen to what happened to me a couple of months ago. I had to drive to the village near our place in Alsace to get something and had just heard that my father died. I adored my father and was upset and trying to figure out how I could get to Santa Barbara for the funeral. Apparently when I drove out of my parking place, I nicked — barely touched — another car — so lightly I didn't even notice it.

"A few days later a gendarme phoned and told me I was a hit and run driver. What? I went to see him. He said that a woman in a house overlooking the square had seen me bump into another car and drive away without leaving a note. She took down my license plate. He gave me the phone number of the other car's driver. She showed me the spot I supposedly hit. You could hardly see it with a magnifying glass. Nothing on my car at all. On hers, a tiny speck of blue on her gray car — a new car, that was the problem. Did I really do it? How can I prove I didn't? She was the Filipino wife of an immigrant. She wanted her car restored to its virginal perfection, and there would be no discussion. I pleaded with her that in six months it would be covered with much worse marks and dents, like all the other cars in France. Nothing doing. I had to pay her garage — 549 euros."

Kate lit a cigarette. It was the first I'd seen her smoke.

"What was the evidence that I'd hit that car? A bored villager looking out the window — not even close. If you get on the wrong side of the law here, it's big trouble," she said. "Do you know they can slam you in prison indefinitely without any sort of trial? I mean, months, years — just on the 'suspicion' of the judge... the *juge d'instruction*. And he can convict you without evidence — just an 'intimate conviction'— *intimate conviction!* Please! No evidence! The 19 suspects in that Outreau pedophilia case in 2006 — who were all finally acquitted — rotted in prison for four years — four years! — without even being able to see a lawyer. Their lives were totally ruined. One of them committed suicide."

Evelyn said she'd read about the bungling of a judge in the case of *"le petit Gregory"* 20 years ago, that it still haunted the country. A little boy of five was found dead in a stream in the Vosges, leading to a series of false confessions, false accusations and a murder.

"And do you remember," Kate added, "a while ago when Robert de Niro was in Paris and suspected of being a pimp... they got him out of bed at 6 am and treated him like a criminal! He said he'd never set foot in France again."

We sat there stunned for a while. People started saying goodbye, more softly than usual.

Then Evelyn said, "Look you all, this has been a hoot, sort of, but I want Lizzie to know that I love France. I love the French. I love living here. Maybe everything isn't perfect, but things are more perfect here than anywhere, and all you have to do is look at everything positively, well, within reason, anyway."

Part III

The Worst Pitfalls

12

Marriage Contracts

I was beginning to get a feel of what was behind Fabrice's riddle at Laura's gargoyle party — the possibility that American wives were the worst news for French husbands. The Lizzie meetings had given clues. When I discussed the subjects we'd talked about with R, he raised his bushy eyebrows and said, "It's a pity that these Americans weren't brought up by an English governess. That would have avoided most of this."

More interviews made it clear that darker storms tormented many American wives than any we'd talked about at our meetings. Remarkably, few were dramatically bothered by the grueling French educational system or ways of bringing up children, both radically different than what they were used to in the U.S. Nor were they bothered by the quarrels blowing up because of different perceptions of how to spend the family income, though Americans have a long history of throw-away-and-replace, buy buy buy. The French, until the 1960's living in an agricultural country, still have the mentality, if not the practice, of making things last forever — socks mended, Christmas wrappings saved, shirt collars turned, and their income stuffed under the mattress.

The storms I now ran into were not about money. They were stirred up by marriage contracts, mothers-in-law, and Other Women.

History took over again.

French marriages since the time of Clovis — meaning 1,500 years ago — and well into the 20th century, were imposed by the parents as alliances to soup up both families' positions vis-à-vis property. Legal division of who had what, and continued to have what, was the formula preferred by the partner who brought the most property to the marriage. Obviously. Eleanor of Aquitaine's contract with Louis VII stipulated that Aquitaine and Poitou, the land she inherited, was her personal, inalienable property, so that when she divorced Louis and married the future Henry II of England, there was no question but that her half of France went with her. Louis was not pleased. Eleanor had a good, tight contract.

Things aren't always so clear. It behooves foreign spouses, particularly Americans, to make sure they are. Marriage contracts can be the joker in the woodpile for untraveled Americans.

Emma, a former fashion model from Atlanta, Georgia, told me this cautionary tale. She met Bertrand, a French executive with Michelin in South Carolina, at a party in Savannah. Bertrand swept her off her feet. They were married in Atlanta, without a marriage contract, which Emma had never heard of, and which is obligatory for French couples when they marry in France. Emma's mother was dead. Her father was an insurance salesman with four children, almost no capital, and as little knowledge and curiosity about the French legal system as Emma.

In a few years Emma and Bertrand moved back to the Michelin headquarters at Clermont-Ferrand in *"la France profonde,"* that is, deep, rural France. Not much modeling for Emma to do there, but she was content to busy herself with gardening, charities and hopes for having children. The children never came. The couple lived near Bertrand's mother; luckily, she liked Emma.

At 60, Bertrand developed a cancerous tumor in his lung. It was operated on, apparently successfully. However, he sank into a depression and started raving about suicide. Emma found out that his family had a history of suicides. Now 60 herself, she began to take an interest in her future… and her legal situation. Bertrand, in his suicidal depression, was hallucinating that he was bankrupt. She knew this couldn't be true, as he had a nice income from securities as well as his salary, and the family had extensive properties. She had assumed it would all come to Bertrand, as an only child. She hadn't yet learned that it is dangerous to assume *anything* in a foreign country.

In any case, she was sufficiently uneasy that she hired an English-speaking lawyer to find out exactly where she stood. She rummaged around in Bertrand's desk until she found a thick file of legal documents to show him.

What Emma's father, had he been French, would have discovered before her marriage was that the estate had been put in Bertrand's name after the death of his father, several years prior to his marriage to Emma.

But, as the estate had come through his mother, a contract had been made stipulating that the properties reverted to his mother should he die before her, without children. There was no provision for a future wife, except that she would then enjoy the French system of "*usufruit*," the right to inhabit, but not own, the big house where his mother lived, 40 kilometers from Clermont-Ferrand. Which in plain language meant that if Bertrand did away with himself as he threatened, Emma had no choice but to live with her mother-in-law in a rather dilapidated house over which she had no control, stranded in the sticks, far from her friends and normal activities. The house where she was then living, in Clermont-Ferrand, was rented.

The lawyer said that there was nothing whatever she could do about this contract. Her best hope, he said, was to convince Bertrand, difficult in his present state, to buy the house where they lived or some other house and put it in her name, along with enough securities for a proper income. If he didn't, and should he die suddenly, she had only two options, as her own parents were now dead: she could marry again or take a rich lover.

Out of many options, French couples usually choose one of the two marriage contracts below before they marry. Each of these has innumerable variations. Roughly they are like this:

1. Communauté des biens réduite aux acquêts: Assets acquired before marriage are separately owned, assets acquired during the marriage are jointly owned.

This statute, *Communauté des biens,* is when everything bought during the marriage belongs to both partners, but property owned before the marriage is not merged. It means that they decide together after the divorce about who gets what of the things acquired since the wedding. This is the situation that most American women usually take for granted will be the case, should the dreaded thing, the divorce, actually happen. Until recently, for an American woman even to think about such things before getting married was considered unfeeling and unethical. She would wonder if a fiancé who insisted on her signing such a contract were not preparing himself a bolt-hole. She might consider this a red flag, proving that he lacked the necessary commitment for entering into this holy state.

2. *Séparation des biens.* All assets are individually owned, including both the assets obtained before the marriage and assets obtained during the marriage

The other most frequently chosen French marriage contract, *Separation des biens,* is most satisfactory when the husband and wife bring equal amounts of capital and property to the marriage, with, perhaps, the complication of children from previous marriages.

Under this contract of permanent separation of assets, everything is clear and quarrels over ownership are avoided if there is a divorce. However, to be smooth, it demands careful bookkeeping during the marriage.

It is not a happy arrangement if the bride is a fortune hunter. It is definitely not to the advantage of the woman of good faith but no or little means who marries a man of some substance. If she contributes little to the joint treasury, she takes little out, and nothing of what was bought during the marriage, except what she can prove she bought herself. An American who marries with her heart in the stars finds this system reprehensible. She will be sure to argue that her labors for the good of the household should mean that she has an equal right to whatever goods are divided up.

As for the inheritance of the American wife, should her husband die before she does, this is a whole other ball game, very different indeed from the inheritance laws in the U.S. She should make it her business to find out about this, ahead of the wedding. French law is not generous to widows, though it is slightly more so than a few years ago.

13

French mothers-in-law

Quiz for husbands:

You're on a cruise with your wife and your mother. The yacht hits an iceberg and sinks. You find a part of a life boat just big enough for you (the only one of the three who can swim) and one — just one — of the women to hang onto. Which do you choose, wife or mother?
American husband: "My wife."
French husband: "My mother, of course. You can always find another wife."

Kate had wriggled out of the subject of mothers-in-law whenever Lizzie wanted to press it. Once I started interviewing other daughters-in-law of French women, I could see why. If you think mothers are revered in the U.S., you should come to France to find out what real mother-reverence means. Again, it's mostly about history, 1,000 years of it.

And if you think mothers-in-law are a dispensable social group, you should come to France to find out what fun they can really be.

For starters, think about this. When French people doing a crossword puzzle come across *voleuse d'enfants*, which means female kidnapper, the only word that fits in the three-letter space is the word for daughter-in-law: *bru*.

Then think a long time about this: in France, the word for mother-in-law is the same as the word for stepmother, *belle-mère*. "Beautiful mother," you call her. Yes. Anything to appease this goddess.

Having the status of mother-in-law in France is the same as the one of stepmother: she doesn't have to account to anyone. The one person who might be expected to curb her power is the one she's already had at least 20 years to work on: your husband.

How did she get so powerful? With tenacity. Like this:

France is a macho society run by men. Right. Threatened with female power, French men circled the power wagons long ago. They had wiped out women's civil rights by 1590. Even now, there are few women in top executive positions in France. Women doctors address each other as if masculine: *"cher collegue."* President Sarkozy has changed the dynamics of government dramatically by including seven women among his 17 cabinet ministers, but there are still relatively few women in Parliament. Women ministers in the government are not quite called "Monsieur" — but almost. They are addressed as Madame *le* Ministre. To be sure, a few of them have begun insisting on being called Madame la Ministre, but the battle is far from won; the Académie Française has impressive reasons for arguing that this is ungrammatical. Most significant is the grammatical rule that one man in any group of women, even thousands of them, changes the collective pronoun in French from feminine to masculine — *ils*. In his *Code Civil*, still the law of the land albeit with a few modifications, Napoleon tried to fix the glass ceiling into granite by pigeon-holing women — and their rights — with children and idiots. French women couldn't vote until 1944, nor have a bank account without their husband's permission until 1960. Until 1972, a wife's adultery was a crime punishable by prison. The husband's? He was slapped on the wrist with a small fine.

Men made a show of adoring women, respecting them, wanting to be with them, making them feel important... so that, the men hoped, women would be lulled into not noticing they'd been had.

However, French women were *not* duped. So the legal system was rigged against them, against even the most elementary civil rights? They cleverly created a parallel power system by inventing the salons, as we saw in Chapter Eight. The salons, run more or less dictatorially by rich, dynamic women, became, amazingly, the arbiters of success for 300 years for authors, poets, artists; often in the 19th century, even for cabinet ministers. But — hold your hats — Frenchwomen's ace in the hole predates the salons by centuries. They understood already back in the Middle Ages that their unassailable fortress was the nursery. Yes. By binding their son to them with a steely lifelong grip, they would have a chance to dictate, or in any case, influence him, perhaps share in his power grabs, and at the very least be confident of his assuring a roof over their heads.

Mothers were as doting as they were ambitious. They suffocated their sons with love: they saw to it that their sons were never far from them. There were no Freudian shrinks around to bully them with guilt feelings. So they simply sailed full steam ahead with their maternal programming. When George Sand's grandmother was unable to scare her son away from his determination to marry a groupie, Baroness Dupin cried, "You mean you love this woman more than *me*?" The mother-in-law of Flaubert's Madame Bovary makes the same furious accusation to her son as she stomps out of his house. George Sand herself, though passionately, even violently in love countless times, consistently described her son Maurice as the "great love of my life."

While the French have written many books about mother-daughter and father-son relationships, few have been written about mothers and sons.

Two have just recently been published, one, *Adultères,* by a bestselling pediatrician, Aldo Naouri, and the other by the psychiatrist Alain Braconnier. Recognizing that this bond is particularly strong in France, Braconnier writes in his new book, *Mère et fils (Mother and Son)* that there is nothing dangerous about this strong bond. On the contrary. He rejects the clichés that a too-close mother risks creating a homosexual son or imprinting her son with the necessity to choose a wife exactly like her.

"Giving birth to a son is the crowning of a mother's desires, whether she realizes it or not," he said in an interview with *Le Figaro.* "It is a source of pride as well a completion of her own self. It gratifies her husband's fondest desires, and those of her own father as well. There are no undertones of rivalry, as there might be with a daughter. On the contrary, the love a mother gives her son is unconditional. If he has a problem of failure at school or of drugs, his mother is often the only person not to discourage him, to still have the courage to love him."

In today's world of the superwoman, Dr. Braconnier feels that it is essential that this bond be as strong as possible — and that the mother also be strong and ambitious for her son. In addition to teaching her son about love, about opening up to others and how to express his emotions, a strong mother can best prepare the son for the rat race out there. He gives examples in history of strong women producing strong sons: Napoleon, Mitterrand, Chirac, Nicolas Sarkozy. And let's not forget Saint Louis and Louis XIV, not to mention the Merovingian kings, totally shaped and ruled by their mothers.

In his recent enlightening Franco-American study, *Français et*

Americains: L'Autre Rive (French and Americans: the Other Shore), Pascal Baudry, the French psychoanalyst turned executive trainer interviewed in Chapter Three, zeroes in on how French mothers develop a culture of son-clinging.

Baudry describes a training process that would seem to be encouraging independence but which in fact is a hidden weapon of possessiveness. French children are put sternly on the potty at one year — even, often, at six months — with the command to perform, no buts. As the baby hardly ever has control so early, this means constant animated exchanges, not to say battles — a special kind of bonding — between mother and son. Decades of screams from psychologists seem to be modifying this practice slightly, but Mediterraneans in general, and the French in particular, do tend nevertheless to do things the way their mothers did, who did things the way their mothers did, and so on.

Two-year-olds are sent to a nursery school — far earlier than Americans — which makes it look as if they're being given early independence. In fact, the mother at the playground with even a five- or six-year-old acts like a general commanding fractious troops. She'll admonish him not to go far, to be careful climbing the jungle bars, not to fall down and get himself dirty, not to talk to strange children, not to share his toys, and so on. He's not allowed to make any decisions for himself. Suffocated by this maternal stranglehold, his adolescent revolt will be stronger than the American's. But while the American will leave home probably for good when he goes to college (*université* in France), the French college student will live at home after the adolescent upheaval — probably until he marries at perhaps 25 or 30 or even later, though this is evolving.

You have to remember that no one tells the French child that he has to stand on his own two feet. What would be the good of that? Nor does anyone tell his mother that she should encourage the child to be independent, strike out on his own, preferably seek an activity as different from his father's as possible. Why on earth should the family disintegrate? On the contrary, French parents encourage the children to continue in the same line of work as their father, presenting a family bulwark against the dark shocks and upheavals of society. Not that the children necessarily comply. How well the parents have formed their children to their own image we've seen in the 2006 demonstrations all over France by high school students marching against modest labor reforms. The most popular first job for them was one that came with lifelong security. Many of the parents marched with their children, though it must be said that some of them marched in order to protect their offspring from the aggressive *casseurs*, or hooligans smashing store windows and burning cars.

With the son's marriage, the family's life changes as little as possible: French mothers have perfected their weapons against the intrusion of the daughter-in-law. First of all, location. The young couple will probably live nearby, in an apartment given to the bridegroom by his parents. Second, habit. French sons are used to being spoiled. No one can cook like their doting mothers. Why not continue to enjoy the family feasts — at least once a week? Woe to the American wife who questions having Sunday lunch, a many-layered affair taking three to four hours, every week with *belle-mère*. Third, the marriage contract. Fourth, perseverance: constant hovering. Fifth, the grandchildren.

Needless to say, the success of the French mother's strategy depends on the daughter-in-law's being French.

As mentioned above, that the French word for mother-in-law, *belle-mère* is the same as the word for stepmother tells you a good deal about the amount of affection expected from this relationship. French fairy tales are even more revealing: for "stepmother," substitute "mother-in-law."

The Queens as mothers-in-law

History (again!) shows us that this has been going on for a long time. French queens, for instance, are a study in what to look out for. Blanche of Castille (1188-1252), granddaughter of Eleanor of Aquitaine and mother of Louis IX, the future Saint Louis, was a capable regent during the minority of her son, fending off greedy barons and leading her troops to battle herself. However, her maternal smothering was enough to make an American mother's heart stop — and foresee a son growing up to be a Mamma's boy hiding in her skirts, not the paragon of goodness and courage, the intrepid leader of Crusades against the terrifying Saracens that he proved to be.

Such was Blanche's adoration of her son that she even did her best to thwart his attempts to find a wife. When he did get married, to Marguerite de Provence, Blanche couldn't bear to think of them alone together. Every night she rushed into their bedroom uninvited and unannounced. (I have an American friend whose French mother-in-law did the same thing when they stayed with her in the country. "She waited outside the door — which had no lock — until she was pretty sure we were making love," said my friend, "and then she barged in.") Louis and Marguerite were polite to Blanche but resourceful. They found privacy in the one place it was available — a staircase. Nevertheless they managed to produce 11

Jealous Mother-in-law
Blanche of Castille discovering Louis IX's love nest

children. And imagine this: Louis was always a devoted and respectful son.

François I's niece, Jeanne d'Albret would no doubt have made a terrifying mother-in-law had she not died (or been poisoned by Catherine de Medici?) two months before her son's wedding. The words describing her usually are "austere" and "iron willed;" she was another smothering mother. Henri IV was apparently none the worse for it. He was not only France's most beloved king, he was also a fearless warrior and an even more fearless peacemaker. Jeanne initiated him into this world by rubbing the baby's lips with garlic and giving him a few drops of Jurançon, the local wine, a tradition in Navarre. She gave him some of his toughest genes. Her own tenacity first became apparent when she refused to marry the Duc de Cleves, a marriage arranged for her by the King of France himself. Instead she married the man she loved, Antoine de Bourbon, King of Navarre, a small kingdom in the Pyrenees, so small in fact that her mother cried her eyes out at her obstinacy. Jeanne loved Antoine passionately throughout their marriage, despite his flagrant womanizing, a propensity he passed on in spades to his son, said to have fathered 55 illegitimate children.

In 1560 Jeanne showed her iron fist again. While Catholic France was being ripped apart by the wars with the Huguenots, she made the scandalous conversion to Protestantism. Her husband vacillated and stayed Catholic, but you can be sure that Jeanne saw to it that little Henri, age seven, was also converted. The Wars of Religion were ended in 1589 by the miracle of this ex-Huguenot crowned King of Catholic France. Henri IV made his famous statement, "Paris is worth a mass," reconverted to Catholicism and issued the Edict of Nantes in 1598, giving the Huguenots the civil rights they had fought for. Paris was reconciled. In a way you can say that Jeanne, though she died 18 years before, was indirectly responsible. She educated her son to appreciate both sides.

The queen who was closest to her son was Anne of Austria, the Spanish mother of Louis XIV. If Anne was overbearing to her dreary and pathetically self-effacing daughter-in-law, Marie Thérèse of Spain, you have to remember that Anne spent the first 22 years of her married life in hell, plagued by a venomous, tempestuous husband, Louis XIII, by the plotting against her of Cardinal Richelieu, who was suspicious of her Spanish relatives, and by being barren.

How did she suddenly become pregnant after 22 years of marriage — in 1638, with no fertility techniques available? And considering that Louis XIII had pretty much given up on his marriage bed years ago? History has given us several explanations. One is that before becoming pregnant, the devout Queen, who spent a great deal of time on her knees praying at the convent of Val de Grace, made a vow to the Virgin Mary to build a magnificent church in thanksgiving, adjoining the convent, should she send her a son. The church that fulfilled the vow is the sublime chapel of Val de Grace, partly designed by Mansart. The second explanation for the astonishing event is that one day the King was out hunting when a storm came up, making it impossible for him to make it back to one of his establishments. The storm got worse and worse. Most reluctantly, but on the insistence of his Master of the Horse, whose job was to see to the welfare of his sovereign, Louis was obliged to stay in the nearby palace of the queen. Protocol ordained that in that case, it had to be in her bedroom. The third account is much less romantic. This one has it that Louis was on his way to Fontainebleau when it was discovered that his bed had been forgotten. The Queen's bedroom was chosen because it was nearby at the convent of Val de Grace.

The little baby that made France explode with joy nine months later was none other than the future Sun King, Louis XIV, *le Dieudonné* (Gift of God). Anne of Austria took care of him herself, hardly letting him out of her sight, and together with the brilliant Cardinal Mazarin, who taught him the skills, duties and complexities of kingship and was most likely his stepfather, they produced France's first dedicated professional ruler. As noted in Chapter Five, the Sun King made France the envy of Europe, its center of art, architecture, science, literature, style — and flamboyance.

And Louis was devoted to his mother for as long as she lived.

Mothers-in-law of Americans

Ambitious French mothers have been taking their cue from these queens for centuries. French daughters-in-law understand how the land lies from the time they're tots. American daughters-in-law reel from this unexpected tornado of power over their husband. The smart, stable ones try to figure out how to outwit *belle-mère*, as if in a game of chess. The others take it personally, and suffer.

I began to realize that the subject of French mothers-in-law was often an open wound among Americans. The subject had flared up at a luncheon of one of the clubs of Americans in Paris.

"My mother-in-law almost broke up our marriage," said Fanny, a widow. "She had two daughters-in-law and would play one against the other. She would tell my sister-in-law that my daughter was more beautiful, or better in school… or she would tell me that Cécile, my sister-in-law, was a better housewife, better cook, better everything…"

"My mother-in-law always goes through my son's closet to see what needs to be ironed — in her opinion," said Betty.

"My mother-in-law always takes my husband's side — and he takes hers. No one ever backs me up," said Dolly.

"Is it any business of my mother-in-law how I potty-train my little boy?" said Lillian. "I mean, he's only three, he has plenty of time! But she's nagging me about it as if he'll be wearing diapers in school. She says she trained all of hers by the age of two. Two!"

And Sylvia, from San Francisco: "It took me a long time to realize that my mother-in-law was really trying to sabotage our marriage. She does it with sarcasm. I'm no good at being nasty back, so she has me every time. I can tell that Jean-Marie secretly admires the way she does it. Ridicule is the favorite sport here. Sometimes it's so clever it takes a while to realize you've been insulted — and then it's too late to react."

Kathleen, from Little Rock: "I hate to say it, but most of the mothers-in-law I've met are really mean. Americans here need to get together and think of ways to get back at them. For instance, serving spinach with ice cream like Gurdijeff. Or putting peanut butter in the mayonnaise."

"I really love my mother-in-law," said Jenny, "but I have to admit there have been times when... well, I'll tell you one story, even though I don't really like telling it because it gives the wrong idea of her. She's a wonderful, loving grandmother and I trust my children with her implicitly. But when we first moved back, we lived with them for about six months. It happened to be the time to potty-train Rita, my daughter, which usually wasn't particularly stressful. But one day I came home from the store and apparently little Rita had had an accident. As I was coming up the stairs I heard my mother-in-law telling her she was going to wipe her face with her peed-in panties. 'Que penses-tu si je débarbouille la figure avec ça?' (What would you think if I washed your face with that?) she said to my little girl. "I was shocked, but all I said was, 'Ça suffit, Monique.' (That's enough, Monique.) And she backed right off, physically. I mean, she just turned and left the room, and I do believe she never did anything like that again. I say that because I could tell that she knew she was wrong, without ever saying so. As she'd rather die than apologize, she let me know that she respected my reaction. That night, I think she probably cooked my favorite meal or something."

Many mothers-in-law of Americans have wreaked havoc with their son's marriage, sometimes bringing it close to ruin. There are exceptions. Charmaine Donnelly's, for instance, whose husband, Gérard Pfanwadel, an Alsatian, is a banker, like Charmaine. He has a mother who hated her own mother-in-law so much that she was determined not to be like her; no matter what, she was going to do what she could to make life easier for her daughter-in-law — regardless of her nationality.

"She doesn't call us — we call her," said Charmaine, "about once a week. She hangs up first. She bends over backwards to be generous to all of us — Gérard has three brothers and three sisters. She is tolerant and generous but rigorous; she has moral weight. No one would think of going against her wishes. She doesn't look for dust in my house, instead she asks for recipes."

Sally's story also is more encouraging. Her mother-in-law did everything she could to sabotage Laurent's wedding plans, but when he went ahead anyway, she came round. "Now she does everything possible for our children. She takes them once a week at least when school is out, and a month in the summer to the mountains."

Ginnie seems to have drawn a particularly trying mother-in-law. This is a conversation she had with her husband:

"Your maman said my hair looked like a zulu and my clothes would just suit Coluche."
"Impossible, Maman would never talk like that."
"Then she said that my makeup made me look like a prostitute."
"No, chérie, impossible."
"And that my meals weren't fit for a goat."

"And do you know what my husband said then? He said, 'Well, darling, all insults can be productive.' He said it!"

14

Infidelity

La vie est un sommeil profond, dont l'amour est le rêve.

Alfred de Musset

The BBC in a recent poll revealed that 60% of British women find more satisfaction in doing housework than in making love. I told this to a 50-something French couple. The husband guffawed and said, *"Pas du tout surprenant pour les Anglais!"* (Not surprising for the English.)

Across the Channel, well, it's different. The good news in France is that French men really do, as noted here already, adore women. They really do like to be with them.

Patrick Poivre d'Arvor, the superstar anchorman of TV 1, said as much in an interview with *Le Figaro*: "I like working with women tremendously. I find them more subtle, more emotional, operating more with seduction than insistence. They get around problems with grace, but they go exactly where they decided to go."

Just flirting, without making love, is fine with Frenchmen. Making love is even finer. All this makes women feel wonderful. It makes women feel like women. Did I say France was the country where women bloomed?

"That's why many married Frenchmen permit themselves to flirt openly at a dinner party. An American man wouldn't dare, he'd be scared to be so brazen in front of his wife," said Shelby Marcus-Ocana. "In fact, I can't even *imagine* a married American husband flirting with his wife present. But Frenchmen do it all the time, since it's not seen as 'serious' but merely a way of interacting."

Well — how far does the flirting go? That's easy. It goes as far as the lady pleases. As to whether it's a sublime trip to the stars, as George

Sand would say…

"Frenchmen love to make love," said Shelby. "They love to make love to their girlfriends, to their wives, to their mistresses; why, sometimes they love to make love to all three of them one right after the other! Flagrant desire is a source of pride and a renewable resource. They have such a good time between the sheets! It's like an amusement park in there!"

Another recent poll, this one by Novatrice-Harris Interactive (*Le Figaro*, 26 July 2007) confirms the delight of Frenchmen in making love. They're ahead of Americans and all their European neighbors in the number of monthly *rapports*: 8.9 for the French, 8 for the Germans, 7.3 for Italians, 5.9 for Americans and 5.8 for Britons. Maybe they're bragging? Who knows? In any case, the same poll has them less fickle than Americans and other Europeans. The French claim to have an average of 11.1 love partners during their lifetime, while with the Germans it's 13, and 12.5 for Americans and Britons.

So it's generally agreed that between the sheets is lovely in France. You could be in for a surprise about what else is there. Early in her film career, Jane Fonda, as already noted, lived with (and later married) Roger Vadim, the French film director. Fonda was crazy about Vadim. In her recently published autobiography, she writes that with a turbulent, difficult childhood behind her, including a mother who committed suicide, she was unsure of her identity, especially her sexual identity. Thus, she was "surprised" rather than shocked, when Vadim came home late (which was not unusual), with another woman and brought her to bed with Jane (which was.) She was a beautiful, high-class call girl working for Madame Claude. It became a recurrent pleasure of Vadim's to bring one or several other women to bed with them. Fonda wrote that she put up with this practice, called a *partouze* in French, in order not to lose Vadim. To please him she felt that she had to do whatever he asked, in order not to seem "bourgeoise," which he loathed.

Apparently there is a pervasive feeling in America that a *partouze* is "typically French." My cousin Tom Platt, a federal judge, told me so last month. Guillemette Faure, in her excellent book *La France — Made in USA*, says so. Well, I couldn't find any American or French women who had been invited by their lovers or husbands to put up with a *partouze*. It's true that Vadim and some others like the Marquis de Sade have special tastes, and that "exchange clubs" exist in Paris (as in New York and Los Angeles). Nevertheless, the lovemaking of most French men seems to be plain vanilla, not kinky, exactly what Vadim would consider "bourgeois," but which women seem to prefer. Movie idol Alain Delon, an assiduous lover of women, said famously, *"La meilleure partouze est la partouze à deux."* (The best orgy is a twosome.)

Shelby Marcus-Ocana's "Seductive Tool No. 3" (Frenchmen love to make love. As often as possible.) is illustrated again and again in French movies. The seducing hero is never at a loss for women. When he meets the new girl, he has to discard the one — or ones — in tow. Or his wife.

• *L'Etudiante (The Student)*: As we saw in Chapter Six, Edouard (Vincent Lindon) takes one look at Valentine (Sophie Marceau) in a ski lift, loses her, spots her in a Métro station and chases after her into a subway car. The day after their first night of love, he leaves on a tour with his band. That night in Strasbourg, the blonde he'd scheduled before he met Valentine is already in her negligée, ready for action, when he realizes he has to tell her he's going to dump her and drive hundreds of kilometers back to Paris to see Valentine again. The blonde is not pleased. She goes with him, back to her husband in Paris.

• In *Un homme qui me plaît (A Man I Like)* a young Jean-Paul Belmondo and Annie Girardot are both involved in the filming of a movie in Los Angeles. Belmondo has a wife at home in Washington whom he telephones a lot. We first saw him in bed with another blonde the night before. That night in the bar, he thinks about Girardot and phones her around midnight. She gets out of bed to join him. Then they go off to Las Vegas together.

• In *Le Professionnel*, Belmondo has two women at the same time, one his wife and one his mistress. You get the feeling he is faithful to both women "in his fashion."

Which reminds me of a television interview given by the actor Pierre Arditi. Asked if he was faithful to his wife, he said, "Often."

Is this an accurate picture of French life? Is a French husband apt to be unfaithful?

Not necessarily. If his parents have a happy marriage, he is likely to wish to follow their example. He is particularly promising as a future husband if he has a deep Christian faith. He will have made the commitment and there is every chance he'll stick to it. Regardless of what people say about empty churches in France, there is a strong core of devout Catholics and Protestants who take their marriage vows extremely seriously.

Otherwise, whether a Frenchman is a safe bet for fidelity depends on a number of things to look out for.

1. His father. Study him with a beady eye. If his father was a womanizer, chances are he will be too, at least to a certain extent. Or else, disgusted at the suffering of his mother, he'll go to the other extreme and be pure as Galahad.

2. You. If you're jealous, hysterical, aggressive or suspicious, you might push an otherwise constant man into those outstretched waiting arms. There is no dearth of those.

3. His character. Some French men just can't help having another love besides their wife. *La rentrée,* usually meaning the end of summer when children go back to school, also means the reunion of a husband with his mistress, after a month with his family at the sea or in the mountains. Keep your eyes and ears open about him and try to figure this out before you settle down with him.

A French psychoanalyst told me, "French husbands aren't adulterers, but of course they do like a little 'adventure' from time to time." Hmm.

4. His age. Did he sow his wild oats before he met you? If he was very young when you got married, in his early twenties, for instance, you may hit some rocks when he gets to his late forties or fifties. He may succumb to the midlife crisis the French call the *"démon du midi,"* or the rage to fall in love with all the other women he missed out on.

5. If he is in politics, watch out. Making political speeches is felt to be an aphrodisiac in France; the politician is making love to his audience. Furthermore, in this Latin country, people seem to demand the assurance of their leaders' virility. See below about two new books detailing the escapades of members of the French government.

6. Other women. If you abandon him in the summer for that house in Deauville with the children, or for a prolonged visit back home to your family in the U.S., you have to realize that you're asking for trouble. Big trouble. Other women will be around to *prendre le relais.* I was told in no uncertain terms by a glamorous French woman that a wife was "mad" to

even consider leaving her husband alone for more than a *week* in Paris.

Who are these women on the prowl for your husband? The ones to be on your guard about are probably single, but not necessarily so. You probably can count on restraint from French women who are close friends, but don't be too sure. There isn't the culture of strict solidarity among friends in France that there is among American and English friends, where it is a big no-no to seduce your best friend's husband. As for other French women who are not really friends but acquaintances, it might be just the game they've been waiting for.

It must be said that the degree of danger from female predators depends to a certain extent on your milieu, where your husband works, and in what field. If he has a pretty, single secretary or colleague he works closely with, expect the worst. If he is in one of the creative professions — opera, theater, music, cinema, publishing, advertising, art exhibitions — both men and women will be *expected* to spice up their marriage with an outside fling from time to time.

Inès de la Fressange, beautiful model, successful dress designer, an aristocrat from an old family, finally found the husband she called *"l'homme de ma vie"* (the man of my life) at age 36. Her husband Luigi, who died suddenly in 2006, was a flamboyant art dealer from Sicily when they met. He had been married once before and had two grown daughters. After great difficulties and every kind of test, Inès at last produced two more children, the joys of her life.

"After I'd been married maybe eight years, friends began asking me who my lover was," she told *Elle*. "When I would say I was married to him, they'd hoot and then gossip among themselves. 'Married eight years and still no lover! What can be the problem?'"

You can't very well put your delicious French lover/husband in a cage. In fact, to keep him interested, you have to do just the opposite.

Yes, but how far does it go — if he's not in a cage? I mean, of course, a cage of guilt, fear, and so forth — the American cage.

I asked R what he thought, and what his friends did. I didn't dare ask him if he went on romps himself. I hoped he would tell me without my asking — and he did. R is very well off, from a patrician family. Constance, his Franco-American wife, is a gorgeous brunette of 41. He's 43, the beginning of the dangerous age; they have three children.

"All my friends stray," he said. "That's just the way it is here. They don't have mistresses in the old-fashioned sense, no one these days has the time or wants the bother of a steady long-term thing, so the word has

come to mean someone not your wife that you sleep with once in a while… maybe you've slept with her more than once, maybe a few times — someone from your own milieu. A fling, a short romance… what's the harm? It doesn't mean anything."
Here we go again. It doesn't mean anything. Of course it does, my American voice tells me. Or anyway, it might. Someone should write a song, "It doesn't mean anything." Maybe someone has.
I waited to see if R, who has a strong Christian faith, would get more personal. After a long silence, he did.
"I don't, myself," he said. "Stray, I mean. But the reason isn't because I'm not tempted, or — like you American Puritans — think it's evil. I honestly don't see the harm, and no Frenchman I know would ever feel guilty. But — if I did, my wife would instantly see it on my nose. I'm one of those people who can't hide anything. And since she would know, and be hurt — and I don't want to hurt her — I realize wives don't like it when their husbands stray. Also, she might begin to play around herself. Well, I couldn't stand that."
It's a moot question what part religion plays in fidelity or infidelity. Some say the Catholics are more apt to stray because they can confess to a priest and be forgiven by the Church. Others say that the only difference is that Protestant strayers feel obliged to confess to their wives.
I brought up this straying problem with a friend, a Frenchman I'll call Bernard, at a dinner party. He is a vigorous 60, a career army officer, and has been married for 34 years. He and his wife are active in the local church. Needless to say, I wouldn't have dreamed of asking him about his own personal point of view, and was surprised and delighted when he volunteered it.
"As for me, being faithful was never one of my problems," he said. "It was a commitment I made when I was young. I don't mean there weren't temptations… but when you make a commitment, that is that."

And what about the wives who stray? A wife's adultery is such a hot and delicate topic from the points of view of male ego, shame and property that it's a taboo subject at dinner parties. French literature and cinema are relatively quiet about it, as are the husbands. Their reactions in both history and literature are varied. Napoleon was sad and distressed about Josephine's lovers; he led his own love life parallel to hers and went on to conquer most of Europe and be crowned Emperor. Charles Bovary quietly expired from grief. King Arthur declared Lancelot his best friend.

A cuckolded French husband's most public show of outrage was made by the Marquis de Montespan, the husband of the gorgeous Athénaïs whom we've already met as the friend of Madame de Maintenon. Athénaïs had finally succeeded in seducing her King, Louis XIV. Her husband was furious, unlike many husbands in similar circumstances at that court, who reacted favorably to the fortunes the alliance could bring. The marquis, however, made terrible scenes. As Nancy Mitford reported in *The Sun King:*

"He boxed his wife's ears. When he was with the King he talked loudly about David and Bathsheba. He drove to Saint-Germain-en-Laye with a pair of antlers wobbling about on the roof of his coach, and there took leave of his friends and relations. Then he went into mourning and referred to the Marquise as his late wife. The King, who very much disliked being embarrassed, was furious."

Guilt isn't exactly a worn-out word in France, since it is usually denied, but if there is any guilt being handed around, it is usually to mothers. For years French mothers were blamed if their children were autistic, for instance. We saw earlier that executive trainer and former psychoanalyst Pascal Baudry blames French mothers for too-early toilet training, which, he says, results in dependent, over-reserved adults who can't communicate.

In a new book mentioned in Chapter Thirteen, *Adultères* (Adulteries), the bestselling pediatrician Dr. Aldo Naouri claims that adultery is mother's fault, too. We've seen how close French mothers are to their sons. In the spirit of Freud, Dr. Naouri writes that sons "fuse" with their mothers at an early age and spend the rest of their lives searching for a woman who can repeat this satisfactory merger. A wife can, at first, but after a while, a few years perhaps, the euphoria wears off. There's no more fusion and the husband has to look for it somewhere else.

Gertrude Stein, who lived in France most of her adult life, from 1903 until after World War II, had an extremely wide and varied acquaintance among various milieus, which she studied with a keen writer's eye. This is what she wrote in *Paris France*, in her inimitable style: "In France a boy is a man of his age the age he is… at every stage of being alive he is completely a man alive at that time. This accounts for the very curious relation of every French man to his mother. Just as he is always alive all the time and every moment of the time as a man so he is all his life continually a son dependent upon his mother. There is no break in that dependence even if a man is sixty years old… there is nothing inevitably different between being a boy and a man in a Frenchman's life and he is always a son because he is always dependent upon his mother for his strength his morality, his hope and his despair, his future and his past. A Frenchman always goes completely to pieces when his mother dies, he is fortunate if another woman has come into his life who is a mother to him."

Describing the narrator in *Une Jeunesse à l'ombre de la lumière (Youth in the Shadow of the Light)*: Jean-Marie Rouart wrote, *"Il y eut et il y aura des femmes, mais la seule fut sa mère... oui, dans le plaisir, dans la tristesse, mon coeur qui bat n'est plus seulement le mien, il bat à l'unisson avec celui de ma mère. Il me semble que désormais c'est avec ses yeux que je regarde le monde."* (There are and there will be other women, but the only one was his mother:.. yes, in pleasure, in sadness, my heartbeat isn't only mine, but beats in unison with that of my mother. It seems that henceforth it is with her eyes that I see the world.)

Roland Dumas, the wavy-haired lady-killer and ex-foreign minister whose romantic scandal with Christine Deviers-Joncour is described below, wrote in *Le Fil et la pelote* (The Thread and the Clew) about his mother: *"Ses joues exhalaient une odeur que je ne retrouverais jamais sur aucune femme."* (Her cheeks had a scent that I would never find in another woman.)

According to Dr. Naouri, this "fusion" becomes serious only when the mother neglects her husband, or companion, and devotes herself entirely to her son. The way for her to avoid bringing up an adulterous son is for her to do everything to help her husband to be a fine father. Above all, she herself must be a demonstrably involved, affectionate and devoted wife/companion.

"Whether it is the husband or wife who is deceived, the pain brought by adultery is terrible," says Dr. Naouri. "It is worse for the husband, for he experiences it as a castration. In this case, transparency, or frankness, is the worst possible thing. If I have any really important advice to give to a husband or wife who is deceiving her partner, it is never, never to tell."

Telling can trigger dangerous outrage as well as wretchedness and despair. In the film *Mariages*, Mathilde Seigner announces her affair to her husband of 10 years, played by Jean Dujardin. He thinks it's a joke, doesn't believe her. He felt that they were happily married. Later, during a wedding feast, the undeniable orgasmic moans of lovemaking upstairs in a baby's bedroom come over the baby's intercom at Dujardin's table. Everyone at the table is partly embarrassed, partly amused, except

Dujardin. He understands that they are hearing the love sounds of his wife, as she is the only person missing at the table. When she reappears, he takes a gun to the head of her lover, who is the uncle of the bride, and obliges him to confess his affair in front of everyone. The violence is cathartic for all the movie's main couples: for the lover's wife, who says she has known about all his affairs all along and now decides to leave him; for the bride, who then assures herself of her bridegroom's commitment by almost jumping off a cliff; and for Mathilde and Jean, who exchange promises to turn over a new leaf and dedicate themselves to their marriage.

But the outrage resulting from telling doesn't always subside gracefully. R reminded me of a story by Guy de Maupassant about a couple of French peasants. They marry at 20. At 25, they go to a dance; the husband lingers, comes home late and his wife accuses him, "You betrayed me with Denise!" He denies it. Every year on his birthday, she accuses him again. He always says no. Then on his 80th birthday, he finally comes clean and confesses. Yes, it's true. She takes a knife and plunges it into his heart.

"The French way," said R. "No long discussions. No shrill nagging. Quiet, swift retaliation. The moral of course is never, never tell."

It seems that Dr. Naouri's counsel would have a wide application in France, in all milieus.

The other day I was at Leclerc, the huge supermarket they call a "hyper-market" in France. There was a long line at the checkout stand, giving me a chance to observe the cashier. She was an interesting-looking young woman. Slim, chic on no money at all, petite, totally in control. Some henna in her carefully bobbed hair. Straightforward big loop earrings, a nose piercing, silver rings on most of her fingers, the requisite gap between her tee shirt and her jeans giving a peek at young skin, a belt sparkling with colored sequins. No makeup except a little eye liner. Wedding ring.

When it was my turn at the *caisse*, I asked her if she would permit an indiscreet question. She laughed. With the line of impatient French people behind me there was no time for a leisurely build up, so I said, right off:

"I see you're married. Do you expect your husband to be faithful to you?"

She laughed again goodnaturedly, and without reflection, shook her head and said, "No."

I guess I looked surprised, so she added, "He's great (*un homme bien*) and I have two adorable children — but life is long, I mean, he travels sometimes and if that gives him pleasure... I'm not the only woman in the world. Anyway, he'd always come back to his family."

I thought, Wow. Things are really different here. Catch an American saying that. I thought of Lynette in the American serial, *Desperate Housewives*. A former career dynamo now the mother of four unruly little children, Lynette comes home to find her father-in-law groping a strange woman in her living room. She throws him out of the house — onto the street with his suitcases — and later, in bed, tells her husband: "If I ever find out that *you* have something to do with another woman, just let me tell you, I'm taking the children, we're out of here and you will NEVER see any of us EVER AGAIN."

Lynette's reaction is not unusual Last year, I met Betsy at a luncheon in Paris. She was the "trailing" wife of an executive transferred to France by one of the big multinationals. She told me she was unable to find a job in France and sick of not working, so she planned to go home to Detroit, back to the advertising job that she'd left. It was still open for her.

"But what about Tom?" I asked. Her husband was 36, handsome and full of fun.

"It's only for a year," she said. "Then Tom will be back home too."

"A year? You're leaving that devastating husband *alone* for a *year*? In Paris? French people tell me that leaving a husband for more than a *week* is asking for trouble. The women here will be fighting for him like puppies over a bone."

"If he's like that," Betsy said, primly, "I don't want him back anyway."

"What do you mean, if he's 'like that'? You mean, if he's a normal male?"

Betsy shrugged. But — she didn't go.

Sarah Shepherd, an American journalist, said that she thinks the strong reaction of American women to a cheating husband is the lack of security it implies in the country of serial monogamy. It means he might leave her. So perhaps she should leave him first.

"The hold of the family is less strong in the U.S. than in France," she said. "It's impossible to generalize, of course, but the level of commitment in a marriage seems to be less, so divorce is more of an option."

In France, infidelity doesn't necessarily imply divorce.

"Tell me," said R, "who would still be married in France if it did?"

"Fidelity goes against the genes," said Jill Bourdais, an American couples-psychotherapist and marriage counselor in Paris. "Man is a roamer. Only if he has a strong religious or moral commitment will he be able to withstand the extra-marital temptations, particularly in France."

According to a recent study by the IFOP (Institute francais d'opinion publique), 35% of French men and 24% of French women admit to infidelity. A little over one in three marriages ends in divorce. And the divorce is almost always initiated by the wife.

"The men can't be bothered to get a divorce," said Dr. Arnold Lamazère, the *branché* geriatric specialist in Paris. "They like their home and see no reason to change... a little adventure now and then is of no consequence. In any case, I see more women than men going down that road."

It must be said that with cell phones, having a life secret from the one you lead with your spouse is made awfully easy. You can make sure that you're the only one answering your phone. You can telephone from anywhere and say you're somewhere quite different. In the movie *La Bûche* one of the husbands, who has been having an affair for 12 years, telephones his wife from his car with the Arc de Triomphe visible in the rear window. He tells her he's in Nîmes.

The opportunity for serving businessmen — and women — interested in a fling totally safe from spouse suspicion was not lost on a clever French female entrepreneur. She founded an agency which organizes bogus seminars, bogus phone connections and every cover-up imaginable for erring spouses of both sexes. It's called Ibila (Alibi spelled backwards).

R had things to add about the straying question, things he felt Americans should be informed about. It's not a free-for-all; there are rules, he said. The French discovered long ago that form is just as important as content. It is indispensable, because it enhances the experience. Variations are possible, but the general form must be respected whether you're making a *blanquette de veau* or a speech to the Parliament. Thus, three groups of women are out of bounds for a married Frenchman: he won't touch the au pair girl or the woman in the apartment next door. Both are too close to home; his wife would be likely to find out. This would hurt her — and his relationship with her. The third group of untouchables is American women.

No Americans? I asked R why.

"She would expect an engagement ring," he said.

Unless he goes against these basic rules, there is no guilt for the French lover.

In *On ne badine pas avec l'amour* (There's no joking around with love) Alfred de Musset — yes, him yet again! — a connoisseur of the subject, sums up the point of view, as he sees it, of the average Frenchman. It could have been written today, not 200 years ago. Camille is a young woman expected to get engaged to Perdican, whom she hasn't seen since she was a little girl. She wants to find out more about him before becoming officially betrothed, so she asks a few questions:

Camille: If the priest of your parish tells me that you will love me all your life, should I believe him?
Perdican: Yes and no.
Camille: What would you advise me to do the day I discover that you don't love me any more?
Perdican: To take a lover.
Camille: And what do I then do when my lover doesn't love me any more?
Perdican: You would take another.
Camille: How much time would all this take?
Perdican: Until all your hair is gray and mine is white.

There is one kind of Frenchman who might very well have a long-standing mistress. This is the Frenchman who travels a lot in France, often to the same places. Like a sailor with a girl in several ports, having a mistress ready to receive him when he's away from home has many advantages. He doesn't have to lie about his whereabouts as he would if the long-standing mistress lived nearby. He has a comforting as well as a passionate presence far from home. But still he needs to be alert. He has to be careful about the cell phone and caution his mistress against strong perfume. It often lingers on his jacket.

One of the problems for broad-minded wives these days is that mistresses are becoming bolder and more demanding. If the husband doesn't seem to be delivering on the promised divorce, she might start telephoning the wife. And harassing her.

Mistresses to the left, wives to the right

A well-known doctor of the fashionable 16th arrondissement of Paris, whom we'll call Pierre, had a harem of girlfriends and a mistress of many years we'll call Amélie. He also had an American wife we'll call Joan. His sister-in-law told me this story: While Joan, the American, knew about Amélie and the others, and that Amélie had had a son by Pierre, she decided against a divorce, though it was said that the son's looks were a dead giveaway of his paternity. When Joan died, Amélie wept copiously. When Pierre, her lover, died two years later, she shed not a tear. She was furious because Pierre had promised to marry her. She was not amused when, arriving at the church, Pierre's daughter, who was managing the service, directed all the friends of her parents to their seats in a loud voice: "Mistresses to the left, wives to the right!"

Some of the employees were surprised when the head of a huge pharmaceutical conglomerate, at a meeting of all his managers in Toulouse, announced that his mistress had just had a son. Everyone congratulated him. His wife was not there.

Diana Holmes gives a Musset-like picture of the French husband. Quoted already in the first part of this chapter, Diana is the gorgeous blonde often seen on the covers of French women's magazines. Except that she doesn't model any more and she's not French. But that's the way Diana looks — French and sleek and elegant and string-bean-slim: 36 bust, 26 1/2 waist, 36 1/2 hips. Yet she's as down-home as they make them in Tennessee, where she grew up being told she was too tall and lanky. When she was 16, a recruiter for a model agency saw her and thought that her height — 5'10" — and those curves were just fine. He entered her in an international modeling competition with 1000 others. She won the prize. It was a trip to Milan, which in a roundabout way brought her to the French community in New York, where she met Michel Levaton, her future husband, owner of his own model agency. If you look at him, you aren't surprised to hear that he had the most beautiful models in New York on his string, or that he managed to sign up Diana after talking to her for about three minutes. Even in a leather jacket and helmet, about to set out on his motorcycle, as he was when I met him, he had a drop-dead-come-hither-I'm-your-man look about him. They've lived in Paris for the last 16 years.

Michel has a stable of 400 models in Paris. Through them and as a member of all the American associations in Paris, Diana has had a ringside seat for observing French and American habits of love.

"For a happy marriage with a Frenchman, the wife must be tender and take good care of him. And never forget this, she must be good in bed," she says. "If he doesn't have sex at home, he'll get it somewhere else. So if you're married to a French guy, you have to protect yourself against the possibility of this happening. As for my own husband — I'm lucky with him. He is 59. It could happen any time — but it's the late 30's and 40's that are dangerous. So many of my friends' husbands have been caught... one with the maid, who is Algerian. The wife stayed because she was pregnant. Well, you know, home life is not very sexy if the children are small. I'm lucky — I have a little boy of five, but I have a maid.

"Just about all the French men I know have mistresses," she added. "It's part of the culture. Americans aren't prepared for this — and when they find out, they usually pack up and go back to the U.S. French men are hard to keep, but worth the work."

Exclusivity is certainly what most American wives think they're bargaining for. Very few can adopt the generous French attitude of the late writer Françoise Sagan: "I can understand if my lover is suddenly struck by a *coup de foudre* (love at first sight), but he just mustn't tell me about it."

"You have to adore your husband," said Gianne de Genevray, from California. "That's what they expect — that's what they got from their mothers — and if you do, you'll have a happy marriage. If not, he'll find someone else to adore him — without any qualms."

When talking about marriage in general, French women tend to be philosophical about infidelity. Mostly they agree with Françoise Sagan: her husband should keep it to himself. "Discreet" is the word they use.

"Life is long," said Marianne. "There are so many other lovely women out there. If you find out that your husband has been unfaithful, the best thing is to exile him to the living room couch for a while, and be awfully flirtatious and merry with other men."

"How can we demand that our husbands be faithful," asked Angélique, "when our Presidents, supposed to set an example of probity and integrity, are obviously carrying on with women not their wives?"

For apostles of purity and exclusivity, it doesn't help that the "happy death" of President Félix Faure in 1899 and the witticism it gave rise to, are solidly anchored in French folklore. Faure died at the Elysée Palace in the arms of his mistress, Marguerite Steinheil, the wife of the palace portraitist. The curé was summoned to give the last rites. On arriving, he asked the maid who let him in, *"Est-ce qu'il a toujours sa connaissance?"* which means in French, "Is he still conscious?" But can also mean, "Is his acquaintance still here?" At which the maid replied, "No, she left by the back door."

"Part of the problem for wives is that the French are proud of the 'success' of their Presidents," said Julie, "success meaning female conquests. We all know about President Giscard d'Estaing's accident with a milk wagon at 5:00 a.m., with a lady in the car, when his wife was known to be somewhere else. And as for President Mitterrand, he had them under every bush, one in Sweden, one in Venice, and at the same time was keeping his official mistress — as well as Mazarine, his daughter by her — in an apartment at taxpayers' expense."

Paying for housing these two women was the only thing that riled French citizens about the situation. When the photo was published of the mistress-mother and illegitimate daughter standing side by side at the grave next to his widow, Danielle Mitterrand, several Frenchwomen commented to me about this graciousness — on the part of both the mistress and the wife.

There are strict privacy laws in France and the press has observed them scrupulously until recently. They kept the secret of Mazarine's existence until a few months before the graveyard scene. She only became public at the request for publicity by Mitterrand himself.

Thus the uproar during the sensational public corruption and "sex scandal" trial in 1987 of Roland Dumas, former foreign minister and, as head of the Constitutional Court, top judge of France. The trial exposed his extra-marital love affair with Christine Deviers-Joncour, who wrote *The Whore of the Republic,* a book about herself, her love affair with Dumas and her involvement as go-between in the "affair of the frigates" sold by France to Taiwan, which netted her $9 million. Dumas was convicted of corruption in connection with the frigates sale, but the conviction was later overturned. *Paris Match* published tender photos of the Deviers-Joncour-Dumas idyll. Dumas took her with him on his official visits to China and to Hong Kong.

Two recent books, *Pas de deux à l'Elysée* by Emilie Aubry and Muriel Pleynet, and *Sexus Politicus* by Christophe Deloire and Christopher Dubois, investigate the connection between sex and politics in France, naming names and situations, suggesting that journalists in the future will be less scrupulous about not mentioning affairs which are obvious to anyone with eyes and ears, such as the duo Dumas-Deviers-Joncour and the new love of François Hollande, the 30-year companion of Ségolène Royal.

The much-respected authors of *Sexus Politicus* quote court records showing that Christine Deviers-Joncour became aware, in the midst of her affair with Dumas, that besides his wife he had had another long-standing mistress since 1968. And she said there were others: *"Dumas ne se contentait pas d'une double vie. Il lui en fallait mille."* (A double life wasn't enough for Dumas. He needed a thousand.)

The authors assert that if their leaders are Casanovas, it's because the French insist on indications of their virility: *"En France, c'est incroyable, mais la puissance politique reste liée à la puissance sexuelle! Ceci remonte au*

16ième siècle, à Henri IV. De tout temps chez nous, le pouvoir politique a eu un parfum aphrodisiaque, même chez beaucoup de ceux qui paraissaient austère." ("In France, it's unbelievable, but power in politics remains linked to sexual prowess! This goes back to the 16th century, to Henri IV. It has ever been so, with us, that political power has an aphrodisiac perfume, even for those who seem to be the most austere.")

The authors note the close watch kept on politicians by the various government agents. Salacious reports, when deemed delicate enough, go straight up to the Minister of the Interior, the Prime Minister and, even, the President. The Pavillon de Musique (music lodge) in the gardens of the Matignon, residence of the Prime Minister, is said to be the scene of choice for various ministerial trysts.

Bernadette Chirac had already gone public in her book *Conversations*, about the escapades of her husband, former President Jacques Chirac. *Sexus Politicus* tells us how close Chirac came to actually divorcing and remarrying a journalist from *Le Figaro* — who accompanied him on many of his official trips as Mayor of Paris. They tell us that former President Valéry Giscard d'Estaing also thought seriously of divorcing and marrying a photo-journalist.

But both Madame Chirac and Madame Giscard d'Estaing, like Madame Mitterrand, stood their ground and upheld the bourgeois values of the Republic, the "three treasures of the past" described by Stephane Denis in a recent *Figaro*: decency, discretion and social conventions.

Soon after, these three treasures of the past were seriously burned, if not buried — for how long? — by two sensational women. First, by Ségolène Royal, the Socialist candidate for president. She announced — the night of the election! — that she was asking her longtime companion, François Hollande, to leave their home and live his "sentimental story" apart from her. The nation gasped in a daze of disbelief. They were the power couple who had it all, and were such a double feature of the political landscape that their permanence as a team of equals was taken for granted. Both had outstanding careers, both were brilliant graduates of the prestigious graduate school for civil servants, the ENA, where they met. They had been together — without marriage — for 30 years and had brought up four children. Hollande is the president of the Socialist Party; Royal is president of the regional council of Poitou-Charente and deputy to the National Assembly. Her 2007 run for President of the Republic was surprisingly popular, with 17 million voters giving her over 46% of the vote. Hollande had repeatedly said that they were one couple with "two liberties." Royal had often rejected the "two liberties."

Beautiful, successful, independent, Ségolène Royal stepped down alone from their pedestal and joined the growing list of French women who, having put up with the Other Woman for quite a while, drew the line of "Enough."

The shock of the Royal-Hollande breakup was a ripple compared to the tsunami set off by Cécilia Sarkozy after her flamboyant husband, Nicolas Sarkozy, was elected President of France in 2007. Cecilia, 49, dark and mysterious, a stunning symbol of French beauty and style, played cat and mouse with the adoring press for six months after the election, breaking long-standing engagements at the last minute, such as lunch with George Bush in Maine; not showing up where she was expected but appearing where she wasn't, until the big question on the front pages was, "Where is Cécilia?" The press kept reminding everyone that she had left Nicolas in 2005 for an amorous escapade with a Moroccan advertising executive, and had only returned in 2006 just before the presidential campaign. Her unpredictable behavior as First Lady was turning the couple's life into a soap opera. Her unofficial, unexpected and unorthodox participation in the negotiations freeing Bulgarian nurses from a Libyan prison, coupled with her absence from the ceremony in Bulgaria welcoming them and honoring Nicolas for his winning strategy, unleashed media tirades. With her picture on magazine covers week after week, the question became, "Will she stay? Will she leave again?"

The French press, pretty much gagged by the law about personal privacy, couldn't do anything more sensational than ask questions, but the English press, delighted at any hiccups across the Channel, had a feeding frenzy. The *Daily Mail* published pictures not only of the Moroccan lover but of the *Figaro* journalist said to have accompanied Nicolas to the Seychelles in Cécilia's absence, and to have been formally introduced to his entourage. Finally, when the suspense was almost becoming boring, their divorce was announced. No comment from the Sarkozys until Cécilia gave a long interview to the *Est Républicain*. "In 2005 I met someone, fell in love, and left, a little impetuously," she said, adding that she and Nicolas had tried very hard to make the marriage work when she came back, but it wasn't possible. She said she couldn't bear the protocol and restrictions of the life of First Lady and wanted to live her life "in the shadows" away from the public eye, so that she could "go shopping in a supermarket" with her little 10 year old son, Louis.

Really? Well, ho hum and good luck, Cécilia, was the general French reaction, which was nothing if not cool, despite the media hysteria. 2006 Polls showed that 90% of French people considered a divorce the

Sarkozys' private matter, and 80% reconfirmed this immediately after the breakup; they didn't think the news was important for the country, nor that it would have an effect on Nicolas's ability to govern. Many saluted Cécilia's "courage" in following her destiny and leaving a pampered life for the great unknown, and for refusing to continue in a marriage where love had flown. Women tended to be exasperated.

The fact remains that the twice-married Nicolas, the first divorced candidate to be elected President of France, a Catholic country, became, in addition, the first to be divorced while holding office. I asked a French psychoanalyst for her take on the situation.

"France has long lagged behind other countries in women's rights," she said. "On the one hand, it is encouraging that a woman in France can now choose to follow her own destiny and not her husband's, even if that husband is the most powerful man in the country. On the other hand, if a woman neglects good manners and protocol to the extent of insulting other heads of state, it is fortunate for the country that Cécilia has left."

Whether the ancient French adage, *Plus ça change, plus c'est la même chose* (the more it changes, the more it stays the same), will hold is a matter of speculation. For some, the startling independence of Royal and Sarkozy could be seen as the dawn of a new age of honesty, no longer hostage to bourgeois morality. To others, that same take-no-prisoners independence could be seen as overkill — the fatal exaggeration of lessons learned from the centuries of French women discussed earlier: beautiful, stylish, smart, strong-minded mothers… and queens of *séduction*. These two beautiful, strong-willed women had robbed France of those three treasures of the past mentioned above, decency, discretion and social conventions.

Part IV

Franco-American Marriages
Case Histories

15

Marriages that failed

No one knows why some marriages hold and some don't, least of all the principals involved. It's a mystery. All you can say is that adding an extra culture to the already uncertain mix is daring, and possibly dangerous overload.

Few observers are helpful. The husband and wife, obviously not. A third party can't possibly know what goes on between the sheets or behind closed doors. Someone like me, interviewing at an even farther removed position, can't pretend to know the truth, even if interviews are detailed and numerous on both sides.

What I can do is present things as I saw and heard them. The details given here can't fully explain what wrecked the marriage, but they're enough to give future brides pause for reflection.

One of the things I found out is that the Americans who are attracted to France are a special lot, whether their dream works out or not. You can even make certain generalizations about them. They have a deep longing to experience with French men what they felt they were missing in the U.S. They're adventurous, obviously, and they're willing to pay the price if things go wrong. They're resilient, innovative and tenacious. They don't give up without a long struggle through the dark night of the soul. Basically you marvel at their guts and achievements. French men who are attracted to Americans are also not typical of their countrymen — but what is typical? Generalizations are, well, densely mined.

If a marriage breaks down, it can be for many reasons; you can be sure that none of them are trivial. The following three case histories show the effects of marriage contracts, frequent infidelities and long separations, but, again, these reasons are only the biggest worms in the woodwork. In each case of these failed marriages, the French husband fell in love with his future wife at first sight — a *coup de foudre* — which in monoculture marriages is often a signpost to success — if there is one.

Of the 11 couples described in the case histories, all met in France except one couple which met in the U.S. and another which met in Austria. After about 15 years, eight of the eleven are holding together happily, albeit one a bit shakily. Of these, one met at work; four were pickups — three met at a café, one on a ski slope; the other three met through friends — one on a blind date, one at a party, one at a wedding.

Sheila, 54 and Hugues, 49

Sheila's trumps: Her chien; her intellectual curiosity; her passion.
Marriage strain: Hugues's conspicuous infidelities.
The last straw: Phone call from Hugues's mistress.

Sheila met her future husband at a bistro in Paris.

"I went to that bistro for dinner alone — it was one of those family type places, long table, everyone sitting at it together and talking to each other," she said. "The kind where if you go often enough, they keep your napkin for you in a little cubbyhole with a napkin ring. I was reading *Le Monde*, minding my own business and two guys on the other side of the table started hitting on me. You could practically hear them thinking 'she must be alone for one reason.' The woman across the table started talking to me so that I could ignore the bonzos. Then I saw her son."

Sheila, now 54 — though she looks 35 — was a stringer for an East Coast newspaper. She grew up a "military brat" who didn't belong anywhere — or belonged everywhere. She took French and modern European history at college, then traveled all over Europe before she went back to the U.S. for graduate school. Along the way, she had found out she could belong somewhere — Europe. After graduate school she got on a freighter and came back.

Why come back?

"Americans come here and say they've 'done France' when they've been to a three-star restaurant and the Louvre... France really is about a bistro and sitting around for four hours chewing the fat. It's a place where

you can talk about Victor Hugo and the *nouveaux philosophes*...
Intellectually you can GROW. I have a hungry mind. I have huge holes
in my French culture and in my American culture... I like being in a
place where you can express yourself passionately... Jacques Brel,
inimitable Serge Lama... *Je suis malade*... everyone sings it with tongue
in cheek. BUT you're allowed to FEEL."

That fateful evening she was dining in her favorite bistro, sitting at
the table with a journalist's slump, feeling sallow and wintry, her limp
mouse-colored hair badly in need of the wash she hadn't had time for.
She hadn't bothered with makeup, which ordinarily gives her an
interesting Modigliani sort of face. She was wearing a leather jacket and
jeans, no necklace, no bracelet, no flirty stuff at all. In other words, the
last thing she was out for was The Look. When she noticed the son of the
woman who had begun talking to her, she decided he was gay.

"He had a short short haircut — what they call white walls (you could
see the skin underneath). He was clearly doing his military service, still
compulsory then, but I didn't know that. I just stared and thought, 'Who
on earth is his coiffeur?' He was younger than I was — I never dated
younger guys — and of all things, he addressed his mother with the
formal pronoun *vous*. His mother! I wasn't interested at all. But his mother
had been nice to me, so I gave her my card when I left. And what do you
know, he took it over and started pursuing me.

"He came on to me intellectually, which was clever... His military
assignment was doing research for the Deuxième Bureau — French
Intelligence — so he had plenty of time to write me the most amazing
letters... We were walking along by the church of St. Germain des Prés,
chatting, and he was appalled that I'd never heard of Apollinaire. So
right then and there he recited his poems to me — passionately. That's
heady stuff. Seductive! You ask an American what is romantic and he'll
say, 'A flower?' and that's it. But a Frenchman is on home ground in
Romanceland. He can go on for hours. Look at Musset reading to George
Sand in that film about them, *The Children of the Century*."

Another time they were walking by one of those Paris restaurants
with an oyster bar out on the sidewalk.

"They were *fines de claires*. He asked me if I liked oysters. I said I
never knew whether to chew them or not. He sat me down at a table
inside the restaurant and ordered a dozen oysters. After sprinkling the
first one with lemon juice he put it in his mouth and then leaned over
and slipped it in my mouth with his tongue. It was the oyster and the
ocean and his saliva all at once. 'Now, chew it,' he said. And it was

wonderful. Did I say the French were romantic? That was the first time anyone ever did anything like that."

Sheila had to return to the U.S. for a stint on the paper, and the day before she left, Hugues sent her a letter to her mailbox marked "to read on the plane."

"Of course I read it right away," she said, "and thought, you fool. But it was such a letter, the poetry was so extraordinary that I decided I was the fool... and I went to his place with a bottle of beaujolais, and we drank it and talked and talked and found out that we had a lot in common... and ended up in bed. I barely made the plane that morning."

Hugues wangled leave and followed her to New York.

"We spent the next month in bed. This was always one of the great things about our life together. Are French men good lovers? You can't answer that because some men are great with some women and not with others. The whole thing has to do with chemistry and whether he gives pleasure to the woman or not. But in general, the French outshine Americans in bed — more fantasy, more imagination — or they can be just silly in bed... you can say, Make love to me with your socks on and he'll say, Sure! Take scent. My husband thought it was nice that I really liked his odor... his armpit smell. Americans smell like soap. Nothing is more attractive than the odor of a man. Well, if he's clean."

Hugues went back to Paris and then Sheila was transferred back, too. By this time things were serious, so, as a foreigner alone in Paris, she expected to be invited to Christmas dinner. His mother had begun to get worried — the last thing this *grande-bourgeoise* from Bordeaux wanted was an American daughter-in-law — and refused to invite her. So Sheila didn't answer the phone for four days.

"I guess Hugues had it out with her because then I was invited," she said. "I always got along well with his father — maybe because I gave him a baseball bat — though we got off on the wrong foot because I would call Hugues sometimes in the middle of the night and couldn't imagine why his phone was often answered by another man. It never occurred to me that a man of 24 was living at home, even if he was still in school. Did you ever?

"Hugues's mother was a big problem in our marriage. She gave the word narcissism a whole new meaning. She was an overbearing ballbuster. When my first baby was born she was insanely jealous that I had a lot of milk, while she never did. So she said it's not a good idea to nurse a child too long — she thought one day was too much. She said that nursing would make a child too attached to its mother. Once she said we should move into the sixth floor of their apartment house. Hugues thought it was a good idea. I said, Over my dead body.

"Imagine this. She gave birthday parties for *herself*, every year, but never for her children or grandchildren. Once when my second son, Thibault, was having his eighth birthday she said she'd bring the cake. But she didn't. So he didn't have a cake that year. Then when she had her next birthday party for herself, she scolded him for not bringing her a present. Thibault said, 'Well, you never give me one.'

"We lived together for two years and got married only when a baby was well on its way. I admit she was cool about this. Of course she knew we'd been living together and what she said was, 'Lots of first babies are born prematurely these days.'

"You know, we were married for 15 years and I had wonderful times with Hugues. We traveled a lot, we discussed everything under the sun, we both loved our children and our house in Normandy, and bed was always wonderful. This was a constant in our marriage... our bodies liked each other. But he used sex as a weapon... he withheld it or used it to avoid confrontation... And he was constantly chasing other women. He'd dangle his dalliances in front of me, made sure I found out. I tried to ignore it all and never said much — our marriage was too important for me."

Once he left a sales slip on top of the fridge from the same store where he had bought Sheila some lacy bras and a garter belt. The slip was for black satin bras and panties dated the same day as the lacy bras and garter belt, but they weren't for Sheila.

"What are the rules for screwing around?" she said. "It isn't a bourgeois thing to have all these girls yet tell your wife that she's the best fuck in town. Anyway, after that I let myself go. It was at our place in Normandy, the children weren't there. I screamed. I screamed whole years of pent-up screaming. He just stood there with his mouth open. He couldn't believe it."

Sheila found that screaming at him was a good idea. It didn't seem to bother him. Maybe in some perverse way he enjoyed it. "Maybe, maybe that's what he wanted!" But she didn't want to play that game. Not with him.

"After that, I went every week for six months to a psychiatrist, to scream and cry and get it all out."

She now thinks that in some primal way, French husbands probably enjoy being screamed at because that's what their mothers did, and they're so close to their mothers. She advises American wives not to hesitate to scream at their French husbands, as opposed to nagging or whining.

But her screaming outbursts didn't change Hugues's life. He carried on in exactly the same way. And then one day, when he had been away for a few days, the phone rang and a woman's voice introduced herself as Hugues's mistress.

"Hugues asked me to call you," said the voice. "I really thought he should, but he said he thought it would be better if I told you he wasn't coming home anymore. The thing is, I've just come back from a few days with him in Geneva. I forgot some clothes and he says he had them sent to you by mistake. Please give them to Hugues when he comes to collect his things. He wants a divorce."

She says now that she thinks Hugues did her a favor by leaving. "I've been able to do things I wouldn't have done if I'd been married. I could never have left him. Three children? How could I bring them up alone? Well, I was forced to, and I did. Hugues helped a lot. They're fine young people."

She hadn't gone back to the U.S. for the 15 years of her marriage. "No money, three kids. Hugues wasn't interested in where I came from. When I did go back for a visit, I was struck by the lack of American curiosity about other places."

Would she go back there to live?

"Never! France is my intellectual and spiritual home, and French is the language of my children. It is a place where you can get excited by an idea without people calling you an intellectual snob. And a place where — well, men and women like each other. No battle of the sexes!

"Yesterday I was crossing the street at a light, on the zebra stripes, and a truck almost ran me down — I mean, it was close. I swore, some really dirty words — I was scared to death — and one of two young men crossing at the same time said, *'Une si jolie bouche!'* or 'Such a pretty mouth saying such things!' It's typical of Paris — it happens in a second, it isn't going anywhere — the young man didn't want to go to bed with me, nor I with him. It's like when they hold the door open for you, or pull out your chair at the table... and I love it."

What next?

Sheila raised her eyebrows. "Plans? If you want to make God laugh, tell him your plans."

Comment: I don't see how Sheila could have foreseen Hugues's turning into a erotomaniacal girl-collector, the male version of a nymphomaniac. With hindsight, Sheila would probably have had a long hard look at his mother and studied her closely before she walked down the aisle. However, I can't think of anyone who turned down a suitor because of his mother. The soothing effect of screaming was interesting.

Victoria, 40 and Edouard, 53

Victoria's trumps: Her beauty and style; her challenging job.
Marriage strains: The marriage contract, communication.
The last straw: The mistress.

When Victoria met Edouard, her future husband, at a party in Paris, he had former Empress Soraya of Iran on one arm and Dewi Sukarno, the former First Lady of Indonesia, on the other. The party was a dinner for about 30 people given by a film director, a mutual friend, in his *hôtel particulier* which translates roughly as townhouse or, often, palace. In other words, a dinner for chic jet-set types.

Edouard took one look at Victoria and changed the place cards so that he could sit next to her.

You can see why Edouard dumped his celebrities. Victoria, now about 40, is a beauty with dramatic coloring — dark dark hair and red lips and clothes that whisper of famous hairdressers and designer clothes — plus a look of shyness and vulnerability that Frenchmen find irresistible. She spoke perfect French and had lived in France for years. At 25, her style and languages had been learned the easy way, changing countries as her father, an energy consultant, changed posts: France, Saudi Arabia, Sweden, Japan and Hong Kong. Finally she spent seven years in the U.S. to become a "very patriotic American." After two years at the Parsons School of Design in Paris, she left for New York. Bloomingdale's had hired her to be a buyer.

"But in New York I missed the French love of romance and adventure," she said. "I fled back to Paris with one suitcase and lived in a 6th-floor walkup in St. Germain des Prés with three models I'd met previously in Paris. I got a job in advertising, assistant to the creative director and met lots of people from the art world, writers, film people ..."

The kind of people at that dinner where she met Edouard. Back in Paris, Victoria blossomed. Her working life with an advertising company

163

was demanding and lively, and her social life was crammed with weekend partridge shoots at châteaux and dancing at the Palace and Regine's.

That night, Victoria was working early the next day, so she got up to leave the party right after coffee was served, and signaled to the girlfriend she came with.

"Edouard told me later he was so happy to see two girls leave, now he could leave too. He invited me to another dinner party, but I refused — he was good company, lots of fun, but he was too handsome, too popular, a playboy type, at 39 too much the most eligible bachelor. I was leery of all that glamour, and had more invitations than I could handle anyway."

A year went by. Victoria went on vacation in Martinique between jobs. She was sunning herself in a deck chair on the beach when she met the president of a publishing group. They chatted, then had lunch together. Presently he invited her to help start a magazine for men. She would do the foreign edition for Japan, Portugal and Spain. Who, me? she thought first and then, why not? It turned out that Edouard was political editor for one of the group's other magazines.

"We kept bumping into each other," she said. "Gradually we started seeing each other more. He began to fascinate me with his knowledge of history — encyclopedic knowledge, really, and not only that. He had the kind of brain that relates something in the deep historical past to something contemporary — such as that the passion of American Protestants for Buddhism is like the French Huguenots swooning over the Bogomils. Or he would say things like the reason Mitterrand had to have so many secret-public mistresses was a sort of rivalry, a Socialist competing with the Don Juans of the Right, Giscard and Chirac.

"I think he was interested in me because I smiled the whole time, and because I was natural and sincere and not out for anything, and the reputation of American women was for being money grabbers. But he wasn't interested in getting married — he was the unavailable, eternal bachelor because of a bad marriage of one year when he was 20. So one evening, on the way to a party at Maxim's, when he said, 'Do you want to marry me?' I started laughing. I thought he was joking. 'Yeah, sure,' I said. 'No, no, I'm really serious,' he said."

At that point Victoria's parents were living in London. Edouard flew over to ask her father for her hand. As he got off the plane he was disconcerted to realize that he'd forgotten something crucial. The ritual for this ceremony was that you arrived at the house of your intended in a top hat and gloves *couleur beurre frais* (the color of fresh butter). No one would wear a top hat anymore, but the gloves were still vital — special gloves that would never be worn twice. Edouard stuttered his apologies. Her father laughed. 'Never mind, the champagne is on ice anyway.'

"It was wonderfully old-fashioned," Victoria said. "I loved it. He was an only child and excited to be part of a big American family — I had four brothers."

They were married at the city hall of the 17th *arrondissement* in Paris, then went on a honeymoon to the Seychelles. With 24 friends. They were there one month.

"We were very happy," she said, "for a few months. And then it all started to unravel, but gradually. I hardly realized how bad things were. We began having children, and I was thinking about them and trying not to think that, really, I was miserable."

She got up to get herself a glass of water and gave me a long look. "If I blame our divorce on one thing, it's that he made me sign that marriage contract, *séparation des biens*. It meant that I wouldn't own anything that was bought during our marriage. I was in tears, but Edouard said I had to sign it, that it was no big deal, brides always signed it and had been signing it for 1000 years.' He added, 'If you don't sign, we won't get married.' Well, so I did, of course. I was in love.

"After we were married, he'd go out and buy something — a lamp, a painting — without asking me. From time to time he'd say, 'Nothing in this house belongs to you.' This really hurt. In my family, we all shared everything. After a while you feel it's not really your home."

They both wanted children, but they wanted them differently. For Edouard, they should be seen but not heard, perfectly educated, perfectly brought up. Coming into the salon to kiss the guests — "Poor children! they have to kiss strangers!" said Victoria — and then leaving almost immediately. Victoria, on the other hand, wanted to include them in everything. In looking back, she feels she may have given the children priority over her husband, something American women are famous for. She says she simply wanted to give them happy childhood memories — and as Edouard refused to participate, she had to create them alone.

"He was from a broken home, his dream was to have a real family, so I thought he would love our holiday celebrations — Christmas, Easter, Thanksgiving — but all this meant nothing to him. At Christmas, he wouldn't even come out of the bedroom in the morning when they were opening presents. I began taking the children to the U.S. to celebrate — my whole family had a lovely time together. He came too, but just once."

What about summer vacations?

Victoria sighed heavily. "I thought I knew about France but honestly… that traditional French family vacation is a real trap, how should I know that? French wives usually go to the sea in July with the children — to stay with the grandmother if she has a big house there — and wait for the husband to join them in August. Instead I went to the States in July. I found out that this July absence from Paris is a clever cover for husbands — a whole month with their mistress."

Mistress? Are you sure? I asked.

"They all have a mistress. They say it doesn't matter because she's not from the same milieu — what difference does that make? Anyway it's not necessarily true — they might be from any milieu. I wish I'd been more French… and had lovers. It would have been more fun."

Victoria doesn't know exactly when things started going disastrously wrong. She was so taken up with the two children that she can't pinpoint it, but soon she began noticing that this *séduisant*, gregarious playboy was turning into a petit bourgeois — a *casanier*, who came home from work and slumped in front of the television set. He didn't want to go anywhere; she couldn't invite people to dinner because their friends were from different worlds that didn't mix. He was criticizing her continually; she couldn't do anything right.

"You suffer, but you don't know it for a long time. You want to talk — and there is less and less communication. TV becomes a priority. Whatever you do is wrong. All of a sudden, you notice you've lost confidence, you're not yourself anymore.

"I wanted to go to a counselor, but he wouldn't let me. He wanted control. 'You have a maid and a window washer,' he said, as if that took care of everything. 'You have all you want.'

" 'But I want you,' I said. I was working at home, longing to talk to him.

" 'Well, I'm here!' he said. But he wasn't. So I thought, we're not going in the same direction."

And then one day he phoned his girlfriend right in front of her.

"So I took the children and left," she said. "When things get really bad, why stay? I never felt it was my home. I was just passing through. When I left, he was shocked. He wanted me to stay, so we could grow old together. Well, I ask you, do you think I should have stayed?"

Victoria has not regretted not staying. She prefers her present, much smaller apartment in a non-chic district to the splendid one in an elegant *quartier* where she lived with Edouard. It's hers. What is in it is hers — it's home, and no one is trying to make her miserable.

"It is much, much better to live alone with the children than with someone who is playing *Gaslight*, tearing me down the whole time. I didn't want my children to suffer. Kids need a father, and they were only seven and eight when I left. So I sent them to him every two weeks. The kids were happy, they had two homes. I was happy — I was free to play when they were off. We did, really, have a 'happy divorce.' He's been a good father. They're bigger now so they don't see him quite so often. I never said anything against him to my children.

"Basically of course you want your marriage to work out. If it doesn't, then you tell yourself, I want to make the best of this. Paris is a fabulous city, so much is going on... Okay, so I'm divorced, but think of the advantages. The ex-husband becomes the perfect father, and I've had several careers since we parted.

"I love my life now. You can do anything as an American woman — I've created several businesses, one an import-export firm, another an antique business on the Internet for wealthy Americans. I look for special *objets* in châteaux in France. I'm living in the arts environment I love, seeing curators and artists and ambassadors and writers and movie directors. I'm a different person — happy."

Edouard saw this — and asked her to marry him again.

"Of course I said no. You don't jump out of the third-story window twice. It's true that as a single woman, I've lost my status, and some women feel I'm a threat. Well, they can keep their husbands!"

When I asked if she had plans to leave France, she looked shocked.

"Leave *France*? And go where? You get used to certain things... I love French men!"

Comment: As I already wrote above, no outsider can have an enlightening opinion on someone else's marriage. However, it is possible to see some red lights flashing in these marriages.

In this case, Edouard's inflexibility about the marriage contract would have scared off a more experienced bride. One could imagine that the inflexibility would extend to other areas, such as not taking part in the holiday celebrations that are of such importance to many Americans. The wounding rudeness of his phoning his mistress from home could not have been foreseen, nor that he would change from a man about town to a couch potato. Like Sheila, Victoria seems to have done all she could to please Edouard, and to keep the marriage going. Maybe she should have let go with some heavy screaming.

Cynthia, 32 and Pierre, 32

Cynthia's trumps: Same family background; helpful mother-in-law.
Marriage strains: Cynthia's homesickness; her failure to make French friends.
The last straw: Cynthia's refusal to accompany Pierre on his restaurant tours.

Cynthia lives in a sumptuous apartment in Paris's 8th *arrondissement*. From one of the founding families of Massachusetts, she was carefully brought up to be an educated American with "culture," and she looks it, with her short brown curly hair and Peter Pan blouses with one string of cultured pearls. Her main feature is huge round brown eyes, clear and warm.

Her first feel of France was a Poiret dress. Her grandmother had bought it on a wild trip to Paris in the Roaring Twenties, long before Cynthia was born. Her mother had loved it and kept it hanging in her closet in case she went to a costume party. It was a shimmering pink-beige thrill of silk taffeta, low cut in front and back, no sleeves, with a long low flapper waist and a skirt of many tiered layers stitched like leaves. Cynthia used to dress up in it when she was little, when her mother was out.

She met Pierre, a freelance journalist in New York, when she was studying design there. Friends of his took him to a party given by friends of hers.

"*Dragged* him is the word, he didn't want to go to the party at all — so he told me later. Then he saw me across the room and told his friend, 'That is the woman I like!' We talked, but just a little because I was leaving; just long enough for him to ask for my phone number.

"I wasn't interested — he seemed scruffy, his hair uncombed, he wore red jeans — he was an intellectual guy, anti-preppy, anti-Hermès and his English was terrible. But then the next day he left a message on my answering machine… with his French accent. It was so heavy, so *romantic*. He wanted me to go to The Laurent on 56th Street to have a drink. So I met him there and ordered a Club Soda. He didn't know what it was, but he ordered one too. Then we went to the Riverside Café overlooking the Brooklyn Bridge. Talk about romance! But after drinks at these two places he couldn't afford dinner!"

He was more careful on their next date. He borrowed some Ralph Lauren clothes from a friend and took her uptown to a place he knew.

"I wore a yellow-and-black plaid Norma Kamali dress… do you know, he kept that dress hanging in his closet for years? Well it was a wonderful evening." Cynthia smiled nostalgically, remembering.

When Pierre went back to France a few days later, they were in love. He telephoned her every day from Paris and sent her tapes of love songs by Jacques Brel and Leo Ferré. He wrote love poems for her. Four months later he sent her an Hermès scarf.

"He really wanted to send me a black lace garter belt, but didn't quite dare. My husband is an *artiste d'amour…* in general, Frenchmen are sexually dynamic. In comparison, American men, the ones I've known anyway, are boring, not poetic at all."

Back in France, Pierre worked himself to death to sell story ideas so that he could come back and see her. Cynthia began to realize that this had become really serious. She thought she'd better come to Paris and check him out in his own country.

"His apartment was a delight, just what a young bachelor should have… two rooms in the Latin Quarter, a walkup in a 16th century house, wonderful beams and a creaky staircase, little secret corners. He also took me to his parents' apartment, on the rue de l'Université, huge and beautiful and oh so elegant. I loved his friends, they were all so nice, I thought seeing them would always be fun."

So Cynthia moved to France. They lived together for 10 months before they were married in 1985.

In the beginning she loved it. She tried to do everything to fit in.

"I took an intensive French course, I was always nicely dressed, I never wore white tennis shoes or jogging clothes. My mother-in-law was a huge help. She was like a friend. She gave me a beautiful sapphire ring after our baby was born and has always helped with her. When Clarisse started school, my mother-in-law would take care of her every Wednesday. She would always support me — sometimes against Pierre. She said she could tell me things she couldn't tell her friends. 'French women don't tell their secrets,' she said.

"She was full of good advice about marriage. 'First of all,' she said, 'always let your husband think whatever you do is his idea. You must manipulate him. Secondly, don't ever let him see you cry. They hate that, it would make him despise you.'"

Nevertheless, Cynthia began to be disappointed in her new country. Gradually her whole attitude changed. What actually happened was that she was homesick, without realizing it.

"I stopped making a huge effort with the shopkeepers, since I got no service. The strikes got me down. Everyone seemed to be manipulating everyone else. The worst was the change in my husband's friends. Before we married, we partied with them all the time, they were fun and I was really looking forward to fitting in with this great group. But after I started living here I saw that the women didn't have the same need of friends as we Americans. The men kept on being men, and nice, but the women were distant.

"I tried to make new friends by standing in line waiting for Clarisse at kindergarten, and then after school. I never could get anyone to speak to me. I became a reverse snob. I gave up on the French and decided to join all the American groups here. I try to do what I can for Franco-American understanding, but the French I see now are usually international, married to Americans or English or some other nationality. At dinner parties our friends now are always mixed. Pierre's friends have become so high-powered that you have to get them months in advance, and I can't deal with that. It's too hard to organize."

Pierre was taken up more and more by his work. They had misunderstandings, wondering if they were "cultural" or personal. Cynthia began to long for the place where she'd grown up. Finally she did find the word for her trouble. Cynthia was homesick. Desperately. For her country, her family and friends, and for the 18th-century farm where she grew up, with its old stones and old oaks and ponds and marshy fields. She left for a month to go back "home" to Massachusetts.

"I came back recharged," she said. "I realized that this was how to keep my sanity — and my good humor."

For the next 15 years, Cynthia had to go back every summer or she felt as if she would suffocate. She had to see her parents and brothers and sisters, ride her horse — just a colt when she left — and see her old friends. She left Pierre for a month every summer.

"A month!" gasped Diana Holmes, when I mentioned this to her. "I was told by my husband's sister never *ever* to leave a French husband alone for more than a *few days!*"

Pierre's extracurricular passion was gastronomy. He liked to go on Hemingway-style drives throughout France on vacation, trying out new restaurants. This bored Cynthia. So while Cynthia was in Massachusetts, Pierre was tooting around France, maybe in the Dordogne, maybe in Strasbourg.

I was saddened, but not really surprised, when Cynthia told me that Pierre had met someone last summer in Lyon on one of his restaurant tours and wanted a divorce.

A year later, close to 50, she is still in Paris and surrounded by would-be boyfriends. She has started a promising business making chocolate cookies in the American way.

"I made a mistake," she says cheerfully. "But Clarisse is fine, and I'm fine and so is Pierre… so now I start a new life. I like it!"

Comment: It's easy enough to say that Cynthia "should have" made French friends that were compatible with Pierre, and that she "should have" gone on his restaurant tours with him, and one can only imagine what else. I suspect that there were quarrels Cynthia didn't want to tell me about, perhaps some kind of shameful family skeleton rattling in the closet, perhaps an embarrassing illness kept out of sight. From a tight-lipped, rigidly disciplined old New England family similar to Pierre's, many things would be left unsaid. Whatever, like Sheila and Victoria, she has kept her balance, her humor and her love of France.

16

Marriages that are holding
– so far

From dozens of interviews I found that the happy Franco-American marriages had at least three of the elements below, maybe more than three, while the divorced couples had two at most, if that:

- Apparent fidelity of both partners
- A wife with a challenging job. This is true of all of the happy marriages below, except one. It is not true of Wendy, a lawyer, only because Daniel's career takes him to places like Chad, where she can't practice.
- A husband who has lived long enough in the U.S. to know where his wife is coming from, to appreciate her culture and to encourage her to keep in touch with it.
- A wife with an optimistic, cheerful disposition.
- A wife with an intellectual and/or emotional excitement about France.
- A husband who backs his wife in any disagreement with his mother, her mother-in-law.
- A husband and wife from the same social class.
- A wife who masters the French language.
- No stepchildren.

Amanda, 45 and Jacques, 48

Trumps: The independence of both of them; their complementarity
English as the common language.

"Marry anyone you want," said Amanda's father, "but not a Frenchman."
If it had to be a southern European, he had nothing against a Spaniard,
for instance. He had a house in Spain. Or an Italian — Amanda's mother
was Italian. But not a Frenchman. "The French are arrogant."

Amanda married Jacques anyway. He was a banker, like her father,
so she knew what that was about. And she herself was already a tycoon-
type with a sky-high salary. How high, exactly? Six or seven digits? I
didn't dare ask. But as she was the international marketing director for
one of the huge American multinational cosmetics firms, it had to be up
there. Jacques was earning about the same salary, so that subtracted some
arrogance possibilities. She met him on a blind date after her transfer to
France.

It turned out that Jacques was not arrogant. I phoned her for an
interview because I'd heard from several people what a happy couple
they were, after 15 years. When I said that on the phone, she laughed.
"That's funny," she said. "We almost kill each other every day."

Amanda is statuesque, almost Wagnerian, tall and imposing, dark-
haired and handsome, with a merry laugh. She grew up in New Jersey.
She invited me to her apartment for coffee. It has a feeling of light and
space and is filled with big wonderful paintings. I asked her how she
had organized their happy life, working full time. She laughed again.

"I figured that we were pretty well-balanced financially, and I'd be
out of the country and up in the air most of the time anyway," she said.
"So if he really was arrogant, I'd be escaping easily. I didn't stop working
to have the children — two girls. I didn't want him or the girls to hold it
against me that I was away a lot, so I organized the house so there were
always two nannies for the girls, and a cook. Dinner was waiting for him
when he got home. He could work late when he wanted. I thought that
wasn't a bad deal, getting married and having children with a wife who
wasn't hanging around all the time."

"You do see each other from time to time?" I asked.

That merry laugh again. "We're both pretty independent. I don't rely
on him. When we moved to this apartment, we argued a lot. Jacques felt
at liberty to make all the decisions. I screamed, I fought. Finally I retreated
— it wasn't worthwhile to spend all that energy fighting over how the
electric outlets were installed. I decided I was lucky to have a husband

who likes details. I hate them."

Amanda stopped working full time a few years ago to be freer and start her own marketing consultancy. She didn't have much time to talk about it. They were moving to a house with a big garden in a few days. Her desk was piled high with the clutter of moving.

"All these decisions again," she said. "Thank heaven Jacques really likes to take care of most of them."

She doesn't speak French. "Well, I do, but without verbs." Another merry laugh. "I haven't had the time or really the need to learn French properly. Jacques's English is perfect. Maybe now with the new house, I'll learn how to garden, become a house person. I have two new friends: the butcher and the cheese vendor. Every day the cheese vendor gives me a lesson in a new kind of cheese, how it's made, where it comes from, what it should be eaten with and when."

Maybe not speaking French, but keeping her English as the language of the family, is one of the tips about this family's *bonheur*. Another might be her sense of humor. A third might be the sense of humor of the non-arrogant Frenchman.

I was able to reach Jacques on the phone and ask him what he thought. "One thing I never doubted when I married Amanda," he said, "is that no matter how old we get to be together, I won't get bored. But this is not because she is American. It's rather her spirit and her *joie de vivre*. I can't say we laugh out loud together all day. But we do share a sense of humor and don't take ourselves too seriously. We actually avoid people who do."

As for being married to an American: no answers from Jacques to Fabrice's question at the gargoyle party. He thinks being married to an American is just fine.

"I think it provides the opportunity to have a wider set of references, as well as the possibility to live in one country or the other, although so far this is not something we have ever tried to achieve."

I asked him what he and Amanda liked to do together.

"We argue," he said.

I got back to Amanda with these quotes. That merry laugh. "The French aren't particularly arrogant," she said. "They're always right. That's different. When I learned that Jacques was always right, even when he was wrong, I gave up and we didn't have any more problems."

Amanda appreciates it that Jacques isn't spoiled. "I don't see my mother-in-law much — she lives in Megève — but once I thanked her for the way she brought him up. He's a Renaissance guy. He can cook, clean, change lightbulbs, you name it. He is steady. I'm all over the place. He's my rock. I wouldn't mind shaking him up a little. One of the things Jacques and I share is appreciation of the world and all the different cultures... and types... recently we went to a party where half the people were Arab. It was fun and interesting.

"An American husband? I'd have to watch football all the time. Americans thinking of marrying a Frenchman should be warned that the French have very strong opinions.

"Another thing. We have two names, two cultures, two religions, two children, we're two different personalities. Jacques is an introvert, I'm an extrovert. He is a detail person, I'm an idea, concept person. I'm perfect, he's not."

Bravos: I'd have had to talk to Amanda for two weeks steadily to find a weak spot where she triumphed. She's that upbeat, a glass-is-half-full woman if there ever was one.

Wendy, 43 and Daniel, 48

Trumps: Their intellectual brilliance
Their curiosity and taste for adventure
Wendy's reaching out to people in distress

Wendy, age 43, is an intellectual with *chien* and a gift for relating to others which has stood her in good stead in her life of constantly pulling up stakes and moving on. She was born in Tokyo and grew up in various countries and various states, mostly Georgia. She graduated from McGill, then studied for a year at the School of Advanced International Studies (SAIS) at Johns Hopkins in Washington. Her father was a distinguished diplomat. For a while, Wendy considered the same career until the day, in class at Johns Hopkins, a teacher, looking at her name, burst out, "Oh? Your father was — !" Wendy was so embarrassed and so annoyed that anyone would think she would have a career on her father's coat-tails that she decided then and there to practice law. She graduated from law school at William and Mary, in Virginia.

For a while she taught English in Brazil, then went to Mozambique as political officer for the UN peacekeeping mission there. Daniel was at the next desk. An *énarque*, or graduate of the elite graduate school for civil servants, the ENA, the French government had appointed him liaison officer between the rebel movement and the U.N. mission. Wendy and

Daniel sweated over the files together, rode into the bush together, dining with the rebel leaders… and eventually married. Wendy gave up her own career and followed Daniel to Zaire and the Dominican Republic. For the past three years they've been living in Brittany with their son and daughter, 12 and 10 years old. It looks as if they'll soon be moving to South Africa.

Daniel is a brilliant Cartesian. That is, he talks in organized paragraphs, with abstractions layered in a perfect synthesis that would take a lesser mortal hours of preparation. Wendy said she fell for his brain first, the best she'd ever met, and then all the rest of him. At the moment her own brain is trying to come to terms with the dark underside of France as well as with all the obvious stumbling blocks. She sent me this email:

I read a study recently about how little time German couples spend talking to each other and I realize that Daniel is always very interesting, and when he decides to discuss something, he has this wonderful European way of reasoning — while his words and discourse are very logical and rational and based on a lot of very neatly synthesized information, his analysis always takes into account the psychological/emotional perspective. It has taken me some time and a bit more exposure to French history than I had before to realize that this collective culture of palace plots and treachery, not to mention the more recent divisions between Résistants and collaborators, has given rise to vast underpinnings of unsaid emotions which color every relationship and create a huge complexity of connotations in what are, on the surface, simple human interactions.

Now I have been trying to think of concrete examples in my married life that reflect this recent discovery, and perhaps the simplest thing I can say is that I sometimes have the feeling that I have let myself be bamboozled at times by taking Daniel's logical arguments about organizing things in the house when, in fact, his reason for doing things is quite different and often more emotionally motivated than he admits. That is as far as I have gotten on this point. I have to think about it some more, but one thing is sure: Daniel has arrogated to himself a certain presumption of credibility, since he has so many times been right about the basic functioning of the society, like when I say we should try to buy something or other after 8 in the evening or at 1 in the afternoon, and Daniel says to me, "Impossible, the store is certainly closed." Then I answer, "You always find an excuse not to do something when you don't want to," and then he says to me, "All right, we'll go to the store and you will see." And then we go, and of course, the store is closed: for lunch, for dinner, for 'congés,' for something.

I preface this by telling you that Mark Twain's Letter to the Recording Angel has helped me formulate my thoughts as I think of the recording angel's answer to the prayers of one devout parishioner by explaining that no matter what he prayed for under his breath, it was the public prayers which took precedence.

Similarly, I think that living intimately with a French husband, at least my French husband, is a sort of eternal effort of interpretation. On one hand, he has internalized the ideal of French education — an impeccable capacity for logic and order. But at the same time, his heritage has imbued him with the subtle art of manipulation which has taken me years to realize. Example: Ever since we bought this house, I have wanted to have a room of my own. This is really based on my own American heritage of personal property being really personal and the need for a larger "bubble" at times than my French family allows me to have.

Although my husband has never said to me that he does not want me to have my own space (he would never say, "Wendy, you don't really need a room of your own, you have the whole house"), he has countered my request by a different argument each time — sometimes perfectly rational. The original idea of putting our different-gender young children in the same room was torpedoed very quickly as he forced me to admit that soon each one of them would need his own space.

But Wendy says that now she has finally scored. She is, in fact, going to have her own office, all prepared and ready to go by next week…

"Just about the time I'll have to start getting ready to move to South Africa," she said. "But that's all right — it will be there to come back to."

Wendy loves living in Brittany. Besides driving the children to school, picking them up for lunch, making lunch, taking them back to school, bringing them home again, Wendy organizes junior tennis teams, lessons for the teams and tournaments; she takes music lessons with her children and plays the piano in the school concerts. She makes a point of consulting the mayor of her village about neighbors in distress. Recently she began a series of four visits a week to a neighbor with cancer. She wants to give her the will to fight.

"One of the things I do with her is order scallops from our local fisherman, a friend," she said. "We get them off the boat and open them together. Last week we each did 22 kilos."

What about the household sweeping, scrubbing, cooking?

Wendy smiles and raises her eyebrow. "Well… it does get done, but I'm not sure when… and luckily, that's okay with Daniel."

Bravos: Wendy has often been isolated in lonely, sometimes dangerous posts with Daniel, without much support when Daniel was traveling on assignments for the Quai d'Orsay, or when Daniel was depressed, as was sometimes the case. She must have very often felt like going to bed and pulling the covers up– but she didn't.

Edith, 37 and Claude, 37

Trumps: Their united stand against Claude's mother
Real satisfaction of both of them with their careers
Their shared experience of the U.S.; their wide travels

Edith is tall and slim and reserved. Her pale face without makeup looks as innocent and plain-spoken as the Arizona desert where she grew up.

Her thick chestnut-colored hair is cut square in the French way, but when she met Claude for the first time, in Washington, D.C., it was just sort of thick and wild. She had never been to France, knew nothing about it and spoke not a word of French. France? Where might that be, anyway? She was studying for her master's in marine biology and environmental engineering.

Claude, halfway through French law school, was doing his year of compulsory French military service at the French Embasssy. They met at a cocktail party given by the World Bank. Claude was talking to two beautiful models. The moment he caught sight of Edith he dropped the models and made a beeline for her.

"I thought he was a lunatic, some kind of aborigine," she said, "the way he rushed me. At the same time, he was this super cool Frenchie. I thought he'd be too cool to call me before Thursday — but he called the very next day and insisted I come out to dinner. I said not then, I was having a party — and purposely didn't invite him. So he crashed it and dragged me out to dinner afterwards."

Claude knew he'd met his future. He was so nervous at dinner he smoked a whole pack of cigarettes.

"He was supposed to leave the U.S. in 54 days — but after we met he invented some reason to get an extension for two years. We both knew there was something there, but it was too soon to talk about it."

Meanwhile Edith transferred to Harvard to get her Ph.D. in

environmental engineering and systems research. Over the next two years she was sent to Japan and the Philippines. Claude flew out to see her twice. Then he wanted to come to Arizona to meet her parents.

Edith's parents were hippies. They grew their own food in a huge vegetable garden. They had 13 children. Edith was the 13th. Chickens, cows, goats wandered around their property. Edith milked the cows with her father. They made butter, cheese and yogurt. Her father ran a cement factory.

"The good thing about being the last child in a big family is that you can do what you want," she said. "The pressure is off. Your parents hardly know you. My parents didn't care if I moved to Paris or Tahiti."

Edith shuffled some papers around and sighed.

"It was the opposite with Claude — he grew up in a château. His mother had been widowed with three children when he was only four. He was the only son. He was her whole life. You can imagine.

"When we decided to get married in France, I moved there — on my first visit. I was as naïve as you can be about what that would mean. I thought, after Asia, what can be the problem with France? I didn't know a word of French or anything about France, nothing at all. And some of the shocks almost threw me."

Being shoved into the shadow of her son's life by a foreign woman — an American! — was not what Claude's mother was prepared to accept, to put it mildly. Edith saw that she was going to need more than the magic of a Ph.D. to get through to her, if indeed she ever could. Claude was going to have to be tough as he had never been. Would he back her up?

It unfolded like a Snow White saga. The first poison the mother-in-law came up with was to insist that Edith sign a marriage contract, the *séparation des biens*, that is, no sharing of their assets.

"I refused. I told her I was going to have an interesting career and make lots of money, which I expected to share with Claude just as he would share whatever he had with me. Then she got nasty. She said I was basically a thief and was going to marry Claude simply to steal his inheritance.

"I talked it over with Claude and he backed me up all the way. I told her again that it was out of the question that I sign that contract. Then she said that if I wouldn't sign it, she wouldn't come to our wedding. This was it for me. Everything was all set for the wedding, the invitations were out and the presents beginning to pour in but I told her, Fine, then we won't be married in France. We'll get married in Arizona. At this she hyperventilated for 10 days, moaning that I was destroying her boy, taking him to the U.S. 'Do you know what you are doing?' she said over and over.

"And then she said she wouldn't speak to her son ever again, adding, believe it or not, that she would convince all Claude's relatives to shun us. Which she did, telling them all that it was clear that we'd be divorced in a year. And — listen to this — his grandmother right away wrote him out of her will.

"Claude was great. He sat down and wrote a letter to 26 relatives. He told them he was ashamed of them, they were living in the 18th century and should wake up; and that if they ever wanted to see him again, they would have to accept me."

So Edith and Claude were married in Arizona in an Indian Mission with all Edith's 12 siblings and relatives. For their honeymoon they bought two motorcycles and roared around Colorado, Idaho and Montana for three weeks. "We had a fabulous time — we laughed and laughed — we were both 27." Claude was hired by a local firm. When little Nicolas was six months old, they decided that, for Claude's career, it was time to move back to France.

"Claude's mother hadn't spoken to him — or me, of course — since we left France. I knew I had to make peace with her. My own mother, who is a wise woman and who knew the whole story, had sat me down for a long talk before the wedding and said, 'You must not marry this man if you can't forgive her, if you can't put all this behind you.' So, before we went back, I wrote Claude's mother a letter. I said, 'I want you to know that you have a place of respect in our family, as Nicolas's grandmother.'

"One week after we got back to Paris, my mother-in-law came for a visit. This is a person who will never say 'I'm sorry.' For my parents, and for me, family is the most important thing. So I practiced my open-arm policy and pretended that the nastiness had never happened. I put the baby in her arms. He looked just like Claude. Well, she melted. She had been afraid I'd put Claude against her. When Nicolas was nine months old, I left him with her for a week and it went well. Somehow she realized I wasn't going to be small-minded."

Edith and Claude gave a party for their second wedding anniversary. They invited the 26 relatives that he'd written his pre-wedding letter to. They all came. His mother made a spectacular turnaround: she gave a toast to their two years of marriage.

"She realized that we were happy," said Edith. "Twice she has told me that she gets along better with me than with her own daughter.

"And now, since Claude and I both travel a lot, we can leave the children — we have three now — with her. We haven't disagreed about much — except potty training. She was really snotty about that, said that Nicolas had to be *propre* (trained) at 18 months. At two, when we still hadn't started it, she was indignant. Claude explained that we thought we'd know when he was ready. In fact, we started it when he was two and a half and it took exactly one week. A little cousin, potty trained at 18 months, is still wetting his bed at nine."

Later one of the relatives came to Edith with advice. "One, learn French. Don't rely on Claude to translate. Two, don't take your mother-in-law's bites too seriously. She has a big heart."

Edith's wisdom and graciousness had resolved the mother-in-law crisis. Her professional life was the next problem. First she had to learn French. She signed up for courses at one of France's leading *Grandes Ecoles*, or graduate schools, the *Ponts et Chaussées*.

"I was a statistic — they only took me because of Harvard," she said. "It was humiliating, really hell. I understood one word in 20. There I was, a Harvard Ph.D. demoted to the level of a baby. At the end of the day I came home with a splitting headache, all that concentration without understanding.

"My first job was with a car company doing innovational research. I had to get a handle on the French mentality — their culture of the abstract. They're not focused on the outcome but on the intellectual exploration. So they invent all kinds of brilliant things without ever making the effort to apply them or market them... like their television, and the Minitel.

"I was kicked out after a year because the French intelligence people told them I must be a spy working for the U.S. Government or U.S. industry. It was depressing to be treated like a pariah! The next job was with a waste management outfit — that was too macho. Then I joined the OECD doing research on environmental performance — how countries manage their environment. It's a sort of audit I do — what are the country's national objectives and if they're achieved. We try to make a level playing field... some countries have an industrial advantage because they don't do what they promised, so we publish a report and try to put peer pressure on them."

If Edith and Claude have kept afloat during their stormy weather, much of the credit goes to Claude, credit which Edith appreciates mightily.

"Every year I have more and more respect for him," she says. "He is constantly doing little things that show he loves me — he doesn't need to say it. For instance, I was having trouble with my visa and called him at the office. He was on the phone with his biggest client, with millions of dollars at risk. He didn't tell me to wait, or that I should call back, instead he told his client, I have something urgent to take care of, can I call you back?

"He told me I didn't have to change my name to his — but I felt it was important to him, so I did.

"I think the fact that he was raised by a tough, strong woman — my mother-in-law — helped. I believe I benefit from that, for many men feel intimidated by strong intelligent women.

"Also, Frenchmen are raised to be both macho and sensitive. They don't have a problem with their sensitive side, so they're perfectly at home with their wife's independence. Claude cooks, changes diapers, whatever is needed. He agrees with me to bring up bi-cultural, bi-lingual children. We have a French au pair during the week and a Filipino during the weekend. And my son Nicolas is going to camp in California this summer."

Edith's advice to an American thinking of marrying a Frenchman is to meet him in the U.S.

"He has to be an enlightened Frenchman; he has to have lived in America, or he can't understand where you're coming from and all your references will be skewed."

Bravos: It's easy enough to see how the attitude of Claude's mother could have shattered their marriage – but it didn't. It's harder for us, outside the marriage, to understand its daily grinding away at their bonds, and to imagine the vision it took on both their parts to stick to their guns. Both Claude and Edith were remarkably – I'm tempted to say sensationally — steadfast in their loyalty to each other. Edith's determination to learn French, not just the rudiments but the structure and complexity of the language and then to undertake the grueling studies of the Ecole des Ponts et Chaussées, when she already had her American Ph.D., must have mightily pleased Claude, in addition to making her highly employable. I have an idea, from the few things Edith said, that her mother contributed much to her strikingly strong backbone.

Deborah, 30 and Michel, 30

Trumps: Deborah's flexibility as a black woman in a new culture
The kindness of Michel's mother
Their shared life in the U.S.

Deborah was fed up with Chicago. She was laid off from her job in the theater and she'd broken off with her boyfriend. She wanted to go somewhere, anywhere, just away from Chicago. But where? She was crazy about French singers, Serge Gainsbourg, Barbara, Yves Montand and Juliette Greco. And what about Johnny Halliday, though Belgian? Maybe she should check out Paris?

Then she heard about Josephine Baker, that the French adored her. What a great time she had in France. That decided it. Deborah is black. If she felt like it, she could give Halle Berry a run for her money. Not when she arrived, straight from Chicago. But when I saw her after six years in France, she was transformed into a dynamo of confidence and French chic. Her devastating smile hits you first, then her beautiful eyes and her hair, framed with a wide brown band, and, finally, her little black dress with a plunging neckline. She spoke excitedly, moving her eyes but hardly ever her hands.

For the first trip of her French destiny, she arrived from Chicago at Charles de Gaulle airport, and met her future husband that very same day. She took a cab with an American called Sally whom she met on the plane, to the only place in Paris she'd heard about, Montmartre. They walked around all day, pinching themselves that they were in Paris. They watched the artists sketching, joined a crowd "marching about something or other," and ate some croissants on a bench on the square, sighing with happiness. Around 5:00 pm they went towards Pigalle, barhopping. They still had their backpacks — finding a hotel could wait.

"We hit all the bars," she said, "and ended up at the Frog and Roast Beef. Sally disappeared — this was a pickup bar, but I didn't know that. There was a rugby game between the Irish and the French on the television — I'd never heard of rugby and was amazed at how excited the guys all were.

"Pretty soon I was tapped on the shoulder by a guy who'd heard me speaking English. He wanted to know where I was from. I thought he was nice so I bought us a couple of drinks. This impressed him — he'd heard that American girls never bought their own drinks. He said his name was Michel. We danced and then another guy asked me to dance the Salsa — Michel didn't mind. When I danced with him again, he said he didn't want me to think he was possessive. By the way, he was a really handsome, natural, fun guy. I liked him.

"Then, suddenly, he left me on the dance floor and ran out the door. Can you imagine? I thought the guy was crazy — until he came back. With my backpack. Someone had stolen it — he'd been keeping an eye on it while we were dancing. Well, I was pretty impressed."

And suddenly very tired. It was time to look for a hotel. She started saying goodbye to Michel — but he insisted on going with her.

"He said we couldn't go to just any hotel — I found out later he meant one of those by-the-hour joints. He took me to a hotel two doors down from the Moulin Rouge, above a Pigalle sex shop. I tell you, Paris!

"Anyway, he seemed like a nice guy — an American would be corny in this situation and move in for the kill — but he didn't and I got no vibes. I thought he didn't like me. We exchanged phone numbers and I saw him again a couple of times. Then I left my things with him when I went to Rotterdam for a couple of days."

Rotterdam? I asked.

"Well, why not?" she said. She wanted to see something else before she went home. She brought him back an antique phone. She stayed in Paris a few weeks more, checking out the racism, among other things.

"It's different than in the U.S., in some ways more natural. They make racist jokes you couldn't make in the U.S., but no one makes you feel uncomfortable. Imagine, they have a kind of pastry called *Tête de Nègre*, which means Head of a Nigger! There are no black television role models and you don't see many black policemen or civil servants... but people don't make you *feel black*, the way they do in the U.S."

Michel, a software designer, was getting serious. He began talking about coming to the U.S.; being with her was part of the plan. Deborah wanted to think about it. She called her mother to send her a ticket home. A month later she and Michel met in San Francisco. They both got jobs and then Deborah got pregnant.

"Michel had been on to me about getting married for a long time — and living in France, of course — but if you look at it, he's French, he's white, and I'm American and I'm black, how is that going to work? How am I going to get on in France? How do I know what it's like to live there? It's one thing to like the food in a country and listen to its songs and go to its plays, but living there, man, that's different and I'm here to tell you about it. I can tell you now, if I'd known then what I know now... well..."

Deborah had a lot of discoveries to make. The first big shock was having a baby.

"Having a baby is all new and scary, and newer and scarier in a foreign country," she said. "If you can make it through the first one, you can make it through anything. When I was about nine months pregnant, I thought I was just going to the hospital for a checkup — and next thing I knew I was in the operating room. No one explained why. It turned out I had to have a Caesarian — but no one told me why I had to have a Caesarian. I only found out when I had Lily two years later. Which was much easier, of course. I knew what was going on, at last."

Breast feeding her first baby was a nightmare. She couldn't find a nurse who knew how to help her, or even one who thought it was a good idea. Finally little Max was hungry enough to figure it out himself.

"There were so many things to learn!" she said. "Mothers are told not to let their babies sleep on their tummies, or they'll suffocate in the pillow or they'll throw up and choke on their vomit. So you have to put them on their back. But that way they don't get to exercise their neck muscles. I had sleepless nights worrying about Max starting school with a floppy head.

"Here they've never heard of Tummy Time, that babies absolutely must spend 10 to 20 minutes a day on their tummies to develop their chest and neck muscles. So of course you can't get a boppy pillow."

A boppy pillow?

"That doughnut-shaped pillow they have in the States with a hole in the middle, so that when you put them on their tummy — for just a little while — their head is free and they can start practicing lifting it, and then lifting their chest. They also don't make that pacifier cleaner they have in the U.S., for when you drop the pacifier in the park.

"Which is just another way you find out that Paris isn't set up for children," she said. "Try and get a stroller on the Metro. All those steps! There are practically no escalators. All right, someone always helps you — always a woman, by the way, and only if you look as if you're handling it alone. The moment you look desperate and helpless, no one helps. And buses... with a stroller, you can only enter at the rear — but you have to pay up front, which means leaving your baby alone in the stroller while you pay.

"As for restaurants, when you enter with a stroller they look at you as if you have smallpox. No high chairs, hardly any no-smoking areas. They send you to the back of the restaurant where they hope no one else will notice. Now, my mom is definitely not a back-of-the-restaurant lady, so when she came for a visit, she managed to change all that in the restaurant near where we live."

Deborah had trouble getting used to the "park culture" in Paris. "In America, the parents are right behind the children in the sandbox. They help them interact with the other kids, admonish them for biting or hitting, or grabbing someone else's toy. The French kids come to the park and sit on the sandbox with a pail — but never talk to the other children. The mother or the governess doesn't seem to pay much attention, just leave their kid alone. It seemed snobbish to me at first, or racist, or something — but then someone told me that's just what it's like here, grownups don't talk to strangers, and neither do children and the children know that, so the grownups don't have to worry.

"But the birthday parties! I tell you. This year, for Max's fourth birthday, I had a dinosaur party for the kids in his kindergarten class, that means I made sandwiches and mini pizzas for all the kids and their parents in dinosaur shapes, and cupcakes with dinosaurs on top, and a big dinosaur instead of a donkey for Pin the Tail on the Donkey. Well, do you know what? The French mothers just dropped off their kids and left! And all the kids bawling! There I was with these kids I'd never seen before, who didn't know Max very well, screaming their heads off. One little girl was petrified — she never said a word.

"I found out that they don't play games at parties here, they don't put balloons on the mail box, they don't pin the tail on the donkey — and whatever you do, you can't blindfold them! They don't serve food at kids' parties here, they stuff them with candy. I don't want my kids having all that candy — so now, when they go to a party I fill them up with a huge lunch so they're not hungry."

Deborah hasn't felt any racism. Nor has she had any mother-in-law unpleasantness. "She's been wonderful — she's hardworking and down to earth and doesn't mind that I'm not a great cleaner. Michel might like the house a bit cleaner, but he didn't marry that girl — if I were cleaning all the time, I wouldn't be me. He prefers the fun times we have, clowning."

Deborah's biggest disappointment has been not being able to make French girlfriends.

"I'd been trying so hard to do things the right way here, yet give my children my own culture at the same time. I've been an Alpha stay-at-home mom — but I really needed French friends to explain everything — and be friends! Not that I didn't try. Every day when I picked up Max at the nursery school, and then at kindergarten, I'd see the same women four times a day — at 8:20, at 11:45, at 1:20 and at 4:20 — and never once did any of them say hello. If I was lucky, I'd get a 'bonjour' in passing. I get the feeling they already have their friends and can't handle anymore. Or maybe they're afraid I'll steal their husband. Is that possible? That's what people say. But I've got my own husband and we're very happy!"

Deborah began to loosen up from the Alpha mom when she discovered Messages, an American support group for mothers with little children. "They tell you which Metros have escalators and where to find them! And that's where I found my best friend. So I figured I was finally all set and could go back to work. Recently I started a public relations company — and it works!" Now that she's figured things out, Deborah is convinced that France is the place for the really blessed to live and that French men are the most charming.

"I keep pinching myself, I can't believe I'm really in Paris, just me from Chicago! I love it here. I love the way they care about how things are done — "'Add a bit of parsley for the color,' Michel will say! He's a great cook, by the way. I love the importance of food and cheese. I love the *Fête de la Musique*. I love the men — they don't travel in packs, as in the U.S., they're not trying to be macho with buddies. I love the importance of style here, and being feminine. The more important women are in a company, the more cleavage they show! And I love the importance of love. Yesterday I saw an old couple walking down the rue de Bourgogne, they must have been in their 80's, she had white hair, bright red lipstick and a scarf tied just so — and they were holding hands!"

Bravos: Michel and Deborah are really "into" the French love of *love*... love for each other, for France, for their lives. This is the only explanation of their happiness in a marriage that is not only cross-cultural but cross-race, and has meant the transplanting of Deborah 3,000 miles from home. Michel's living for a long moment in the U.S. and Deborah's creation of her own business have a lot to do with their happiness, as do the visits of Deborah's mother and the helpfulness of Michel's mother.

Eleanor, 42 and Bruno, 43

Trumps: Similar family backgrounds
Close-knit extended family
Eleanor's cross-cultural competence.

Eleanor, 42, looks back on meeting and marrying Bruno as "pure Kismet." She grew up in Minnesota as a francophobe. She couldn't bear the French because her mother, a passionate francophile, had frequent French visitors speaking French. Eleanor couldn't understand them and resented it. She rather liked England — her father was English — and as she had studied German in college, she had a good feeling about Germany. Working for 3M in Boston after college, she was quite pleased when, after three years, she was transferred to Germany.

She was back in Boston when her brother, who was studying for a degree in international business in Fontainebleau at INSEAD, decided to get married in France. The wedding was to be in Milly-la-Forêt, a little village on the Seine, which would be easy for the English cousins to get to. Eleanor was 28 then, slim and pretty and dating lots of different men. She had planned to go to the wedding with one of them. He backed out at the last minute, so -- first sign of Kismet — she went alone.

"The wedding was in a beautiful little *auberge*," she said. "During the reception I went on a long walk along the Seine with Bruno. It was dark and he was impressing me mightily, talking about Greek philosophy. I thought he was so educated! Later I found out that he had learned all that from a comic book. It was a romantic walk until suddenly a huge German shepherd bounded out of nowhere. I jumped into Bruno's arms... it was our first physical contact."

It felt good. But there was someone else in her thoughts too. When Bruno phoned and suggested meeting her for Christmas, she surprised herself by saying, "Fine!" They spent a week in Florence together.

"Everything seemed to show a future paved for us, but then I flew back to the U.S. and things looked different. This love was lovely but impractical. He was too far away. Then I was transferred to Germany again and after one and a half years of seeing him every other weekend, I moved to France. We were married six months later."

Now Eleanor, in full bloom, seems to have it all: a super husband, three children, a roomy family house with a garden in an elegant suburb and a job she loves, marketing for a computer company .

She invited me to lunch to talk about what makes it work.

"Similar backgrounds, first of all," she said. "Being from a similar class is more important than being from the same country. Our families are both Catholic, our fathers both high-powered engineers. Both our fathers worked up from simple backgrounds, both in contrast to their slightly-snazzier wives, who had more money and more social clout."

All of them put family and the intellect high up among sacred principles. Eleanor's mother-in-law is a research scientist, one of the first women to graduate from Agro, the agricultural engineering Grande École. She speaks to Eleanor's father in English on his visits.

"She recognized the similarities of our two families right away. And she has always been sweet to me," Eleanor added with a smile.

That doesn't mean the ground wasn't mined with cultural traps. She wasn't prepared for them at all:

"The lack of acceptance and standoffishness, the difficulty in making female friends overwhelmed me at first. Minnesota has a huge French influence — Champlain and other explorers are very evident — but this didn't help. You know what happened? I got so upset that I put on a lot of weight. Me! I'd always been Miss Slim — and I got fat! I finally understood that many of my problems with Bruno came from his being the oldest, and so terribly close to his mother. As I said, she was always supportive to me, but — I mean, imagine this, his socks had to be ironed — ironed! — to make sure they were really dry. I still have to iron all his underwear.

"And meals. There is no question of giving him a sandwich at lunch — it must be a warm, three-course meal. He can't function without it. On Saturdays and Sundays, our whole family and his parents and sometimes his brothers and their families, we all sit around for hours preparing lunch, eating it, cleaning up. Bruno often cooks it."

Their different time perceptions upset them both. How late is late?

"In the U.S. and Germany, being five minutes ahead of time is about right. In Mediterranean countries you can be half an hour or so late, maybe an hour, no problem. In France it's somewhere between the two, depending on the region and the family. I'd come from Germany, where I'd been officially scolded for being seven minutes late. Bruno would say he'd meet me in front of FNAC at 2:00 and at 2:45 he showed up. I was in floods at this — I thought this was his way of leaving me. If he said I'll see you in a minute, it would be 20 minutes. *Tout à l'heure* would be three hours.

"Also, he'd leave me every Sunday to go rock climbing in Fontainebleau — saying he'd be back 'soon.' I was alone and would be in floods when he came back... four hours later.

"Now we're a couple with the same time system — I've decided the French way is better. I've taken it on, I've soaked up this way of taking one's time over a cup of coffee or a walk. It's refreshing to come here after Germany. Here, if you arrive at a meeting late because you have a sick child or something, no one scolds you."

Eleanor is such a positive person that I wanted to know how she fared living with the French religion of criticism and negativism.

"The *esprit critique*! It drives me crazy. It's one of our main problems. I want enthusiasm and I get all the reasons why such and such won't work," she said. "I promise you, American women aren't prepared for this — and they should know that if you change this in a Frenchman, you disarm him for living in France.

"Bruno and I have discussed this 100 times. I tell him, I only want you to say just once, 'What a great idea!' He tries hard not to say no — he realizes it's a problem for me. And he has told me that he really understands that some of my ideas he pooh-poohed led to decisions that were good. The worst is that I get this negativism from the kids too. It's called culture."

Eleanor's little girl, Claudine, age 12, joined us at lunch. Eleanor began talking about male-female relations in France.

"Being a woman is special here. Men and women are not on the same page. The men are more gallant, attentive to your wishes, respectful of women. They're more at home with their bodies, more relaxed. In the States, men are never happy with their bodies unless they're an Adonis. Here, they're more accepting of imperfections — in their own bodies and in a woman's body. On a weekend once, staying with English friends in Normandy, Bruno stripped naked for a shower under a hose on a tree. 'We can tell he's French,' said our friend."

"What about being a girl," I asked Claudine. "Would you rather be a boy?"

Claudine frowned and said, "I'm proud of being a woman. I'd hate being a man."

Not food — mirrors.

"Girls here are females in training," said Eleanor. "If you have a party of girls and boys of Claudine's age, you don't need food for the girls, you just need mirrors. I'm fascinated to watch them, the way they move. If you go to a park you see them dressed in jeans just as tight and form-fitting as their mothers', moving their bodies just the way their mothers do. They have a sense of their bodies that American girls don't have, and

"She's not naked, Jake, she's French."

they carry themselves better. There is pride in being a woman here. Women are at ease being women."

And the men?

"That's just it, the men are wonderful to them. I really love French men. Whether you're beautiful or not, size six or size 18, they don't care. Whatever, they're respectful. I think French men are 'nice' — they feel protective and chivalrous. I don't think this is limiting. At work they look on me as a colleague and as a woman — not just a colleague with breasts. Someone at work said something one day that made me burst into tears; no one said, 'Pull yourself together' or, 'That's not professional behavior.' Men came to see me and said, 'Don't worry about it.' American colleagues would say 'Pull yourself together' or 'That's not my problem.' They're very harsh and hard."

Eleanor then rhapsodized about France, including the attitude to children, which she finds light-years away from Deborah's experience.

"I love having children here. You understand the strong French notion of family best when you're pregnant. People I barely knew visited me

191

with generous presents when the baby was born. In Germany, children are fashion accessories. In France, they're accepted in every aspect of life. Children are always at a French wedding; if they weren't, it wouldn't be any fun. They sit through a late dinner at home or at a restaurant quietly, without complaining. But at the same time, life here recognizes that they're not grownups. They're not always included in grownup activities. For instance, they're not with guests at the dinner table, as is often the case in the U.S. The generation gap is not a concept here, because French children are closer to their parents, nicer to them, there is less of 'us' and 'them.' They stay close to their parents all their lives, without being choked. You feel the respect on both sides. French people have their children for life. They can't be disinherited. There is a lot of love, a lot of tenderness and at the same time, a lot of firm discipline.

"My brothers and sisters in America cater to their children — you don't see much discipline and there is a lot of noise and disorder over there that you don't see here. Here, there are rules the children have to obey — they're not given a 'prison-free' card."

Eleanor has one big frustration: making jokes in French. "I can't make throw-away comments and put Bruno in stitches like my brother. For this you have to have the same references, the same fairy tales since kindergarten."

Bravos: I don't have a clear idea of Bruno except that he is deliciously, exasperatingly French and that Eleanor loves it, even ironing his underclothes. Eleanor comes across clear and strong: flexible (she adapted her time-perception to Bruno's) an enthusiastic francophile mother as well as wife, daughter and daughter–in–law, with as strong family ties as Bruno. She is a keen observer of their cross-cultural differences and labors to smooth them over or enhance them, if she thinks one culture does something better than the other.

Juliet, 39 and Xavier, 43

Trumps: Juliet's mastery of French etiquette
Shared spare-time interests

You'd imagine Juliet meeting her husband in white tulle and lace at a dance, waltzing around one of the ballrooms in Pittsburgh, where she grew up. In fact, she met him in Paris standing in line at the post office. Juliet had come for a summer course at the Sorbonne after surviving excruciating studies in microbiology and health economics, to relax before she went job hunting. She chose Paris mainly to spite her mother, a virulent francophobe, and arrived with very little French and not the faintest idea of French history. That day, she was having trouble explaining to the clerk how she wanted to send a package to the U.S. Xavier, behind her in line, offered to translate. She can't remember much about that meeting except that he was tall, something a tall girl always notices. She ran into him again the next day at a café she liked near the Pantheon, and again the day after that. It began to be a joke.

Finally he took his coffee to her table. "May I?" he asked. "This place is near my office and has the best coffee in the Latin Quarter. What's your excuse?"

Juliet had learned a little about French banter. "I came looking for you," she said.

"Good. Are you free for tennis this evening? The Luxembourg courts are nearby and not bad."

"Except that my tennis racket is about 3,000 miles from here. How do you know I play?"

"It's obvious. Those long legs. Seven o'clock then? I'll meet you there, with a racket."

Tennis was fun. They played a few more times, separating each time without sharing so much as a cup of coffee. Juliet found it a very odd courtship, if that's what it was. She didn't even know his name. The day before she left for home they finally exchanged cards. She didn't recognize the name itself, that it was one of France's oldest, made illustrious over centuries by marshals and scientists, but she did recognize the title. Then she heard the bartender addressing him as *Monsieur le Prince.*"

"Hmm," she said, looking at him. "Shouldn't I have met you first as a frog?"

"No, since you didn't kiss me yet," he said. "In any case, all Frenchmen are frogs, aren't we?"

Juliet went back to Pittsburgh and a job. In due course Xavier came to visit her. Apparently he also thought she would look wonderful serving tea from an antique silver teapot in an elegant setting. A year later they were married and she moved to France, where weekends would indeed be spent in — another surprise for her — the family château.

"That summer at the Sorbonne did nothing to prepare me for living in France, so my mother-in-law took me in hand," said Juliet. "She was always nice to me, that is, proper, but unbelievably strict, stricter than my own mother ever was. Not exactly warm, but helpful. I'm sure I was lucky that Xavier was the youngest of her three sons."

What sort of things did she correct you about?

"The rules! The rules! I grew up with rules; behavior and manners were taken very seriously in my family — but the French! They've been thinking them up, adding and changing them for 1,000 years. You mustn't say *bien mangé* (eaten well), but *bien diné*. Never invite someone to come and visit *chez nous*, but *à la maison*. Never never never say 'cheers' and never never *bon appetit*! Put someone's title on the envelope — a prince also gets an SAS *(son altesse sérénissime)*, meaning his serene highness, before the title. Did you ever? Always spell out Madame and Monsieur on the envelope. In a letter, never address someone you don't know as 'Dear' but Monsieur or Madame, or Monsieur plus the title, like *Monsieur l'Ambassadeur*. Be careful how you end the letter, there are 26 formulas and the one you choose depends on whether you're a woman writing to a man or to a woman, and on your rank and on his or her rank. Imagine! I'm still lost with it.

"Do you know, sometimes a future mother-in-law will make a little test for her son's intended, not that the fiancée in question knows she's being tested. A pear will be served at lunch after the cheese, to see if she knows how to peel it. With a knife and fork, of course. Do you know that the French —well, the French upper classes — peel *all* their fruit with a knife and fork? Even a banana! And practically everything else — an English friend at dinner almost fainted to see Xavier decorticating *shrimp* with his knife and fork. When I invited him another time, he asked me to serve shrimp so that he could watch Xavier go at it again.

"The only exception is asparagus — which they eat with their fingers! It seems Edward VII did, when he visited France as the Prince of Wales, so all the Parisians rushed to take it up.

"The rules at table are endless. No hands in your lap — the host will think you're up to something with your neighbor under the table. As for the seating arrangement — even in the family you're always placed. Who gets the seat of honor, and the next-to seat of honor and on down. And listen to this, I have a friend who has been married to her French husband for 17 years, but not in church, and so her mother-in-law doesn't let them share a bedroom when they visit her!"

I asked if there were tips for château visits that Americans probably didn't know — and would be better off knowing ahead of time. Juliet had a lot to say on the subject. Some of them repeated what Evelyn had told us at the Lizzie meetings.

"Never ever read a book, except in your bed trying to sleep at night.

Magazines, yes, books, no. This was my aunt-in-law's tip when I got married. I didn't believe her, but it's true. The *maîtresse de maison* is obviously not entertaining you properly if you have to open a book. I actually overheard one of my hostesses say this: 'When she stayed with us she did nothing but read books. I don't have any, of course; I don't have time to read, so she brought her own.'

"My mother-in-law has often told me very proudly that she hasn't read a book since she was married. 'I haven't had the time, but if you really do want a book to read,' she told me once, 'there are three in my bedroom.' They were the *Bottin Mondain* (a sort of French *Social Register*), a Bible and a Prayer Book.

"Never ever say that you're a Protestant if you're in a Catholic family. Protestants, in France, are Calvinists and they have a very different form of religion indeed. My mother-in-law, at a funeral in London, with the usual horror of Calvinism that French Catholics have, was stunned when she realized that the words there, and also at an English wedding she went to later, were exactly the same as in a Catholic funeral and wedding. She couldn't get over it, and still tells all her relations, in front of me, when she gets the chance.

"Never, never, ever, say that your father is a Freemason, even if he is terribly important. It is different in France — the Catholics and the Freemasons don't get along — to put it mildly.

"Never, never, never help yourself to a drink of any kind while staying with a French family, yours or someone else's. Whisky, gin, wine are fairly obvious, as you'll be branded an alcoholic, but if it's very hot, and you're properly panting and no one offers you anything even if you ask, you do NOT go and find a glass and fill it up with water from the tap and drink it. 'Do you know what she did?' I overheard my mother-in-law say. 'She simply helped herself from the tap! And not just once, but she had at least three glasses. I mean, we were going to have dinner in half an hour and she could have had as much wine as she wanted. But no, she doesn't drink wine. She only drinks water. And always SO MUCH. Poor François has only just put the bottle back on the sideboard when she wants more.'

"Then there's privacy. Don't expect people to be friendly in the village next to the château — or any other village. I have a friend who says that she's been living in the same little village in the Sarthe for five years without anyone greeting her. Americans may interpret this as rudeness, or that the villagers or the people in the park don't like Americans or the color of your hair, but it's just the rule. Greeting people you don't know is considered an intrusion."

The French resistance to accepting blame is the cultural bump she has had the hardest time with.

"The children take it on, of course," she said, "it's all around them. They can't help it, much as I try to tell them that their American half absolutely insists not only on people taking blame for their mistakes, but also, often, taking blame for things they didn't do, providing everyone else involved knows they didn't do it. They simply must accept our ballet of 'I'm sorry, it's my fault' and the response, 'No no, it's my fault.' I really never lose my temper, but I lost it yesterday when a crayon fell on the floor and my son blamed me."

Juliet and Xavier sing in a choir. They both love horseback riding as well as tennis. When the children were all old enough to be in kindergarten or in school, Juliet found a job she loves in a neuroscience research company.

"When we go home after work," she said, "the outside world STOPS. That is when the real fun begins."

Bravos: Juliet and Xavier seem to have had smooth sailing all the way. I know this can't be true, but to give that impression – of any marriage, not to mention a cross-cultural marriage — is a singular triumph.

Pauline, 29 and Etienne, 34

Trumps: Pauline's journalistic love of discovery
Her appreciation of old things
Her wise handling of her mother-in-law

France first beckoned to Pauline when she was a little girl. Now 29, her earliest memories are of her French grandmother reading her bewitching tales about France. She grew up hero worshipping Jacques Cousteau, the underwater sea explorer and environmentalist. She took four years of French in high school with a view to reveling in all things French on a short trip to Paris after graduation. However, she discovered that she couldn't speak "worth a damn." Parisians couldn't understand her, nor could she figure out a word they said. So, after college she signed up for the torture-the-foreigners-with-funny-accents program at the Sorbonne. She made friends with a girl in her youth hostel. Several days after her arrival they set out together to explore the city.

She met her future husband at a café-brasserie on the rue Mouffetard that first night on the town. Etienne was on a bar stool right in front of the door. He turned around as they walked in and smiled, a huge ear-to-ear grin.

"French people don't smile, even at young women they're checking out," she said. "But it wasn't a leer; it was a genuine, happy-to-be-alive smile and I was so relieved to see someone smiling at me that I immediately felt comfortable talking to him in my hopeless French. My girlfriend and I went to that bar a few times over the next week or two. He was always there and pretty soon he'd decided he liked me more than my girlfriend because I knew about computers and he was a software engineer.

"By that time, however, I had also noticed a certain jittery excitement that kept him moving around all the time and he was so thin I wondered out loud to my friend if he was snorting cocaine. It turned out that, no, he's just a ball of nerves. He still irritates me by always jangling his keys or tapping his pencil or making some other repetitive, annoying noise."

When she had to move to another youth hostel far from that bar, she realized she wouldn't be showing up there again… which meant not seeing Etienne again. He had no way to reach her. She wasn't sure exactly how she felt about him, but she didn't want to just disappear; she liked him enough to not want to be rude. She knew where he worked, in the *Institut du Monde Arabe* building, so she decided to wander by at quitting time on the chance that she might bump into him.

"The place was deserted," she said, "and I felt like an idiot waiting for him, so I turned to go, and there he was, walking across the courtyard, all alone. He headed directly for me, looking completely unsurprised to find me there, as if we had a date already arranged. And that was that. A couple of weeks later he introduced me as his 'fiancée' to his parents. I know that doesn't mean the same thing as in English, but it seemed nonetheless to pretty much seal the deal for everybody."

A few months later, they moved in together. The next summer Pauline ran out of money and returned home, telling him to come to San Francisco if he wanted to see her. After he visited, she said, well, you have to move here if you want to live with me, which he also did. After about a year of Etienne looking unsuccessfully for a job without papers, they decided to get married in a quickie ceremony in Las Vegas. They moved back to France after the arrival of their second child.

"Even today, older and wiser, Etienne is still a smiler (and still skinny), only now I can see when his enthusiasm is sometimes off-putting to other

French people," she said. "He's just a little over the top for them; but his 'un-Frenchness' is what I was attracted to. The other French men I met seemed so broody to me; I didn't find it sexy or romantic. I was intimidated by their seriousness.

"On the other hand, one of the things I was looking for in a man was someone who could teach me something; I hate to get bored. And so his 'foreignness' has been one of things keeping us together because we always have more to find out about each other."

Pauline is philosophical about France. She enjoyed being in Japan as a summer exchange student and was more excited by Rome and Barcelona at first sight than by Paris. She prefers Italian to French food. She feels pressure to be more domesticated here than she wants to be. She appreciates good food and admires others who are great cooks, she has learned how to iron a dress shirt in less than five minutes, but, a freelance journalist, she is not ambitious to be seen as a "perfect homemaker."

"I know French women my own age and younger who are still ironing their sheets!" she said. "Is this a waste of one's precious human resources, like time, or what?"

She is happy here, but thinks she could as easily have ended up marrying an American or someone from some other country.

"I do admire the mental and physical discipline in France. I like the way they really care about intellect and language and the way they're committed to identifying and upholding principles. Just like General de Gaulle, really. I like the way they insist on privacy. But the way they're tickled by scatological jokes… I mean, grown men, my husband included, laughing at pee-pee and ca-ca jokes. It shows up in those comic books they read too. Well, I just roll my eyes.

"Another plus about France, I love old things. I love objects that other people have lived with. You don't throw out the old stuff here, you build on top of it. I love that feeling that everywhere around you are reminders of the past. Not just monuments and historical stuff but things that belonged to someone's grandmother.

"Other stuff too. But my feelings for France aren't about France per se, but about Etienne. And his family and oh God, about all the knowledge of Frenchness I've had to sweat over. I guess it's not Etienne's Frenchness that is my big joy, or the American stuff he adopted when living in the States, but our own special sort of sub-culture we've developed for our family."

I asked her about her in-laws.

"Well, you may faint at this, but I love my mother-in-law! And I know she loves me... even though she doesn't like foreigners, including Americans."

Pauline's successful mother-in-law technique? "I really love her," she says adamantly. "We've always gotten along wonderfully well." In the next sentence she confesses, "She's an overbearing know-it-all." After a minute, she adds, "But she's also very observant, and generous, and helpful. She always comes through for you. Of course, this being on her own terms, which means basically telling you what to do. But if you accept that, as I do, then there's nothing she wouldn't do for you.

"The trouble is, there are all these things that French women seem to have in their genes, and we Americans don't. So of course we can't pass them along to our children, which of course is one reason we're not popular. I mean, my mother-in-law knows a lot of things I don't, not just the French language and culture, but also she's a great cook and can iron like nobody's business and knows when you're supposed to plant stuff in the garden and things like that.

"At some point I may snarl at her to stop starting every visit by walking around the house inventorying 'Everything Pauline is doing wrong.' You can bet that when I question her opinion — oh, very rarely! — that I'm 200 percent sure I'm right before I open my mouth. Yes, it's mildly crazy-making. But I go along with it because I know that her obsessive nitpicking, and most French parents' nagging, isn't a lack of compassion or disrespect; that's just what they think their role is. Their job in life is to be the setter-of-standards until they die. They can never relax; it's exhausting to be a French parent. And my mother-in-law in particular needs to be needed; she loves me because I really have needed her help, and I had no pre-conceptions about how to do anything here. And I trust her judgment, more often than not, anyway. I know my mother-in-law knows how hard I've tried to learn French and to fit in and she's proud of my efforts. I have no doubt of that.

"The only minor conflicts have been over the kids, of course. She's a wonderful loving grandmother, and I trust my children with her implicitly. You can't ever expect a French mother-in-law to say 'I'm sorry.' But that doesn't mean they never feel sorry or want to make amends. French is an implicit culture; you have to listen for a lot of important stuff in between the words. My husband I expect to adapt, to a certain extent, to my ways; we're married, and so, therefore, he can damn well learn to say 'I'm sorry' just because it's important to me — it makes me feel better to hear it. But I can't ask that of my other French relatives."

We were talking in a Paris café not far from the one where she met

Etienne. She ordered another *café crème* and stirred it thoughtfully before she mentioned her biggest disappointment.

"It's strange, but the real disconnect is with my sisters-in-law. They're perfectly pleasant to me — it's not that we don't get along — but we've never become friends in all this time. I still don't know why; I sometimes feel they just find me ridiculous — they exchange little looks when I mispronounce something. Or maybe it's just too tiring to be my friend because the foreign thing does mean they have to make more of an effort. Or maybe it's them... maybe they're the kind of French women who don't really make female friends and they're already being as friendly to me as they possibly can be."

I tell her that I've noticed that French women who have sisters rarely have close women friends. Probably they don't need them.

"Yes, maybe that's it. It's hard to know, and that's another thing about French families. Love and intimacy don't necessarily go together for them. My own family doesn't know what the word 'secret' means. Sharing pretty much everything is expected as a sign of love. Holding back is rejection. But French families do keep secrets and it doesn't mean they don't love each other or aren't close."

Isn't that part of their famous discretion?

"Well, discretion is fine, but when does it become ridiculous — or insulting? Important stuff like who is a closet alcoholic or what they paid for their house, fine, but when they're ruffled — and think you're prying — because you asked about the weather in Cannes? For instance, my sister-in-law is moving this summer from Paris to Saint-Nazaire. She just spent a week there on vacation and I asked my mother-in-law, 'Did she get a chance to see any houses for rent?' And she replied, 'I didn't think to ask, but here's what they ate on the way home.' And then she listed every meal they had for the whole week."

Pauline can even be philosophical about the French "preoccupation with food."

"I made the mistake of being bored by all the talk about it, but I think I've finally understood. It isn't just about food. The food talk takes up room while they're waiting for the other person to reveal something more important." Other Americans repeat this idea too: that French families can spend an enormous amount of time together and talk and talk and talk and yet never share a single really personal piece of information.

Pauline added: "I have right now a group of French girlfriends mixed with American women and the difference is striking. The French women talk about movies and politics and the next vacation, but without talking about their feelings. They never mention their husbands or their families. American women only give you enough facts to set the stage for a discussion about their feelings.

"I miss my girlfriends back in the States that I used to talk with this way... but I can now see this trait from a French point of view too. Americans really are open books. I'm not saying that's bad, it's kind of like catching a view of yourself from the back in a mirror. Is that what I really look like?

"Anyway, because what I do is write in English, it's hard for me to share what I'm good at with my in-laws or even my friends, and that's sometimes frustrating. All they can see is the stuff I suck at. Since the French tend to focus on the negative anyway, sometimes I get defensive. I think writing has really saved me in this way; because I have an outlet where I can make sense of it all, make light of it all, including myself."

Bravos: Pauline is younger than the other Americans interviewed and as a journalist is acutely alert to cultural anomalies as well as to her own shortcomings, as seen by the French. As a gifted, articulate writer, she pinpoints things that have bothered other Americans without their realizing what they were annoyed at. She has come culturally very far, in an isolated part of France without any cultural guides nearby to help, and is on her way to being not only bilingual but bicultural. Bravo Pauline, and bravo, Etienne, for not getting angry when Pauline asks you about cultural anomalies she doesn't understand, but for standing by her and helping. I'm looking forward to a book that Pauline will certainly write about her experiences here.

Susan, 47 and Jean-Paul, 49

Trumps: Their passion for skiing
But — this couple's marriage is going over bumps
and it's not sure they'll make it.

Jean-Paul couldn't believe his eyes. The girl with the fur hat on the chairlift ahead had just jumped off. Skis and all. Five meters, he figured. Into deep snow. Dangerous as hell. But she landed as if it were nothing and skied on down the mountain. Why did she jump? He almost jumped too, to follow and find out. He'd already noticed her standing ahead of him in the lift line, tall and beanpole-slim like a French woman and nervously squeezing ahead of other people in the line. Good looking, as far as he could tell behind her huge goggles. Blond, apparently, from the wisps of hair straggling out of her hat. That hat! He'd never seen anything so pretty. It was the rich red-orange of a healthy fox, so smooth and fluffy you wanted to caress it. What nationality could she be? In Kitzbühel she could be anything. Northern, not Austrian, he decided. She seemed to be alone...

Susan was pleased with her jump. She climbed out of the deep snow and wedeled downhill on the piste as fast as she could to catch up with her ski class, six top skiers from Germany and a terrible one from England. In fact, Otmar had seen her jump and had stopped his class a bit farther down the slope. He grinned, wagging his finger at her. "Crazy Americans! You could have broken both legs and your back."

"But I didn't. And it was fun. Let's go! Why are you stopping?"

Otmar laughed and shook his head, winking at the others in the class. "How shall we punish her?"

"By going really slowly," said the Englishman. Everyone laughed and then Otmar headed off piste to the deep snow.

Susan told me she liked remembering the details of that afternoon. I had met her for the interview at the Café de Flore in Paris and found a slim, cheerfully athletic looking woman with keen brown eyes and a high wide forehead somewhat hidden by low bangs. Not very French looking by a long shot, but not dramatically un-French, either. She had suggested meeting in a café because she thought her apartment was too small and stuffy. It wasn't, I found out later. I also found out that "small" was a subjective judgment, depending on what you were used to. Most people in France would find Susan's apartment perfectly adequate. Not particularly charming, as if no one was thinking much about it, but comfortable, in an interesting part of old Paris, the Marais.

She told me about being late for ski class and desperate not to miss it. It was a perfect day for skiing. The sun was bright, the sky a deep blue, the air crisp and clear. Several inches of made-in-heaven powder snow had fallen during the night. She saw the class ski by under her. She told me about considering the distance of her seat from the slope. Pretty far, but the heck with it. The jump. The fast run with the class in deep powder, soaring like a bird, the Englishman left far behind after a fall. Then, waiting for the next chairlift, the annoying man who walked on her skis — with his skis. "Excusez-moi," he said. French? She grimaced at him. She couldn't see what he looked like under the goggles except for curly black hair, no cap — and anyway she didn't care. The French were as bad as the Germans in ski lines, no discipline. She had to concentrate on keeping up with Otmar.

"I think maybe he stepped on my skis on purpose — so that I'd notice him. He's too polite and too good a skier to do it accidentally," she said. "But of course he doesn't admit that. The next day I was walking back to my hotel with my skis on my shoulder when this guy comes bounding up to me in a red cap with a tassel — no skis — and asks me out for dinner. Of course I didn't recognize him, as I'd never really seen him. I wasn't used to being picked up by strange men. In New York, you'd get the police. Well, it wasn't exactly New York, right? So I couldn't very well get the police. I guess I made a face or something, because then he burst out laughing and took off his cap and dark glasses. When I saw that curly black hair again..."

Did she go out to dinner, I asked.

"Dinner? With a stranger? I certainly didn't intend to. But — I was 29 and a pretty toughened-up New Yorker — and this was supposedly one of the great ski-and-play spots of the world. I found it almost ridiculously quaint, yet somehow captivating – its crooked streets and many-colored houses with frescoes on the walls, and yodeling locals in lederhosen. Since I was in London on business, I'd flown over for a few days between meetings — I was an options trader — and I hadn't met a soul, except the jerks in my ski class, so I thought, for heaven's sake, I'd been there for two days and all I had to look forward to was dinner alone on a tray in my hotel room. It seemed like a terrible waste not to at least do something. I'd just had a hot chocolate in one of those Hansel-and-Gretel-type places with an orchestra where they dance at tea time and everyone was having a great time except me... and I guess I was feeling kind of left out. The guy was polite and looked like fun and he turned out to be French! If he'd been German, I don't know. Luckily he spoke English."

Jean-Paul came to get her at her hotel. Their feet crunching in the new snow, a full moon just rising over the peaked rooftops with the mountains behind profiled in the sky, they walked down the street to the *Hotel Goldene Greif* (The Golden Griffin).

"What a place," she said. "I wouldn't have missed it for the world. A hotel, not big but sumptuous. White and gold with thick green carpets and stags' antlers everywhere. We had the dinner of my life — well, my life up until then. Venison! With a fabulous cream sauce, and champagne and then a chocolate cake to end chocolate cakes... and afterwards we went to a small bar upstairs with dancing, and a zither playing — just like that old movie, *The Third Man* about Vienna after the Second World War, did you ever see it?

"As for the next evening — I was leaving in the morning — he said some friends had invited him to a party in a nearby village. Do you believe this, he took me there in a horse-drawn sleigh! Across snow-covered fields! There we were, sitting in the sleigh, with the horse's bells jingling and a fur blanket over our knees — it wasn't at all cold — and driving towards the *Wilde Kaiser*, that's the name of a big craggy mountain there — it means Wild Emperor — with the full moon — and the snow — I mean! If I ever felt like a hick from Worcester, Massachusetts, that was it.

"His friend was Austrian and had a chalet, a wooden sort of log-cabin-type house hundreds of years old, but this one was really big, high ceilings and beautiful paneling, everything. The guy who opened the door was dressed in one of those Tyrolean green velvety jackets and black trousers. It looked like evening dress to me — an Austrian dinner jacket — so I stuck out my hand and shook hands with him." She laughed, remembering her gaffe. "He was the butler. I'd completely forgotten that scene in *Sound of Music* where the new nun-governess does the same thing."

She took a long sip of her *café crème*.

"What a group at that place, I never," she went on. "Silk dirndls with long skirts on the women. And the men, you can't imagine how good looking. One of them was some kind of an aristo, a count I guess," she went on, "at least two yards tall with masses of silvery hair, about 50, devastating looking, craggy and boney, and he had on the most gorgeous jacket you ever saw — two complete rows of silver buttons on black velvet... apparently he was in a couple of movies in Hollywood. I mean, this was a new world for me, pretty interesting."

"Sounds like a promising start for a romance," I said.

"Well I thought it was one of those vacation flirts, although we did have fun. What impressed me about Jean-Paul was that he didn't try anything — you know, not even a hand sneaking under the blanket in the sleigh. I didn't expect to see him again. When I left he gave me his card and said I should call him in Paris. I didn't call guys. They could call me, go to a little trouble, or the heck with it. But when I told this story to a French colleague in London, she said, 'Ecoutez-moi. French bachelors don't hand out their numbers unless they're really interested. In fact, they don't have *dates* the way you do. Call him.' So I did and we were married a few months later. Gosh, 18 years ago, I can't believe it."

"So you dropped everything, your family, friends, career..."

Susan raised her eyebrows and made a grimace. For a while she didn't say anything.

"The funny thing is," she said then, "before I left on that trip I went to an astrologer. I was a little nervous about going to Europe all by myself for the first time, not speaking any foreign languages, and I wanted to know what my horoscope said. The astrologer told me I was going to get married to a foreigner and live in a foreign country. Me! In those days I could hardly find Europe on the map."

I asked her how she started out. Did she find a job?

"A job? Doing what? As an au pair? I didn't have anything except a BA, no French. Jean-Paul said I'd learn French in no time — but this language is hell! It's so difficult! I never had it in school. I took lessons here for years. I couldn't even think about getting a job because the babies started coming. Three of them, pretty close together.

"But we had a few wonderful years. Jean-Paul has a hilarious sense of humor and we're both passionate skiers. He said he could tell right away I was a real skier because my skis were the best make, and all beat up, really been used. Well I guess watching me jump helped. That really impressed him."

"Why did you say 'a few' wonderful years? Just a few?"

Susan dropped her cheerful banter and began oddly babbling.

"I like his parents and his friends, his mother has been really nice to me, not like the other mothers-in-law I hear about — she's great about looking after the kids when we're off skiing — luckily Jean-Paul is the younger son... if he'd been the oldest... he has a job he loves in the civil service, he's an *ingénieur*, that's the cat's whiskers here — he's an X, you know, he's been to the Polytechnique, that tiptop engineering school. At the moment he's head of the cabinet of the minister of transportation, he gets lots of vacations and he'll probably be ambassador one of these days... that could be fun — it could also be terrible, depending where..."

I tried to bring her back to her marriage. "What happened, Susan? Why were the later years less wonderful?"

Susan rolled her eyes and gave a low hoot. "Have you talked to any American married to a French guy who wasn't on the point of leaving him 20 times?"

I asked her to tell me about the 20 times. She went round and round, circling whatever it was she didn't want to talk about. She said that it was being an at-home mom which just about had her flying back over the Atlantic. She repeated that the power and glory of her banking job in New York was like a tulip bulb in her heart, ready to flower the moment her three babies were a bit older. She said that one of the problems was that Jean-Paul's parents bought a weekend place in Senlis for them. Near to their own place. Susan and Jean-Paul still had the Marais apartment, but that meant that now, Jean-Paul wanted to go out to the country every Friday. And that meant every Sunday lunch with the in-laws sitting around half the day over the table.

"It drove me nuts," she said. "I grew up in Massachusetts. There, Sunday lunch takes about 20 minutes and then everyone rushes off to some kind of sport — tennis, hockey, squash, swimming. Well, I could handle the in-law lunches, they were no big deal really, but what really got to me was not having a job. When the littlest, Olivia, was five, I started seriously looking for work. Plenty frustrating, I can tell you. Jean-Paul was nice about it, he didn't say 'But look, honey, we have a nice life, why not just enjoy yourself,' as you might expect…"

She didn't want to go back to banking. She tried teaching English as a second language, but found she didn't want to teach. She tried to import special toys from Japan that didn't exist in France, but couldn't get a license. By now her French was pretty good so she tried being a buyer for the Galéries Lafayette, the department store. She found out she "didn't know beans" about retailing and didn't really want to find out, either.

"I was feeling run into the ground by the French," she added, "and their peculiar ways of doing things and their negativism, so I decided to build on that. I started a consultancy for foreigners, part showing them real estate, and part showing them how to get along with the French. And that works."

I prodded. I pointed out that until now she'd given me a totally rosy picture of her life in France. Her husband seemed to be pretty wonderful. She hadn't once criticized him, or the country, or her parents-in-law, and her children all seemed to be winners, so what soured her?

"Did something dreadful happen?" I asked.

She looked around the Flore before she went on. She smiled at someone she knew. Pushed her bangs up her forehead. And then:

"I guess you could say that. A slinky predator happened… I almost left. Why not? My mother would have been delighted to get me back, except that… with the kids…"

Susan's voice trailed off. She lit a cigarette and made a face. Her tone changed from her usual half-jest to dead serious.

"I never smoked before. I took it up when I found out that Jean-Paul was… doing that."

"How did you find out?" I asked.

"She telephoned when I came back from a visit to the States earlier than expected. I answered the phone."

She inhaled a couple of times. "I decided to tell you this so that you'll get the message out to Americans planning to marry Frenchmen. It is 95 percent sure that there will be other women in his life. If you know that ahead of time, you're better able to cope with it. Or get out while you still can."

"How can you be so sure?" I said. "Some polls say that 35 percent of French men admit to being unfaithful and 24 percent of French wives. That leaves a lot of faithful husbands... and even more, according to some other polls. And how can we be sure these men are telling the truth? They may be boasting and the women pretending." I tried to play the devil's advocate. "Besides... life is long, I mean, so Jean-Paul had a moment of weakness..."

"It changes everything, that's all. And he doesn't see it that way!"

"How does he see it?"

"When I asked him at the time if there had been others, he said, 'One or two but it doesn't mean anything.' So I went into a tailspin. Should I leave him? And go where? The truth is that my mother is frail. She's lived alone since my father left her. I'm an only child. My so-called good news is what keeps her alive. It would kill her if my marriage failed. And my children? They adore Jean-Paul. He's a good father. I talked to my mother-in-law — who by the way, as I said, has always supported me in the nicest way, even slipping me extra bills of 500 euros. She laughed it off and said that Jean-Paul was just like his father, and I should realize that it had no importance."

She put her coffee cup down vehemently, spilling it. "Don't you see? Jean-Paul has no sense of guilt!" she went on. "How am I supposed to live with that? He couldn't see the problem. I guess if everyone jumps from bungee cords, then you do too. He told me that when he had dinner with a woman colleague it was just 'normal' to sleep with her afterwards. He kept repeating that it didn't 'mean anything.' That he would 'always come back to his family.' Maybe all *ingénieurs* are like that? So I decided that what's good for the goose is good for the gander."

"You mean you took lovers?"

"One. I met him walking my dog. He was married and wanted me to invest in his software company, besides being a terrible lover. That really cured me. Jean-Paul is a marvel in bed, by the way. It wasn't as if he was neglecting *me*. So... I took a look at my kids, my apartment in Paris and the house in the country and decided that if I could teach Jean-Paul to say 'I'm sorry,' I would be the winner of the million dollar lottery."

"Did you?"

"They can't. In their culture they don't have the right to make mistakes. So they don't make them. How can they say they're sorry for something that didn't happen? But there is a little progress."

Susan laughed and took back her habitual tone of banter. "We've pretty much figured it out. We keep our working lives separate. I give him a nice family dinner with the children every evening, unless he is away on a business trip. He goes on weekends to the country with the kids or without them, and I stay in Paris without anyone bugging me to go out there too. We go on vacations together. We ski a lot — I love that. If he has other women, he goes to great lengths to keep it from me. That's the deal. It's good enough, don't you think?"

When I said I thought it sounded very mature, to my distress and discomfort, she burst into tears.

"It's not good enough at all!" she sobbed. "It's empty, don't you see? Empty!"

"But Susan — " I groped for something to say that wouldn't upset her. "He hasn't left you!"

Now she screamed at me. It came from her depths, a primal scream if I ever heard one. People were looking. "You're defending him! You're not supposed to agree with me! You're supposed to say he's a fucking bastard and I should go home where the men are decent!"

"I'm not sure that would be wise at all… your children…"

"You don't realize! He is *sinning*! It's sin against me, a sin against himself, a sin against our children conceived of God! And me — I sinned too, just like him!"

She went on sobbing. "I should have known better than to marry a foreigner! But I was almost 30 by that time — my mother was dying for me to marry and give her grandchildren — but you can't marry someone who picked you up in a ski resort — I can't bear thinking of these other women…"

I thought of what the divorced Americans I'd interviewed had gone through. If it were an American movie, I guessed Susan could pick up, take her three girls, move back to America and magically find a Sir Galahad stepfather who would be perfect in all ways. In the real world, she probably wouldn't even be able to get her children out of France. If she did, it would be years of grind without household help before she found a husband ready to take her on with all her baggage, if indeed she did find one. And if she did, would he be a gentleman with her daughters? Or maybe nasty to them? Or — horrors — some kind of sexual pervert with them? Was I looking at it straight, or was I becoming French myself?

But there was something else nagging at me about the depth of Susan's pain. Then it came to me: *The Scarlet Letter*. Susan, whose mother's family had roots in Worcester, Massachusetts going way back, was living through a ghostly displacement of the religious single-mindedness of her New England ancestors, without knowing it. Hawthorne's poison pen had gotten to her, 150 years later, with the power of shame and the anguish of being cut off from God. Hester Prynne wore the scarlet letter long after her sentence was purged; her lover, the preacher Arthur Dimmesdale, was in permanent hell. "As matters stand with my soul," he tells Hester, "whatever of good capacity there was in me, all of God's gifts that were the choicest have become the ministers of spiritual torment." Southern American women didn't have this heritage. It was certainly one of their advantages.

I tried to find a lighter note. "Now you're being silly," I said, finally. "Desire and love are two different things. Jean-Paul obviously loves you — and isn't hooked on another woman, and doesn't have some Faustian relationship with his mother, like so many. Now listen to me," I went on, beginning to feel like a guru myself after all these interviews. "A ski resort is as good a place as any to meet a husband, maybe one of the best. You were both doing what you love. You still are. You have a devoted husband who has given you three healthy daughters, who is committed to you and to his family, who supports you, leaves you free to do your own thing. I gather he doesn't gamble or drink and he's not abusive — nor does he have a contagious disease; or put you down in public or private and his in-laws treat you well! For God's sake, Susan. Count your blessings. You're not 25 anymore... close to 50?"

She let out a shriek. "You sound like my mother! That's just what she would say!"

I stayed until she had pulled herself together. When I left her I was feeling shaken. Sorry for her, sorry for women and human beings in general, but dizzy with a feeling of having understood — I thought — why that Frenchman at Laura's dinner thought an American wife might be disastrous news. And I wondered when someone was going to write a great song called, "It doesn't mean anything."

But I still needed to talk to more people.

Tentative bravos to Susan and Paul: Nothing is harder for an American to accept than a husband's philandering, and nothing is harder for a Frenchman to understand than this misery about something which "doesn't mean anything." (I really will write that song.) Bravo to them both for trying hard to work it out and be really committed to each other.

Part V

Deciphering the Riddle

17

Advice about French husbands
from French wives

And what about *French* wives of Frenchmen – not actresses, not royal mistresses, not politicians, but the kind of women who might have married the French husbands of the Americans in the last chapters: what do they say about making French husbands happy?

I went to see them where they lived. The interviews made me think of an American home organizer of the sixties — immaculate, *soignée*, her house beautifully kept, the dinner prepared in the kitchen, the table set in the dining room, the children fed and tucked in bed, the housewife fresh and lovely as she waits to receive her husband. Needless to say, no job.

But this is the 21st century.

The current vintage of Frenchwomen, like their mothers and grandmothers, are proud of being the heirs of the Marquise de Rambouillet and Jeanne de Loynes, women whose point in life was first of all to please men, and secondly, to run a complicated operation. While they, these 21st century women, may have grown up in a house full of servants and a leisure-time mother who spent her time organizing church bazaars, having facials and manicures and relaxing at uplifting concerts and exhibitions, they themselves have little help – but a husband, children and a flourishing career. The operation they run is fully as complex as Madame de Rambouillet's or that of Jeanne de Loynes, and is still organized around pleasing men. Pleasing men in the 21st century is as much based on form and style as in the Renaissance, these contemporary charmers told me. Tradition demands both. That their primary focus in life really is, as always, on their man and on love came through loud and clear. French men in love are imaginative and tender, they said, and, also, very cerebral. Their minds never stop reasoning, analyzing, comparing. To keep their men happy, women have to place them first in their heart. Then the children. Then the career. If they don't drop dead first, I thought, as I listened to their lives.

Talking with American women, on the other hand, the children seem to come first. Then the career. Then the husband.

"American women marry for a partnership in life," said Shelby Marcus-Ocana. "That means that when managing the children and the household, everything is shared and up for negotiation. An American man gets married because he falls in love. A Frenchman gets married, as does his wife, to found a family."

Pascaline Malfait
Be tender, protect him from trivia, and have family dinners

Tall, slim, radiantly young-looking and vibrant at 46, Pascaline Malfait is a French whirlwind with a fulltime day job and an overtime job as mother of three adolescents, and, above all, as the wife of Luc, the French director of a Japanese multinational. Time is something she always needs more of, but that doesn't seem to spoil her good humor. I haven't even mentioned her handicapped sister and aging mother in Germany.

During the day she is a real estate agent, taking foreigners, usually company transfers, around to apartments for rent and explaining the labyrinthine French laws about renting, insurance, taxes and so forth. On the way home after work she does the shopping. At home, still in her spike heels and Ralph Lauren pants suit, her makeup perfect, she checks on her children's homework, then prepares a three-course family dinner for whenever her husband arrives. Like many Frenchmen in the private sector, he rarely gets home before 9:30 or 10:00 pm. When everything is ready, she lights the candles on the dining room table.

The family also has breakfast together.

This lady is organized.

"We don't talk much at breakfast — we're still pretty sleepy," she said, "but at dinner everyone, my husband and all the children, tell us about their day. French women keep their husbands happy by keeping the life of the family together. And when our oldest gets married, then we'll find a way to dine or lunch together on the weekend."

Pascaline said that her oldest child had been part of an exchange program last summer with a school in Charleston, South Carolina. She loved America, but some things did shock her, like the air conditioning everywhere, even when it was unnecessary.

"Above all, she was shocked that the family didn't dine together," she said. "They all had their separate schedules; the children simply went to the fridge whenever they wanted to and took out whatever they pleased. That is unheard of here. I wouldn't like it a bit if other people were helping themselves to my refrigerator. How would you be able to plan a dinner?"

She feels there is no doubt that the mother is the core of the happy family. "Home sweet home is very important," she said, "and it's the mother who makes it sweet. Men are strengthened when they feel reassured by their wife and the mother of their children."

French men particularly?

"Yes, perhaps. I feel that French men are fragile and need the nest of their childhood when they get married... and a wife who mothers them. French women mother their husbands. I feel that I have four children — my three teenagers and Luc.

"Another French habit that helps families to stick together is the summer vacation. In America there are short vacations and the cousins often live too far apart to be together in the summer. Here in France with our five weeks vacation, we can spend two weeks at the mountains at Christmastime and another three weeks at the shore or somewhere in the summer, most likely in a grandmother's big house or in one rented so that we can all be together."

I asked why there are so many divorces: one in three couples in France.

"Yes — women have more independence now — but we're still nowhere near the U.S. rate of one in two couples divorcing," she said. "As it is usually the wife, in France, who initiates the divorce, there are three possible reasons. One, the husband is always cheating on her. Two, the husband is too stingy. Or, three, the husband is irresponsible — with money, or with the children, or something important."

I asked Pascaline how she went about mothering Luc.

"It's a matter of being tender," she said. "Giving a kind of authenticity to your love. Maybe it's doing what they do in the comic strips — like getting his slippers when he comes home from work exhausted. Partly, I guess, it's not bothering him with trivia — what the plumber forgot to do, or the bad grades of one of the children, or the nastiness of a neighbor — unless it was a funny incident. And not confronting him with problems and decisions at the wrong time.

"French men don't like hanging out with other men — going to clubs or playing squash after work like the English or Americans. They prefer to be with women. So you want to make sure it is you he prefers being with, and not some other woman or women. It's a fulltime job, being a French wife.

"And then it is doing little things for him that show you care. I put out Luc's clothes for him every evening, for instance, for the next day."

There is no marriage-contract problem, nor a mother-in-law problem. Lovers on the side? Not something you ask, not something you're told, but highly unlikely. No time, for one thing, but above all, they are a united family with Christian values.

Monique Raimond
Be subtle, tender and a good cook

I first met Monique Raimond at a luncheon at the American Embassy. It was given for French women who had been part of the Alliance Française's 150 year anniversary celebration. I had no idea who she was. What I saw was one of those French women whose beauty and glamour are sensational and ageless. Blond hair and blue eyes and subtle elegance are just the beginning.

After that luncheon, her face kept cropping up in the French glossies. If there was a celebrity fundraiser for destitute Biafrans or a gala premiere at the Opéra, Madame Raimond was there. I made inquiries. "One of France's most able ambassadresses," I was told. Her much older husband, Jean-Bernard Raimond, was a former foreign minister and is one of France's four permanent Ambassadeurs de France. His posts took them to Morocco, Poland, Russia and Rome with their twin daughters. "Now that her husband is retired," continued my informant, "she's Cardin's ambassadress — he says she's his best."

Obviously this official ambassadress of French elegance would have things to say about French women in general. I went to see her in her office at the Cardin headquarters in Paris where she presides over public and press relations. That is, she's the communication impresario for the Cardin conglomerate employing 175,000 people around the world. In addition, in 1991, she was elected municipal counselor of Lyon, where she was born and grew up in an intellectual family. She studied law, then got her doctorate. When she met her husband, he was a young diplomatic counselor at the Elysée, the French White House. Soon after they were married, he was appointed to Rabat.

I said I'd come to talk about French women and their men. Our interview was brief but revealing. She synthesized in a few paragraphs the wisdom of the ages.

"French women are Latin," she said, "and Latin women are very feminine. They know that men have a horror of powerful women — when they show it. French women don't demand things, they get them subtly. Mediterranean women all have the power, but they're careful not to show it."

She smiled a glowing smile. It sounded as if Kate's theory really was on the right track.

"French men are romantic and sentimental, and a little... how shall I say it?" she continued. "Perhaps that they are... delicate. They need to be reassured, constantly. You have to take care of your French husband — *il faut vous occuper de lui*. Tell him he is the most handsome, the most brilliant, the most marvelous of men. French men are roosters but they're tender, and they need tenderness. They're faithful, if you take care of them.

"If I have one bit of advice for American wives of French men, it is to learn how to cook. How to cook really well. Better than their mothers."

Micheline Guez
Respect, trust, good will – and a secret garden

Like Monique Raimond, Micheline Guez has impressive degrees (HEC, the prestigious business school, and Sciences Po). She has been married for over 25 years and has two grown daughters, also with impressive academic degrees. Both before and after her marriage she had demanding jobs as treasurer for BSN and Danone, until her parents' illness obliged her to resign. His position as a partner of Accenture often obliged her husband, Jean-Claude, a retired Polytechnicien workaholic interviewed in Chapter Three, to leave home on long trips to countries around the world. Micheline had to deal with these frequent absences on top of her working and parenting. She has managed to keep the marriage bonds close. How?

She says it boils down to respect, trust and good will.

"Respect for your 'other half' is crucial," she said. "That means never playing the shrew, never being overly vehement but, on the contrary, using soft language under all circumstances."

"Part of showing respect is giving freedom to your spouse for what the French call their secret garden. You must also have your own secret garden: this is a place where each of you is free to be spontaneous, to do what you like without considering anyone else. You have to have trust that your spouse will not use his secret garden in a way to dismay you. He must have the same trust in you."

A secret garden requires a stash of gold, she added. Your husband being presumably a wage earner, will not have a problem with that. If you don't have an independent income, and you're not working, you must be sure that your allowance for household expenses is enough to cover also a modest stash. This is important to settle before you get married, as the French flee money discussions like the plague.

"A marriage can't work unless the mutual respect extends to differences of opinion, perhaps strong differences," she said. "The difference can be about the friends we like, the restaurant one of us wants to go to but not the other — and it can also be about politics. Sometimes you have to agree to disagree — and that's not always easy, if you're a passionate sort of person with strong opinions. But this gets easier with time. I've noticed that when a couple has been married for 25 or 30 years, they usually begin to share each other's opinions.

"On the other hand, if it's about where to buy a house, for instance, that can be very difficult. Then you both have to make concessions to come to some sort of compromise.

"One of the things people don't mention, but which is essential, is the importance of jumping in to help whenever your husband is having a crisis. You'd think that would go without saying, but I've seen wives simply standing by, wringing their hands, or not even that, when the husband has suddenly lost his job, or a beloved brother, or has some kind of sudden health problem..."

Micheline insists on interests in common being vital for spouses' continued delight in each other.

"If you don't have any in the beginning, then you must sit down and think what they might be," she said. "Perhaps one of you will have to learn something new — or both of you. It could be bridge or bird watching or combing the flea markets or, but this takes longer to develop, a sport like tennis. We have our house in Corsica which provides endless possibilities for working together. We're now trying to agree on an addition, to accommodate our newest grandchild. One of our daughters made it very clear that if we wanted to have both daughters and their families with us at the same time — which we do — we'd have to enlarge the house. Jean-Claude, with his computer expertise, discovered a software program which enables you to put together what you want three-dimensionally. We're both having fun with this."

Working together with Jean-Claude for something they both believe in is Micheline's recipe for a marriage which is continually refreshing and stimulating, the opposite of monotonous. It keeps them both on their toes. Their latest project is founding, with two friends, a non-profit association called One Thousand Fountains for Tomorrow, which funds a system — invented by the father of one of these friends — for solar cell-powered water purification mini-factories in remote villages in Cambodia. The system works so well that their goal now is to raise funds for installing it in other remote, poor and unsanitary villages in Vietnam and Madagascar.

Claire Gallois
Don't marry him!

Claire Gallois is one of those quintessential Frenchwomen who, if you see her on the street, make you want to rush home and throw all your clothes in the trash basket. It's partly that she is petite, stick-slim and perfectly coiffed; mostly it is that casual *je ne sais quoi* of throwaway, excruciating style, a mixture of things from Saint Laurent and the nearest supermarket that you'd never think of putting together.

She is a successful novelist, a member of the jury of the coveted Femina prize — she was its president for years — and an astonished grandmother. "I know that other people have grandchildren but it just seems amazing." She is also a dedicated member of the the CNCDH, the *Commission Nationale Consultative des Droits de L'Homme*, a Council of Europe watchdog for legislation affecting racism, the rights of children and teenage delinquents.

Her appearance and her achievements intimidated me until I met one of her neighbors, who said that Madame Gallois is the only person in her building on the rue de Bourgogne who keeps in touch with the elderly occupants.

"She is very kind. We don't have a concierge, and Madame Gallois is the only one who calls on me to see if I'm dead or alive," said Madame Abrate, 79, a neighbor on the ground floor whose only close relative, her daughter, lives in Morocco.

I was delighted that Claire Gallois accepted being interviewed in her apartment, on the floor above Madame Abrate. It is a happy place, full of light and color and bursts of joy, mirrors, a comfortable bright red sofa, white curtains, period chairs, marble busts, a Greek column and in the dining room, a mural of a Tuscan landscape.

I was settling in to the red sofa, poised for erudite advice from this gifted, elegant Frenchwoman on the subject of marriage when she dropped her bombshell. The advice Gallois has to give on the subject of marrying a Frenchman is to not marry.

What's that? Yes, you heard me.

This grande dame of French letters, this ultra-elegant blond grandmother thinks marriage is, well, to put it mildly, overrated.

The thing she resents most about marriage is the continual need for concessions.

"When you're young, you're happy to make concessions, but after a while, you lose yourself in them," she said. "Too many compromises, too many concessions and a woman fades away. Principally, with all the power problems and constant concessions, you don't have a chance to really pay attention to the one you love, and perceive what he needs.

"French men are charming. They're probably the most charming men in the world, except maybe for Italians. Perhaps Austrians? I haven't had experience with non-Europeans. But you can't compare Frenchmen with Englishmen, or Scandinavians — too reserved — or with Spaniards or Greeks or Germans. The French really want to please, to give a woman pleasure."

Gallois thinks marriage is an institution that has outlived its usefulness. She has tried it twice.

"My first marriage was a mistake. I was too young — I just wanted to get away from home," she said. "If I hadn't married my second husband, I'd probably still be with him. People complain that I'm too independent — I reject that. Women have finally got the right to live as they wish, and should do so. What I have the most trouble with is conceding power constantly to a husband. It is always my chair, my bed, my wife. I'm the chef. Why haven't the dishes been washed?

"If you're not married, he has no right to ask why the dishes aren't washed. In a real couple, there is no need of marriage. The power problem isn't there anymore. Instead, every day you make the decision to stay together because you want to, not because of legal or social constrictions. Isn't that much more beautiful? You don't keep your cat in prison, why keep the person you love there? Of course if there are children, that changes things."

Gallois points out that in former times, marriage was above all a question of patrimony. A peasant would marry a neighbor with good land so that he would have another hundred acres. Married or unmarried, women had no rights. Nowadays, women are more secure. They have won back their civil rights, so they can take or leave marriage, and that is a real step forward. They don't have to put up with a brute or a lush or a lecher.

"So they're exercising the right to freedom," she said. "More than two thirds of the divorces in France are initiated by women. I know lots of men who cheat on their wives continually but are too lazy to take any steps like that. Women are stronger than men, by far. They don't need sexual harassment laws — if a man puts his hand where he shouldn't, or makes offensive remarks, a French woman can put him in his place. She can take care of herself."

18

French husbands' comments

What did French husbands have to say about their American wives or ex-wives? Not enough! They were unfailingly gracious about them. Of the many I talked to who were divorced from Americans, there were mild, saddened comments on an incompatibility not obvious at first. I heard no tales of frigidity or being cudgeled with a rolling pin or spat at by a shrieking shrew. Nor, not surprisingly, did I hear of a husband's violence or infidelity.

Most of the complaints were mild and looped around communication itself — different cultural references from different educational systems, different childhood fairy tales, different norms of behavior. There were veiled references to mothers-in-law, both French and American. Most of these Frenchmen couldn't imagine why an American wife might be the "worst thing" that could happen to a Frenchman. The politeness went so far that one of them, a doctor, said, "But I had always thought that an American wife would be happiness itself (*le bonheur*)."

And then I talked to Jean-Marc. He was the roguish young *ingénieur* at the gargoyle party, who had been so bitter about his prim American ex-wife from Vermont. He seemed to be in a better humor now.

"How can you live with someone who interminably wants to talk about feelings?" he said, during lunch at a brasserie. "Joan always wanted to know if I loved her. If you're asked that a hundred times, you begin to wonder. But the most difficult was her lack of *esprit* (wit). I would tease her and she'd be offended. Teasing is vital, like spring water, for us French."

What did he tease her about?

Jean-Marc reflected for a while. "About her constant insistence on her rights for this and that. Everything had to be talked to death."

"At Laura's dinner you seemed to be irritated by the direct way Americans always come out with everything, instead of being a little more subtle about the *non-dit*."

Jean-Marc laughed. "That was part of it. But look, when two people are that totally different in the way they live their lives, it doesn't work. I got married with idealism, I was crazy about her, I admired her and wanted us to be faithful to each other all our lives, but with Joan... I couldn't handle all the friction. Little things turned into monsters of irritation, like her constant big smile on the street. I told her people would think she was a half wit or a hooker, but she said looking cheerful was necessary and kept on grinning. I got the feeling she was bringing Vermont to Paris and not making any effort to fit in. I began to see that it really couldn't be." He lightened up with a little rumble of a laugh. "I worried about bringing up grinning children."

Vermonters could be pretty stubborn, but that didn't explain anything — which maybe was the point. I pursued.

"Was there one incident that determined you not to go on?"

Jean-Marc bit his lower lip and narrowed his eyes. It looked as if he was going to clam up. But then he said, "I didn't like it when she threw a glass of Scotch at me. Including the ice."

Violence. Now we were getting somewhere. For a long time I wondered who started it and what it was about and what he did after that. Did he hit her? Break a few ribs? Ask for forgiveness for whatever had caused this apparently quiet, prim young woman to lose it? He had a bad reputation with women... But he said not another word.

I decided to concentrate on the happy French husbands of the Americans I'd interviewed. Surely they would have a slant on why their compatriot had such a dark view of American wives. However, I soon gave up. They talked about Napoleon and somehow slid over into the 35-hour work week. They talked about politics. But about their marriage? Silence. To give you an idea, I asked one of them what he liked to do with his wife. "We discuss global warming," he said.

I finally got the message from these Frenchmen that their private life was private, and none of my business, and I should get lost.

Fair enough.

However, when I heard through the grapevine that a Parisian was willing, even amused, to talk about his marriage and his American wife, I rushed over.

He was tall and slim, with a beaky nose and graying hair. A healthy 56 or so, I decided. Immaculately dressed in a dark suit and a striped blue-and-white shirt. Almost military bearing. Married about 30 years. He was just as skittish as the others, but did talk, after he was reassured that I had NOT talked to, and WOULD NOT talk to his wife, nor mention where I saw him, where he lived or in what kind of a residence.

I had to agree not only not to use his name — I'll call him Alexandre — but also not to use any — ANY — detail which would make it possible for a friend to spot him.

So I can't tell you where he met his wife, although this was unusual to the point of being unique. It wasn't in Katmandu, but that kind of place, where young people go for an exotic vacation and mix easily. (Yes, I was allowed to say they were young, though not how young.)

I can't tell you how many children they have or of what sex, or where they're living, but I can say that there are several, and that they all — get this!! — married Americans. Alexandre doesn't find this disloyal to his country. On the contrary, he says his children are all very French and speak perfect French and act as ambassadors for France. "Which we need," he said. "One of my sons-in-law has even learned French." Aha! I'm allowed to say that he has two daughters... Actually, more than two. At least one isn't married.

Alexandre was born in Paris. He went through the French education system and came out on top. His wife, I'll call her Melanie, is from the South (never mind what part; not Texas). And that, he says is the key. His analysis was much like Kate's.

"It's much easier for a Southern girl to move to Paris than to New York," he said. "The way she has grown up, with rules of etiquette and politeness, of how to be a lady, is *vieille France,* quite similar to how we do things here. So I think it is a mistake to talk about Franco-American marriages — it's really a matter of regions.

"Another thing about Southerners is that the women are very feminine, they're not aggressive about women's rights and so forth, as they tend to be in the North. French women are relaxed about being feminine, probably because they have had power, real power, ever since the 17th century when they created the salons. They don't need to be aggressive about it. They have a strong role in social life here — they do everything with men. At a dinner party, there is none of this barbaric Anglo-Saxon separation of men and women after dinner, for instance.

And golf — I never heard of a husband and wife playing golf together in the U.S., but here, they do.

"I realize that we have a terrible record about the number of women in Parliament, but nevertheless I do feel that women are more respected in France. Don't forget that in recent years, more women than men have been getting their degrees in medicine and law. And what do you think about having a beautiful woman running as candidate of one of the major parties for president?"

Alexandre thinks that mixed-culture couples have an intellectual decision to make which can ease or pollute their life together.

"There are two possibilities for a mixed couple," he went on. "You can make it a subtraction or an addition. If a subtraction, then one of the two forgets his culture and adopts the spouse's culture 100 percent. I think this is a very sad path, and probably dangerous. The one who has sacrificed his culture will ultimately miss it too much. The other way is to add your spouse's culture to your own — and to learn as much as you can about it, which is enriching."

Alexandre is Roman Catholic and Melanie is Protestant. Instead of one of them changing his or her religious practices for his/her spouse's, or continuing in their separate liturgies, Alex and Melanie have each embraced the other. Sometimes they go to a Catholic church, sometimes to the American Cathedral in Paris, which is Episcopalian.

"It's the same with America and France," Alex said. "There is a lot I appreciate about America, particularly in connection with the way they do business. Americans are more explicit — not to say blunt — in their instructions and expectations, while the French are generally implicit. You have to be French to know what they mean. For instance, a French colleague of mine told his American subordinate that *il faut regarder cette question* (one must look into this subject). The American had no clue that this implied urgency and did nothing about it. My French colleague was very put out, until I explained it to him.

"Another aspect of American business I find excellent is their insistence on praise. I try to hand this on. When I give seminars for Frenchmen about to work with Americans, I ask them to mark down on a piece of paper whom they praised that day."

I plucked up my nerve and asked him if Melanie got along well with his mother — her mother-in-law.

"Melanie adores my mother! Southern families are generally very close, and Melanie's is especially close. She talks to her own mother every day on the telephone, but she misses her, it's not the same as having her here. So she is very happy to have my mother living near by. She confides in her. It is Melanie who initiates going to see her. We have lunch or dinner with her at least twice a month, if not more. We spend the summer together — in France or in the United States." Alex and Melanie have a house in the U.S. (Don't ask where.)

In fact, Melanie seems to do all the right things. She's a great cook, French cuisine as well as Southern. She loves going to museums, movies, plays and operas with Alex. She loves traveling with him. Like him, she loves to read biography.

I tried to catch him admitting something, anything that they disagreed about. He cited *Evidences Invisibles*, by Raymonde Carroll, a classic contrasting American and French cultures by a French cultural anthropologist married to an American. Alexandre said that anyone who had read that excellent book shouldn't have any trouble ascribing curious reactions to a culture without reacting angrily.

"Does she object that you don't say you're sorry?"

He seemed confused. "Sorry? For what?"

"Well, for anything," I said. "If you stepped on her foot in the kitchen by mistake, for instance. We Americans say it all the time, even for things we don't do. Most French people have a real problem with this — as it's not part of the culture to do anything wrong."

"Ah. But you know, Southern girls are not confrontational, they're very soft, so she would probably say it so that I wouldn't notice."

Melanie was looking more and more like Marianne, radiant symbol of France. I braced myself for the big one. I brought up the delicate subject of *"les petites aventures"* — philandering.

He didn't understand me at first and made some unintelligible murmurs.

I tried to be more explicit. "Frenchmen are known to have an eye for the ladies, even if they're married… and sometimes… Well, look at your presidents, for instance… I'm just wondering how you feel… if it's quite normal…"

He dismissed this. "Oh, politicians. Politics is a sort of aphrodisiac, but… really… for the rest of us, that's rubbish."

I persisted. "Your friends… they're not tempted to stray?"

"Certainly not!" He frowned thunderously. "Nor am I! I'm very much in love with my wife!"

I didn't say anything for a while, to give him time to calm down.

Then, I said: "I wouldn't have dreamed of asking you such an indiscreet question — I was sure that was not your style. And it seems clear that the era of the long-term mistress is over... men just don't have the time anymore. But the temptations are still there, *les petites aventures* seem to be as much a part of the culture as ever, according to sociologists and psychoanalysts, so I'm wondering how you explain your fidelity."

"I told you," he said, more quietly, "I'm very much in love with my wife."

"Do you think that religion plays a big part in your commitment?"

He thought for a while. "Well, of course it does. Marriage is sacred. It is a sacrament."

19

Vice-versa Marriages

What about vice-versa marriages — American men to French women? Is a French wife the best thing that can happen to an American man? The answer is maybe — if they live in France. Sometimes, even if they don't. If they live in the U.S. with an American husband, French women may be thrilled with the friendliness, the pace, the anything-goes style. After a while they may find the friendliness superficial or commercial, the fast pace unnerving, the anything-goes style sloppy and ugly. That's when they admit that they hate the food and miss the sounds of their native tongue and the things they can say in it. They miss the intense discussions — arguments! — over a four-hour Sunday lunch. They miss the beauty of old buildings. They miss the steps of churches worn smooth by hundreds of years of people treading on them. They miss the smells of Paris... instead of the smells of fresh bread, of lilies and daffodils, and chickens roasting on a spit, they smell ketchup and pickles.

Perhaps most of all, they miss the French game of seduction, the highly charged male-female exchanges of *non-dit* between casual acquaintances of "I am interesting and so are you," and the alert, approving stares of men on the street or at a party. The lack of them makes them feel invisible, as if they're not there.

American men may think at first that they have the best of all worlds with their stylish, sensuous, competent, responsive French wife and her delectable cuisine, her satiny creamed skin, but after a while they may miss the direct talk, apologies, sportiness and vocabulary they were used to with an American. If they live in France, there are other endless possibilities for friction.

On the other hand, the French bride may feel that California, or Alabama or Maine is where she feels more alive than anywhere in France. Her American husband may find himself rejoicing every day at his brilliant choice of a Gallic mate.

Judson Gooding, an editor and author who grew up in the Midwest has lived for several years in France and southern Vermont with his lovely Françoise, is one of these. For 30 years he has reveled in her delectable cooking, her sense of proportion, her style and her softness; and her unflappable competence in managing their family, their 20-room house and her art-restoration business.

"It's impossible to describe all her amazing qualities," said this happy husband. "There are so many of them."

Jack Miller, a divorced New Yorker, met his French wife when he was in the U.S. army in Vietnam. He brought Anne-Marie to New York and feels the same way as Judson Gooding. "My first wife used to cope with crises. Anne-Marie prevents them."

And what about the French woman who won the sweepstakes, that is, the heart of America's superstar heartthrob, Johnny Depp? As astoundingly popular as he is offbeat and uninterested in the Hollywood circus, Depp settled on a beautiful, sensuous *French* pop singer and movie star, Vanessa Paradis, for the mother of his children. America's young women can only pine for him in vain and ask, why her, why not me?

You might as well ask the wind. Johnny Depp does not like to talk to the press. He's too busy filming, for one thing, back to back, one movie after another. If trapped, he seems to disappear, he becomes invisible. If he does talk to the press, which is very, very rare, he does not talk about Vanessa. Did you say discreet? Tight-lipped, uncommunicative, reserved really don't convey the problem. Vanessa is like a sacred lake with still waters that you don't fish in.

He is on record just twice about Vanessa. The first time was a while ago when someone accused him of breaking off with Kate Moss because Vanessa was pregnant. When Depp heard that, he hit the roof. "I would never do that," he said. "That would be a terrible way to start your life as a father."

The second time was a few words to *Allure* magazine about what he called his Paradis — Vanessa in all her Frenchness. In a few words he described a sublime love, one that he himself is obviously moved and amazed by:

"She cooks for me, she waits up for me at night, no matter when I get back from the set, even if it's 3 am. She runs my bath for me… I don't say a woman has to cook for her man, but she takes care of me. It's the first time."

When Vanessa mentions Johnny, it's always *mon amoureux*. On television she said, "The love of your life is also your best friend. I've fallen in love before, but, before, I spent more time with my friends than with him. Now, not anymore."

Both these stars had restless, turbulent lives before they met. Now they've come home, and home is their farmhouse in the south of France in the Var, not far from the sea and St. Tropez.

They say just hearing a French accent turns Americans on. In her book, *La France /Made in USA*, about her observations during her posting in the U.S. for *Le Figaro*, Guillemette Faure quotes an American ex-girlfriend of a famous French politician, saying, more or less, just that. "When he speaks French to me on the pillow, I can't help it, I just melt. I don't have any idea what he's saying, but it doesn't matter. It's the sounds."

Maurice Chevalier and Yves Montand knew all about those sounds in song and their effect on Americans. Other languages just don't have it. *Amour amour amour toujours,* goes one of Vanessa's songs. *Que ça dure jusqu'au dernier jour…*

20

Three lives unfolding

I hadn't seen Lizzie for months when she called me up after Christmas and asked to come by.

She flopped on my sofa, as usual, but everything else was different. Gone were the sneakers. She had on *escarpins* — pumps — slim, sleek but low-heeled and suitable for bicycling, and paint-on jeans that almost covered the heel. On top she wore a white turtleneck sweater and tweed jacket. Her blond hair was loose, without the barrette, cut in a stylish square shape; and her lipstick was pearlish and colorless. "Nooly" was gone from her vocabulary. She now lived in *Neuilly* — which is sort of pronounced nuh-yeeye.

She looked great.

"What's up?" I said.

She sat up straight with a little bounce and crossed her legs. She gave me a radiant smile. "I've got a job."

"Wonderful. Where? Doing what?"

"It's the old job I had, pre-babies, but over here. I had to go to the States last month — my mother was sick, she seems better now — I wanted to be free to see her all the time, so I went alone, no kids. Guess what, my mother-in-law took care of them. And Thierry, of course. On the plane going over I thought about those meetings we had and suddenly I realized — boom, like that — that the reason all those Americans were happy here had nothing to do with changing themselves inside out, like you said, but with one simple fact: they had a job. It suddenly hit me that there was no reason on God's green earth that I couldn't get one too. Get out of the house! See people! Have a goal besides making a perfect *blanquette de veau!* My work was three quarters of my life — what am I saying? *All* my life! — before I married. It was okay to drop it when we were in the U.S. and the kids were small, but to come here and have that great big gap plus all the craziness of this country — well, it was too much. So, simple as pie, I went back to my old company, and asked them if they could use me over here — I'd been in marketing — and they said fine."

"Sounds great," I said, "but don't you think a major reason those women, as you call them, are happier here is because they've learned how to please their husbands?"

Lizzie snorted, with a vigorous shake of the head.

"Maybe partly, but another thing I figured out over there is that I have the word independence tattooed on my brain. Call me ungrateful, but I hate being subsidized by a man. It's okay when you're all fuzzy and breathless with love, but after a few years of diapers and vacuuming, you start dreaming of the days when things were more challenging than getting the children to school on time. Now that I know when I get up that I'm going to be driving my own car to my own job, where I'll find a group brainstorming with me about how to promote one of our new brands, well, I can tell you I'm much more open to all those things they talked about at our meetings — pleasing my husband by being serene, not argumentative, not prickly, nicely groomed, not grumpy at night when he wants to make love, not blowing up because my mother-in-law has been nasty to me — again. Really, all that talk about identity — if you ask me, most American women get their identity from their job and all the rest follows."

She really was different. I tried to figure it out. Maybe the marriage was going better.

Lizzie continued: "I talked to my married friends at home — you know, in Nebraska. Yes I know, that word 'home.' Well there it is, it's still home. Anyway, their kids, like mine, are out of diapers and they're all — all — back at work. They have a different system, because the men over there have been so ground down — or trained to be cooperative, if you like — that they have this partnership of who does what in the house, sort of half and half. Who gets the broom and who gets the dishcloth. My best friend says that she wasn't born pushing a vacuum cleaner anymore than her husband was, and that she's supporting the household as much as he — so if her husband doesn't shape up and do his part, she's out the door. Thierry says that that would never work in France."

"Why not?"

"I don't know. Thierry says that French women don't want their men to become women. That they'd faint if they saw their husband in an apron. *Vive la différence*, all that. It's okay if he wants to help with cooking the strawberries for putting up jam, but not the everyday tedium of housework. Maybe that's changing with younger couples, but I wonder."

I marveled at the change in her. *Vive la différence* indeed — between Lizzie before her trip and Lizzie post-trip. The clothes, the hair, her general pulled-togetherness. Her exuberance seemed to be back, without her startling effervescence that threatened to spill over into some embarrassing loud outburst.

"How did you like being 'home?'" I asked her.

"Wonderful." She paused, then looked down at her lap. "Wonderful. But — I have to admit, things I used to take for granted got on my nerves. Strangers grinning at me in stores if our eyes happened to meet. Music everywhere — noise. Loud voices. Loud laughs. Fat people. Women in sweatsuits at the supermarket — and not only track suits — curlers in their hair! Television movies and news being interrupted every 10 seconds for an ad. Kleenex everywhere. Ads about bowel movements — heaven save me! The suffocating chumminess of waiters. The mountains of food, hidden under unrecognizable sauces, shoveled onto restaurant plates. But what really got me..."

She paused to pour herself a glass of water from a side table.

"What really got me," she went on, sitting down again, "was the children. My friends' children were like savages."

"They didn't get up when you came in the room?"

"Get up! You're dreaming! They ignored me completely. Went on playing Game Boy or watching television — which no one turned off so that I could chat comfortably with my friend... As for shaking hands, a girl of 15, one of my friend's daughters, said she thought that was really cool and how did I learn to do it. A high school boy, when we were sitting around at his parents' place, heard me talking about the Second World War. He said, 'You mean there was a first one?'"

She paused again and gave me a long look. "I was almost glad to get back to this straitjacket of rules, rules, rules. I mean, for instance, I was asked to a friend's house for dinner. She handed the serving dishes around and then, since the table was big enough, left them on the table. I was actually shocked to see the way the other guests helped themselves to second helpings, before being invited by the hostess. Same with the wine — they'd pour it themselves. Sometimes they even got up during dinner for a pee. I decided — believe it or not — that the straitjacket of rules isn't a straitjacket at all. It's choreography so that the dance will be pleasing and not chaos."

I had lost track of Kate for the last few months, the way you do in a big city. But after seeing Lizzie I phoned her right away. Soon after, we met on the rue Mouffetard at a café we both liked, though it was a little too near the fishmonger's for my taste. Kate looked even showier than usual, more eye-liner, redder hair, more jangling bracelets. When I told her about the dazzling change in Lizzie, she couldn't resist playing the pedant.

"Good," she said. "I thought she had it in her. That's normal, of course, when you zigzag between countries. For a few years, whichever country you're in gets on your nerves and you want to be in the other one. Then after a few years, you stop noticing and simply switch your automatic pilot subconsciously to the country you're in. Everything seems normal and fine."

Kate studied her coffee cup for a long time. Finally she said, "Needless to say, that's if your marriage is going well." Another long pause. "Listen, I have something to tell you."

I hate it when people say that. If it's a child or a husband, it is sure to be bad news. "Mummy, I'm pregnant." Or, "Darling, believe me, I don't know how it happened, but I'm in love with someone else." Or, "I have to tell you something very sad. Your brother is in the hospital."

"What is it, Kate?"

"I'm leaving Geoffroy." Another pause. "He's just too much of a stick. It's no big deal, really, since we don't have any children."

"But I thought — for heaven's sake, you're supposed to be the guru who gets it right and tells us all how to live happily ever after."

"Well, I thought I had it figured, but he found out. Actually, to tell the truth, he's throwing me out. Just as well."

"Found out what? Not an affair! No — don't tell me. For heaven's sake, Kate, that is too adolescent to be found out." I felt angry. Also cheated. "It's a big deal for all of us, even if it isn't for you. I mean, you're the shrink. Are you going to leave France?"

She laughed. "Heavens no, after all this investment. I love it here."

"But you said — you told Lizzie…"

"I know, and it's true what I said, but every marriage is different, every combination of these two cultures is like a bomb waiting to go off after about 20 years of both spouses becoming someone they're not. That is, unless by some miracle they've rounded off each other's annoying edges and yet stayed themselves. They're the blessed ones, I guess. Anyway, I'm not one. I picked the wrong husband, that's for sure. I really don't think I'll have any trouble finding another."

"But what about Geoffroy?"

"He's devastated. I was his alter ego — you know, the show-off extrovert to his introvert. I think marriage with a foreigner should be against the law. Really." She paused again. "You better call Laura. She has some news, too."

"Oh no. Laura has been playing around too?"

"No. It's the irresistible Fabrice."

"Irresistible to whom?" I thought of Fabrice's merry eyes that could seem to be saying, "Try me."

"Don't tell me it's Fabrice?" I said.

Kate looked around and jangled the bracelets on her wrist. Another long silence.

Finally I said, "So how did Geoffroy find out?"

"It's the classic rat these days — the cell phone. Laura smelled it and sneaked a look at Fabrice's. I'd told him a million times to delete everything, and usually he did, but once he didn't. He said the message was too tender, he couldn't bear to delete it. So when Laura heard it, she forwarded it to Geoffroy."

I began to feel really sick. I said, "Well, you can't just leave me up in the air like this. What was wrong with you and Geoffroy? You always said how much you admired his brain and principles, you always seemed happy…"

"Happy, happy. I know, I'm the shrink supposed to know all about it, but I always wonder what people mean. Content? Thrilled? Content isn't good enough, you know that, and you can't live on the plane of thrilled for very long. Anyway, with Geoffroy, it's the old, old story. In the beginning I was excited by his conservatism, his discipline and his encyclopedic knowledge. He always had something to teach me — I was always a sucker for smart men who knew more than I did. He fell for my wacky offbeatness. Then I guess we both hankered for something more like ourselves, but we hid it — even from ourselves. But I could see that deep down he really didn't approve of me — and after all these years he still treated me more or less like a nincompoop. I got sort of tired of always being taught, if you see what I mean — tired of the very thing that had attracted me. I found out that it had a dark side."

"So go ahead and tell me he's a lousy lover."

"No, actually, that was never a problem."

"Then — I don't know, you seemed like such a good couple. Of course, one never really knows. Appearances..."

She sat up straight and gave me a long hard look. I was reminded of a cobra suddenly uncoiling to it full height. "All right I'll tell you. But you probably won't understand. One can't convey the daily piling up of resentment... It's a kind of grinding that gets you. Listen. If your French husband corrects you about everything... if he imposes his political and cultural views even to the point of explaining *America* to friends... or colleagues... do you get an idea of the frustration of the American wife? Since she's not French — the French expect happy spouses to contradict each other in public — but, instead, she's from a culture where a well-brought-up 'lady' doesn't disagree with her husband except in private, do you see that this carries over into the rest of their life together? She won't retaliate in public, but she'll be seething internally... and her retaliation — perhaps unconsciously — will be coldness in the bedroom. And that, for a Frenchman, is unforgivable."

I called Laura the next day. We met for lunch at a restaurant opposite Notre Dame. I was a little early. The usual crowds were milling about on the square as I went by. The gargoyles seemed to be leering down at me.

Laura showed up smiling as usual, serenely smashing as usual.

"Never get an apartment near gargoyles," I said, as she sat down. "Bad luck."

"What on earth?"

"Kate told me. Well, I guess it's no wonder, the way she goes around in those slinky tight trousers. What are you going to do? Leave?"

Laura ordered a *tajin* and rolled her eyes. "Listen. I always knew there might be trouble when I married a brilliant, fun guy like Fabrice, who was not only handsomer than God but looked sexy just sitting in a chair. His bursting bank account was a nice bonus. When I found out that his father was a well-known womanizer, not a great role model for a son, I asked myself if I was tough enough. I'm sure Kate isn't the first."

"But Laura, *quand même*... she's your best friend."

"Not really. She's not the friend you have heart-to-hearts with late at night. Anyway, it's no big deal, it was only a one-night stand, or almost. Maybe a few *cinq à septs*. We were all skiing together one weekend at Courchevel. Fabrice hurt his ankle. You know how men are, they're terrible *malades*, patients. He was insisting on skiing anyway. That would have been curtains for his ankle. So Kate said she'd stay with him. Well, it was nice of her to give up a day of skiing, not that she skis very well. They only saw each other a few times after that… I don't think Fabrice really liked her. She comes on very strong, you know. When she's after a man, she practically rapes him. And there's a lot of vulgar language…"

"In other words, she's amoral, huh? How did you find out?"

"My cell phone didn't work. Fabrice was in the tub, getting dressed, so I borrowed his. I found a very, very sexy message from her, modeled on George Sand's to Musset. I didn't tell Fabrice, of course. I sent it to Geoffroy."

"You didn't!"

"I did. After all, the way she lords it over us all the whole time."

"So you'll just carry on like normal? You're not even going to mention it to Fabrice?"

Laura's setup sounded so much like Susan's, both of them in marriages that seemed like the luckiest of all, and now this. Yet their reactions were worlds apart. Was it their different backgrounds? Or the different backgrounds of their husbands? Or the difference of growing up in New England or Philadelphia? Or was it a matter of childhood happiness — or self esteem — or just character? Was Laura just tougher or less sensitive than Susan?

"Mention it to Fabrice? No, why should I? Accusations and shrieks of jealousy? What would be the point — it would just make a horrible atmosphere. Of course I'm going to 'carry on.' The children would suffer terribly if we separated. They adore Fabrice. He's a great father! I don't want to break all this up. I don't want to go back to work. I don't want to live alone. And I love Fabrice. How many years have we been together? Counting before we were married, 22."

"And it's fun being a countess," I said. "Or is it sort of silly, in this day and age?"

Laura laughed. "It gets you a table faster in a restaurant. Honestly, I don't wake up in the morning thinking 'Whee! I'm a countess!' All the family baggage can be a real drag, but, you know, I like the oldness of it, it goes way back. You and I have talked about that, how our families brought us up to respect things that have been around a long, long time, tradition, all that… which makes it easier to fit in, in France." She looked off into the distance. "But it all boils down to Fabrice. He is one in a million. He's spoiled me for other men. He's *fun*."

She frowned, leaned forward on her elbows and gave me a long, intense look. "And there is something else about Frenchmen like Fabrice. They're superb lovers, yes, and part of the reason is that they're poets.

Real poets with their language, the moment they write a letter. Not just any letter, but a letter of condolence or congratulations on a birthday, something personal... I can't even describe their love letters. Their words are so beautiful, they are such a winged song that it makes you want to cry. I feel that they live in a different dimension, a place I can't really reach. It's not a matter of talent, they all write like this. Fabrice doesn't understand why it moves me so. He takes it for granted. I read somewhere that it's a matter of soul, of old souls. I think it must be hundreds and hundreds of years — a thousand, really — of troubadours. Or maybe it's just a matter of technique and literary education. But I don't think so. I think they're on a different plane altogether."

One of her children interrupted us on her cell phone. I mused on about our conversation and about Laura. Her patrician roots probably gave her a head start with grace and confidence, but you'd have to catch her being rude or cruelly sarcastic with people of different milieus to accuse her of snobbery. I never had. She saved her wit and puns on the ridiculous for her friends. She did the flowers for the church, was constantly visiting frail, ill old ladies and sending packages to babies in Africa. She was always ready to pitch in for the various American groups in Paris, whose members fell into about every category you could think of. So how come she could stroke Fabrice's cheek and ignore his follies... while Susan was drowning in tears? Had Susan chosen to be a victim? Or was Laura a sleepwalker in a virtual world? Where was love in all that? Susan didn't mention it. Laura did. And Laura was not only not in tears, she had a radiance about her.

She hung up her cell phone and turned back to me. "If you ask me, Kate has been looking for an exit excuse for ages. Would you stay with Geoffroy? Cold fish, no matter how you look at him. And that apartment, no charm whatever — on the street, noisy, terrible furniture..."

"You know, Laura, you've become — well, French!"

She finished her coffee and gave me a long look. "Isn't that the point? Is it maybe a matter of being grown up?"

I couldn't help saying what Susan had said to me. Maybe her answer would help me to straighten out Susan. "But doesn't it mean your life is sort of — empty? fake? I don't know —"

"Fake? What's fake about it? Are you still stuck in *Sleeping Beauty*... insisting on the pure Prince who loves his princess passionately and single-mindedly forever? That's perfect — if everyone really is asleep. I grant you it's a nice dream — although I can imagine it might get tedious

— and perhaps it exists — somewhere, for some people — but I promise you, without going into sentimental blobbiness, marriage can be fulfilling and all those big words as long as there is commitment. And commitment doesn't have to mean total fidelity. What you can demand is discretion… and dignity. Not to be humiliated. If you love to be with your husband, if you.. *like the way he is*, like talking to him, like doing things with him, like what he does with the children… and if he doesn't have any of those devastating problems like alcoholism or gambling… well, then, you're pretty lucky. Which means, I'm pretty lucky."

The waiter had long since served our lunch. We'd hardly noticed. Now Laura dug into her tajin. I had a couple of other questions — not for Susan's benefit, but for this book.

"Laura, does anything Fabrice do irritate you - I mean, something French, that the French do and Americans don't?"

"Yes *et comment!* He teases me and I really don't like it. I guess because I want to be perfect. For him, of course!"

"About what?"

"Mostly dropping things. We all do, in my family."

"Can I ask you another question? Does Fabrice tell you what he loves about you? I mean, as an American… or as a woman?"

She'd just taken a bite of her tajin. She sipped her glass of wine, then laughed. "Not really. I can tell more by his criticisms of other women — which seem to have the subtext that he's glad I'm not like that."

"For instance?"

"You know something, this is getting too personal. I'll just say that I think he likes me as I am, just as I like him as he is."

I thought, Bravo, Laura, to myself. She wasn't wearing her soul on her sleeve. She was together, not spilling over her borders, but gathered. Her husband was a joy to be with; he loved her and was committed to her. They had children. What he did with that part of his anatomy with someone else was beside the point. She was American: she'd made her French bed and was lying in it. And she loved lying in it.

21

Are there conclusions?

*Will you be "glücklich wie Gott in Frankreich"
— as happy as God in France?*

(Old German saying)

None of the people I interviewed had really said it, but one possible answer to the riddle at the beginning of this book was sneaking up on me.

Perhaps the reason a Frenchman thought that an American wife was the worst thing that could happen to him was that she was in danger of taking on the qualities perceived as male. *Vive la différence* has always been the battle cry of French men and women. Testosterone is fine with them — in men.

I was reminded of my honeymoon years ago in Greece. At the Athens airport, my European bridegroom was pained to see an American woman shrieking at her husband in public. She was a big woman and vulgar looking, with huge breasts, bright red lipstick and a too-short skirt. Her husband looked like a beetle. Small and hung like a coat rack with cameras, binoculars and his wife's handbag, he was trying to maneuver two enormous suitcases. After that, for years, every time I started to get adamant about something, my husband would smile wanly and murmur, "Athens airport."

Ted Stanger writes about a similar couple of American seniors in *Sacrés Américains*. They were trading insults on what appeared to be a sort of second honeymoon in Paris. The tone of the wife was so loud and shrill that Ted, at the next table, couldn't help overhearing it. Finally the wife shrieked that her 40 years of marriage were far from being a bowl of cherries. Her husband tried to calm her, saying that they were in Paris to enjoy themselves, not dig up old quarrels. She screamed louder that of course he preferred to bury all his dirty two-timing. Then she brought up the disagreeable subject of Rosa. He admitted that Rosa had certain attractions. The screaming went from loud to piercing.

R had told me that if there is anything a Frenchman is allergic to, it's being bossed around by a woman. It simply doesn't happen. Or, if it does, it isn't part of the folklore. There is no Mr. Milquetoast or Dagwood Bumstead in French comic strips. The caricature of the European male has the man on the donkey, his wife following behind carrying the suitcases. The caricature of the American tourist couple is the opposite. The wife carries nothing; her husband carries everything, including her handbag, as at the Athens airport.

I wanted to know what Jill Bourdais, the couples-psychotherapist and marriage counselor, thought about all this. Jill was married to a French executive and had lived in France for 25 years.

We met at a pizzeria near St. Germain des Prés.

"It's obvious," she said. "We're seen as overbearing. All the cartoons show us like that, the big strong wife with the meek, frail-looking husband carrying her handbag. Frenchmen know the reputation of American women for being overbearing and aggressive. They usually don't know the reason for it… our pioneering heritage. Our female ancestors had to be tough in the Wild West. They had to be able to pick up and move on a moment's notice in those covered wagons. They had to protect the house and the children from marauders — perhaps Indians — when their husband was away. If the husband was killed in one of the Indian wars, they had to fend for themselves, alone.

"An American woman can change, but not overnight. She has to explain her heritage to her future French husband so that he understands. He has to explain to her that female loud voices and loud displays of enthusiasm on seeing old friends, or loud arguments in public or private are just not on in France. Otherwise it will take her quite a while to figure it out for herself, and by that time he may have given up."

So, is a Frenchman happiest with the steel magnolia Southerner?

"Not necessarily. That depends on the Frenchman. It's one of the zillions of paradoxes about the French: they want subtle talk, full of nuance and the *non-dit,* but they also spoil for good tough verbal sparring. You can see this on the street or in any office, two men arguing vehemently. You think the knives are about to come out and then suddenly it's over, they're shaking hands and saying, 'That was a very interesting conversation, we must do it again sometime soon.'"

Dara Teste, the antiques book vendor from Connecticut, mentioned earlier, couldn't adapt to this.

"I never imagined that conflict could be what my husband would want," she told me. "That's not me at all — I wanted quiet support and agreement. All this conflict was destabilizing for me. American women expect a partner. It took me a long time to see that we would have gotten along a lot better if I had been more hysterical, demanding. He liked confrontation, which I saw as an attack. I'm thin-skinned — so I closed up instead of going to battle. I'd left my environment, my city, my friends and family, all that defines me. In France, I spent years trying to recreate myself — but my marriage suffered. In the end, I lost the support of my husband."

So, is catching and keeping a Frenchman's heart maybe not about being a Southern steel magnolia, but a confident screamer like Sophie Marceau in *L'Etudiante*? Or Mathilde Seigner in *Tout pour plaire*? Or as Sheila (case history no. 1) discovered when she finally screamed at Hugues for 10 solid minutes? Maybe. But you won't find anyone admitting it.

I was stumped. I had trailed the Frenchman's heart through the do's and don'ts of the wife of his dreams. I had found out that she was mysterious, voluptuous, erotic, elegant, witty, practical. She bathed in the *non-dit*, wore lacy black garter belts, ignored his *petites aventures*. When he teased her, she teased him back. She was uncomplaining, independent, a sublime cook, sympathetic and resourceful in a crisis and, above all, tender. She knew how to handle his mother. She soaked up French culture and made sure that her children triumphed in the French educational system. She screamed if the situation called for it, she obeyed when it seemed important. She was seductive with everyone all day long. Above all, she put her husband first.

Fine. It was a pretty challenging persona but not beyond the reach of a determined American woman… we met several of these paragons in the case history section. So what was the fatal flaw of the American wife of Fabrice's riddle?

I had just about given up when, softly, with a significant pause, Jill dropped the answer in my lap. Clearly, in detail, she described the glass mountain that very, very few American women would be able to scale. It sounded like a minor bump on the road, prosaic, mundane, no red flags, nothing to attract your attention. It was like a rusty key that only special people knew was solid gold. If someone told you that this was the root of the daily misery of many Franco-American marriages, who would believe you? Ah, but listen: if you pay attention, you pick up on the fateful reality that this skill is linked with the goddess of the French husband, his mother.

"From my patients," said Jill, "I've understood that one thing that exasperates a French husband is being continually asked by his wife to take care of the family paperwork: paying the EDF (electricity) and the telephone bills, filling out the social security papers, paying the rent, the taxes, dealing with the French *Administration*."

Jill paused for emphasis. "You have to realize that all this was always done by his mother."

Another pause. "So, naturally, he expects his wife to take care of it."

Jill continued: "As a new bride the American wife is totally confused by all those documents, particularly if she doesn't know French, but even if she does. She has to run to her husband for help about everything, including tickets to the theater and vacation reservations. At first, bursting with love, that's fine. But before long, he becomes resentful and impatient. This is when it is dangerous for the marriage. The husband falls back on his previous autonomy, but the wife has nothing to fall back on.

"In the first phase of a bi-cultural marriage, both partners find the differences intriguing and refreshing. They enjoy the wider horizons. But then once settled, when the bloom is off, the reaction sets in and they turn back into what was familiar. This is when the American wife, obviously, is at a disadvantage. The French husband wants to turn her into a French wife."

Jill added that sometimes the wife consciously prolongs her dependency on her husband for all these details. He comes home bushed from work, calls for his dinner, and afterwards flops in front of the television set. She has been waiting all day for him to come home. She is longing to talk and finds that she can't get his attention... so she falls back on asking his help with paying the EDF bill.

To help bi-cultural couples, Jill often asks them to sit down and list on a piece of paper the 10 things they would like to have from their spouse to make them feel more cared for.

"The husband's list never mentions anything about sex," she said. "It's always about his wife taking on these duties and showing her independence. Frenchmen don't want to be bogged down in these details they consider women's work."

I had an example near home of Jill Bourdais' perfect French paperwork-champion wife. My cousin's French daughter-in-law, is a writer who just finished her fourth novel while also taking care of their three sons, ages 9 to 15, getting the youngest at school, taking the others to music lessons. She prepares a three-course family dinner, and usually serves it at 10 p.m. when her husband finally comes home. She organizes their social life, and arranges for the children's doctors' appointments when necessary. She always looks fresh as a daisy and as *branchée* as if she just stepped out of *Elle*, with big shiny earrings and ropes of beads and the *dernier cri* in the cut of her pants. And somehow she calculates and pays their taxes, their rent and all the other bills, and takes care of all the official papers for her handicapped sister-in-law.

So, what is my conclusion?

That, as Bette Davis said about old age, marriage to a Frenchman is not for sissies.

You can train for it, as you can for old age. You can first of all decide whether you're a slave to what I call the Hester Prynne syndrome. *The Scarlet Letter* may not be at the top of school reading lists anymore, but the Puritanism of the Hester Prynne predicament is visible immediately to Europeans visiting America. They understand that for us, men as well as women, adultery is the ultimate sin in marriage, the betrayal of our soul. Decide how you will handle this, if it should be your lot. You can and should read about other likely bumps and pitfalls, the precipices others before you have fallen off. You can learn — and had better learn — the language, the history and the codes of etiquette. You can go to French movies. You can read the novels of Balzac and Victor Hugo. Get French DVDs — with subtitles to begin with, that makes it easier. You can read George Sand's correspondence and be exhilarated by the paths she trod 200 years ago, paths of lovers, children, family, writing, friends and activism for women's rights. You can study Chanel and learn about style, real style, so that your *chien* is such that you can hold your own with any French woman. You can go to Japan for a year, learn about the rigors behind the charms of geishas, and subject yourself to codes of behavior that will make living in France seem like a vacation cruise. Determined to master that fatal flaw, you can go to your local town hall and sign up for a course in how to deal with all the papers and documents of the French *administration*.

Now you're ready for Olivier Todd's recipe for being a French husband's lover, friend, ally and pride, which is the same as his recipe for making love: that there is no recipe, there is only attention to the other person. As Laura put it, if your skin likes his skin, if you like the way he is, if you like talking to him and doing things with him, and if you are both *committed*, then you have the beginnings of a chance at basking in *le bonheur*... one of those French words full of nuances and the *non-dit*, which basically means "happiness." You're at the top of the highest peak. The view is lovely.

Bibliography

Appert, Valérie, *Trouver un Jules à Paris*, Ed. Parigramme, 2001

Baudry, Pascal, *Français et Américains, L'autre rive*, Village Mondial, 2004

Beaton, Cecil, *The Unexpurgated Beaton: The Cecil Beaton Diaries*,
Phoenix/Orion Books, 2003

Braconnier, Alain, *Mère et Fils*, Odile Jacob, 2007

Brem, Anne-Marie, *George Sand, Un diable de femme*, Gallimard, 2004

Buron, Nicole de, *Mais t'as tout pour être heureuse*, Flammarion, 1996

Buron, Nicole de, *Docteur, puis-je vous voir ... avant six mois?*, Flammarion, 2003

Chandernagor, Françoise, *L'Allée du roi*, Gallimard, 2006

Chevalier, Tracy, *The Lady and the Unicorn*, Harper Collins, 2003

Clerc, Christine, *Le bonheur d'être français*, Grasset, 1982

Cronin, Vincent, *Napoleon*, Harper Collins, 1971

Dejean, Joan, *The Essence of Style*, Free Press, 2005

Dicks, Diane, ed, *Cupid's Wild Arrows*, Weggis, 1993

Downie, David, *Paris, Paris, Journey into the City of Light*,
Transatlantic Press, 2005

Delorme, Philippe, *Blanche de Castille*, Pygmalion/Gérard Watelet, 2002

Dubois, Jean-Paul, *Une vie française*, Editions de l'Olivier/LeSeuil, 2004

Dulong, Claude, *Anne d'Autriche*, Perrin/Hachette, 1980

Faure, Guillemette, *La France made in USA*, Editions Jacob-Duvernet, 2005

Fonda, Jane, *My Life So Far*, Random House, 2005

Forlani, Séverine, *George Sand*, Jasmin, 2004

Fraser, Antonia, *Love and Louis XIV, The Women in the Life of the Sun King*,
Doubleday, 2006

Giroud, Françoise, *Les Françaises: de la gauloise à la pillule*, Fayard, 1999

Hawthorne, Nathaniel, *The Scarlet Letter*,
Prestwick House/Literary Touchstone Classics, 2005

Heyden-Rynsch, Verena von der, *La passion de séduire*, Gallimard, 2004

Johnson, Diane, *Le Divorce*, Plume Books, 1998

Joubert, Catherine et Stern, Sarah, *Déshabillez-moi*, Hachette, 2005

Kale, Steven, *French Salons*, Johns Hopkins University Press, 2004,

Kelly, Amy, *Eleanor of Aquitaine and the Four Kings*, Vintage Books, 1957

Kleinman, Ruth, *Anne of Austria, Queen of France*,
Ohio State University Press, 1985

Kunz, Edith, *Fatale: How French Women Do It*, Bridgewood Press, 2000

Lipschitz, Aronna, *La Voie de l'amoureux*, Robert Lafont, 2006

Lurçat, Hélène, *Comment devenir une vraie Parisienne*, Parigramme, 1999

Mansel, Philip, *Paris Between Empires, 1814-1852*, John Murray, 2001

Messinger, Joseph, *Les gestes qui vous séduisent*, First Editions, 2004

Mitford, Nancy, *The Sun King*, Hamish Hamilton, 1966

Maurois, André, *Lélia ou la vie de George Sand*, Livre de Poche, 1952

Musset, Alfred de, *Il ne faut jurer de rien*, Larousse, 2001

Musset, Alfred de, *On ne badine pas avec l'amour*, Livre de Poche, 1999

Naouri, Aldo, *Adultères*, Odile Jacob, 2007

Ozouf, Mona, *Les mots des femmes*, Fayard, 1995

Pernoud, Régine, *Aliénor d'Aquitaine*, Albin Michel, 1965

Pernoud, Régine, *La femme au temps des cathédrales*, Stock, 1980

Pernoud, Régine, *La Reine Blanche*, Albin Michel, 1972

Poirier, Agnès Catherine, *Touché, A Frenchwoman's Take on the English*,
    Weidenfeld & Nicolson, 2006

Powell, Helena Frith, *Two Lipsticks and a Lover*, Gibson Square, 2006

Rouart, Jean-Marie, *Adieu à la France qui s'en va*, Grasset, 2003

Rouart, Jean-Marie, *Nous ne savons pas aimer*, Gallimard, 2002

Sand, George, *Lélia*, Edition Garnier, Gallimard, 1960 and 1985

Sand, George, *Elle et lui*, Seuil, 1999

Sand, George, *Mauprat*, Crémille, 1972

Sosral, Alain, *Sociologie du dragueur*, Editions Blanche, 2004

Soublard, Thierry, *Où s'embrasser à Paris*, Parigramme, 2004

Stanger, Ted, *Sacrés Américains*, Gallimard, 2004

Stanger, Ted, *Sacrés Français*, Editions Michalon, 2003

Stein, Gertrude, *The Autobiography of Alice B. Toklas*,
    Alfred A.Knopf and Random House, 1933

Stein, Gertrude, *Paris France*, Liveright/W.W.Norton, 1996

Travers, Susan, *Tomorrow to be brave*, Bantam Press, 2001

Todd, Olivier, *Carte d'identités*, Plon, 2005

Tuchman, Barbara, *A Distant Mirror*, Ballantine Books, 1978

Turnbull, Sarah, *Almost French*, Nicolas Brealey, 2003

Vaillant, Maryse, *Comment aiment les femmes*, Seuil, 2006

Varro, Gabrielle, *La femme transplantée*, Presse Universitaire de Lillle, 1984

Warner, Mariana, *Joan of Arc, The Image of Female Heroism*,
    University of California Press, 1981

Wolf, John B., *Louis XIV*, W.W.Norton, 1968

Index